The Rita Lila

(say Ree-tuh Lee-luh)

A Western Yogini's Journey to Bliss

By Rita Ann Shankara

The Rita Lila: A Western Yogini's Journey to Bliss is a true story, with most
names changed to protect individual identities.

Cover design by Gaelyn Larrick, Copyright © 2009.
(www.book-covers-that-sell.com)

Published by Bliss Press.

Printed by Lulu, Inc., www.lulu.com.

ISBN 978-0-578-01131-8

For dear Basil,
*   who showed me the pathways to Bliss.*

And for my beloved, adorable Gurus, Amma and Neem Karoli Baba,
*   who shower me with Protection and Grace.*

Contents

Chapter 1 – Meeting Basil and Kali

At age thirty-three, I realized three important things about myself. One, I was a yogini, a woman who seeks yoga, or "union," with her highest Self and with God. Two, I had an addictive love pattern that I could trace back to the age of nine. Three, I was burning through life's emotional ups and downs with the intensity of water sizzling on a hot griddle.

On the surface, the lila, or divine play, of my life had seemed rather ordinary. I grew up Catholic in the Midwest, moved to the West Coast after college, got married, bought a house and had two kids. Although I had enjoyed some adventures, traveling in foreign countries and such, after half a decade of being a wife and mother in a small town near Mt. Shasta, in northern-most California, my life had acquired a rather bland tone. Appearances were everything to me. My husband and I threw great parties. Everyone thought that we were such a wonderful couple.

Beneath the happy family face we wore, the truth was that the misery of our marriage was wearing us down. We argued almost continuously over ridiculously trivial matters. Being at home with young children all day left me feeling bored, frustrated, and increasingly depressed and anxious. I don't know how that might have been different if the marriage was harmonious, but as it was, the strain of daily arguing with my husband compounded the stresses of managing the home and caring for the boys.

I somehow functioned in constant stress, but the strain of living in the survival part of my brain began to cause irritable bowel syndrome, difficulty sleeping, extreme fatigue, fear of being alone at night, and frequent migraine headaches. I wasn't sure which was worse – the fear of getting a migraine or actually having one.

Two years into the migraines, my husband and I started sleeping in separate bedrooms. At that time, on Valentine's Day, 2003, I noticed that I had a little crush on a woman who babysat for our boys. Her name was Anastasie. She had golden brown hair and a smile that melted my heart. This was not the first time that I had fallen in love with a woman.

The first time I had fallen for a woman she was involved with a man, but this time the woman was actually gay. Shortly after I noticed my feelings for Anastasie, I found out that she was in a serious long-term relationship with Sina.

Since Anastasie was not available, my feelings quickly evolved from a crush into an obsession – with no satisfying outlet for the passion. I grieved over the reality that I was unhappily married with two sons while Anastasie was happily living with her woman lover.

To keep from going totally insane, I confided my secret lust to a few close friends. One friend clapped her hands and said, "Oh, this is richly exciting!" She encouraged me to seize the opportunity to learn from whatever the woman was mirroring for me.

1

I thought about that and I realized how much Anastasie reminded me of my Dad – she embodied a similar fun and playful spirit. Recently I had been working with a therapist to find ways to be more fun and playful myself. Could my friend be right? Was my obsession with this woman rooted in my desire to be like her, to be more like my Dad?

During that time, I wrote several poems to Anastasie. I imagined myself one day reading them aloud at a buzzing coffee shop event. Here are a few of those poems:

thick maple syrup
drips down
the mountain
and i climb
like i will never
be able to climb
again
and i am hiding
my desires
for complete
and utter wildness
inside a cave
which is dark
and the honey
drips into my
mouth and the
tears flow
from my eyes
like rivers into
ponds with fat croaking frogs
and i just want to be free again
free to slide down
the muddy bank
laughing
and choking
on the salty tears
which explode
from these glassy stars
i call eyes
and at that moment
i want to see you
your big brown eyes
your smiling heart
splashing in the water
washing your hair
cracking open your heart & soul
and reaching out to mine.

2

****

Patience
is a calm girl
with tidy pigtails
standing beside
her mother
at a tea party.
I am a wild woman
with wild spiked hair –
sparkling silver strands
rippling through it.
and in my sex
i could swallow
a bold river.
there is no patience here.
and, yet,
THERE MUST BE.
i must straighten my skirt
and wait.

****

so raw
so real
you are rough
i see the tumble-bumble
in you
and I want to roll with you
down grassy slopes
into a flower meadow
where the sun drops
on pink star flowers
make us cry
and I get to touch you
your soft, delicate hands
your rough face lines
your juicy center.
i get to touch you
to melt into you
and I cannot
distinguish
between pain

and pleasure.

****

While the fantasies tumbled around in my mind, I reluctantly attended counseling sessions with my husband, Bryan. The counselor asked us to do nice things for each other in the evenings, like giving massages and making tea. I tried to make myself do the assignments, but I didn't *want* to do them. After the boys fell asleep, all I wanted was some peaceful time to write – alone.

I just wanted to be alone. Or did I? I was thinking about her more than I wanted to admit. How could I stop obsessing about her? How could I focus on my marriage? How could I save my life from falling apart?

Not knowing what else to do, I poured myself into dancing and writing. In addition to my regular modern dance class, I signed up to take classical Indian dance. Simultaneously, the idea for my first novel came through, so I carved out some regular times for writing.

At that point Bryan announced that he was moving out. At first I felt rage, but then I resigned myself to the reality of having two houses. With the boys over at papa's house halftime, I could focus more time on writing.

And then I met my teacher. A few weeks before Bryan moved out, one of my best friends, Luna, called to say that she would be returning to town soon with her new partner, Basil. She had met him at one of his spiritual retreats. Over the past thirty years, several hundred people had studied with him in small group settings across the country.

Luna explained that Basil draws from the Lakota wisdom that he received from John Fire Lame Deer, and from the ancient Yogic teachings that he learned in India from a Guru named Baba Muktananda. Through creative teaching methods such as chanting, storytelling, 'reading' peoples' energies, and meditation instruction, he leads participants through processes of deep self-inquiry. Luna told me that Basil would give a concert of poetry and chanting the following week in Mt. Shasta City, and she hoped that I would be able to attend.

There was no question as to whether or not I would be able to attend. Although I did not know it yet, Providence had assigned that evening to be the time when I would meet my spiritual teacher. There is a saying that *when the student is ready, the teacher appears.* Apparently I was ready, because when I met Basil I knew immediately that he was my teacher.

Basil and I greeted each other with a hug. We liked each other instantly. I felt as though we had met before.

I really enjoyed the evening. I especially loved listening to Basil tell the life story of Jelauddin Rumi, a great mystical Persian poet of the twelfth century. My favorite line of Rumi's poetry was, "*God picks up his reed flute world and blows.*" (*The Essential Rumi*, by Jalal Al-Din Rumi (Author), Et Al Coleman Barks (Translator), HarperCollins Publishers.)

4

The next morning, about thirty people gathered for brunch to welcome Basil to town. Luna offered a beautiful blessing and then asked each of us to share something about gratitude. I said, "I have gratitude for being in love with life again after a dark period. I feel beauty and trust being here – I know I am in the right place."

I *was* in the right place – that much was true. However, I did not yet realize how many dark periods were still to come.

After we ate, Luna and I sipped hot tea together. She asked Basil to work with me on my headaches. He tuned in to me energetically and then he said that the problem was in my throat chakra and also a bit in my womb. He said that my sexual energy needed to be very clean and clear. I asked what that meant and he said that my opening and shutting of 'I want her, but no, I can't have her' was *not* good for me.

Basil assigned a mantra for me to sing regularly: *Shree Om Kali Ma.* Kali is the Hindu goddess who destroys the illusions of our egos. Basil then explained, "Rita, you have been running too hot. You need to bring your focus down to your womb. There lies your power."

I told him, "So much wants to come through me," and he said, "Welcome to the Universe." Basil then said that I had built up all these deflectors to protect myself, but he and Luna got in and saw me where no one had ever seen me. He said, "You need to let yourself be seen." Luna told him, "Rita thinks that she is too much for the world." Basil looked at me and said very seriously, "You are not too much. You need to make peace with yourself." I took my tea out into the sunshine. I sat alone stretching, and the autumn sun felt gloriously warm. Internally I felt calm and still.

The next day Luna and Basil left a message on my answering machine. Luna said, "We just wanted you to know that we are thinking of you and holding the container for you." Then Basil said, "Rita, there is no such thing as too much complexity – there is only this myriad diversity of life unfolding through its precise and deeply feminine streams of manifestation – so, go for it, girl. Have a good day, Rita."

I felt so blessed and so held. A few nights later I had an interesting dream:

> *Looking out the window, I saw lightening and a dark grey storm cloud straight up in the sky. I was cold and shivering and I felt unprepared for the storm. But then I noticed that there were little jewels and crystals hanging down all along the bottom edges of the big storm cloud! The jewels and crystals were so beautiful and sparkling, like colorful lights.*

A friend at my dance class said that the dream's message was to trust. Trust Spirit. Maybe I felt cold and unprepared for the storm ahead, but I could trust that there would be jewels in it.

I thought of those jewels often as I chanted to Kali and summoned the courage to face Bryan moving out. The week before he moved out, just before Halloween, we sat at the table with our boys, Joshua and Benjamin.

Just as Bryan opened his mouth to tell the boys about the other house, I saw a bat flying around in the garden yard. It flew around right outside the window the whole time he was telling them the news. In our seven years in that house, we had never seen a bat in that yard! The bat felt somehow auspicious as we told the boys that we were still going to be a family, just a different kind of family. Even though we would live in two different houses, we would always love them and take care of them.

Later I looked up Bat in *Medicine Cards* by Sams and Carson. According to them, bat is a symbol of rebirth. Bat signals the rebirth of some part of yourself or the death of old patterns. They write, "If you resist your destiny, it can be a long, drawn out, or painful death. The universe is always asking you to grow and become your future."

That was fitting. I reached into the Halloween basket and chose a black plastic bat ring. With the bat on my finger, I chanted *Shree Om Kali Ma*, and breathed in a new level of trust for my place in the universe.

Chapter 2 – My first workshop with Basil

I felt so ashamed when my husband moved out. I felt like such a failure. Then I attended my first one-day workshop with Basil. First, he strummed his guitar while we sang a beautiful Sanskrit chant. Next, he tuned in to each of the dozen beings gathered in the round retreat center room with the plush green carpet.

To me, he said, "Rita, you have suffered long enough. Go get the best pen and paper in town and write down everything that you think you have done wrong in your life. Meditate on each thing, from your essential soul self, and then let it go. When you are ready, write at the bottom of the page, "I forgive myself." And while you are going through this, be meticulous about your diet. Really contemplate what foods will best support you now."

Basil then explained that we are streaming beings – we are not the content of stories that we are immersed in. He reminded us that we are not in control. He said, "We should let what IS *create us*, instead of us trying to create what is. We have to open to what wants to come through us, but not get arrogant. We should always remember the Source of the creativity flowing through us."

Despite Basil's teaching that we are not the content of our stories, I kept thinking about Anastasie. I thought about her a lot. I felt so in love with her. I judged it as irrational, but then I thought that love doesn't care what is rational or what is practical. Love doesn't care about what "makes sense." And love certainly doesn't care whether I am gay, bi, or straight.

As I cooked the daily meals, washed the laundry, and struggled with the boys' sibling rivalry, I felt exhausted and I wondered how I would ever survive single mothering. Somehow I got up each day – the will to live must have pushed me along. Also, a repressed creative fire stirred within, the embers of which sustained me during the dark times.

Luna said that if I painted, my paintings would look like Frida Kahlo's – like bright puzzle pieces put together. I actually have a lot in common with Frida. Like her, I am colorful, appreciative of Beauty, attracted to both sexes, alone a lot, and a soul who falls in love deeply and hungers to create. I even look like her, and I desire to decorate myself like her. Could I have been Frida – or touched on her essence – on my way here from the stars?

The attraction to Anastasie was so strong. I was tempted to tell her, but I couldn't do that because she was in a relationship. I *had* to act with integrity. I looked up *integrity* in the dictionary. It said 1. steadfast adherence to a strict ethical code. 2. the state of being un-impaired; soundness. 3. the quality or condition of being whole or undivided; completeness.

I had to act with integrity. I could not tell her. So I distracted myself as often as possible. One evening, I went to a lecture. The speaker explained his enlightenment theory – that before you can become expanded, you have to work through your personality and get to know all of your sub-selves. I found that interesting, but it didn't jive with Basil's teaching – that if you work *with* your sub-selves, it solidifies them and gives them form, and then they can lock down, making them more difficult to release.

I resonated with Basil's teaching: if you live in your essential self, vibrating to your essential soul field, and you feel connected to the Source of life, then all of the personality parts just naturally settle down. I liked that philosophy – just go straight to God and all else will eventually fall into place.

Even though I intellectually understood what Basil taught, emotionally I was still flailing around. I wondered how many married women found themselves attracted to women. How widespread was it?

I was asking myself that question the night I went to see Luna sing in a musical. After the performance, she and Basil invited me to join them for tea and pie. Basil gave me some insight from his incredible well of wisdom that I was beginning to see was like immense stars and shattering lights shooting through the universe. He said that the way Bryan had been using me in his psyche was the same way I was using *Anastasie* in my psyche. He very seriously cautioned me to watch out because there was a lot of projection going on and it was very seductive.

I didn't really understand what he meant. Basil said that I was transferring what was happening with Bryan onto Anastasie. He said that she and I were having some connection of our higher selves, but it was unclear for him to read since I was projecting so much.

I wondered aloud what I could do to remedy the situation. Basil said that first I needed to clean things up with Bryan, by not getting mad at him and not wanting, needing, or expecting his approval. He said that if I didn't clean up the situation with Bryan first, then it would just spill over into my next relationship.

As we parted on that chilly night, Basil cautioned me again: "Be careful. Remember that you and Bryan are still bound. You are binding through conflict. You have to truly let go and truly separate from him before you can be with someone else."

In the days that followed, the power of courage swelled from deep in my belly. Yes! I could do this! I now had more courage to face the pain of separation.

Chapter 3 – A Thanksgiving that rang with the bells of honesty

A few days before Thanksgiving, my Dad sent me an email, saying that he wished he could wave a magic wand and eliminate my sadness. I felt like a princess in a fairy tale, having him say such things to me! I felt immense gratitude that my conservative Catholic parents were offering me love and support even though I was getting a divorce.

My Dad told me that in their belief system, Christ is the head of the marriage – thus the marriage is indissoluble. He said that he wished that I shared their Catholic faith, but he acknowledged and accepted that I had chosen a different spiritual path.

That night I went to a chanting concert with Luna and Basil. A stunning couple named Deva Premal and Miten led beautiful songs. I cried as the men all sang *"There is so much magnificence, near the ocean,"* and the women responded, *"Hallelujah!"*

On Thanksgiving morning, I chanted songs from the concert while I cooked. My heart swelled with gratitude. After preparing the vegetables for the stuffing, I took a break to have tea and toast with Eliza, a very special friend from my past. A few weeks prior, I had called her to see if we might meet soon because I had something to tell her. She said that she would be in town to visit relatives for only two days, but she would squeeze in some time for a brief visit with me.

As the visit with Eliza drew near, I felt both nervous and excited. I kept remembering the night we had met in that dark train station. We had shared a large peanut butter cookie while telling our life stories. An hour later, when we boarded the train for San Francisco, we both already knew that the roots of our deep soul connection reached far into the past. Just recalling those first hours of our meeting sent a little shiver through my heart… and through my yoni.

We had not talked for almost two years. We sat down on my red couch and I told Eliza the truth. She was the woman I had fallen in love with so many years ago. She said she *knew* that was what I wanted to tell her. She said that we always know these things on some level.

Eliza responded to my confession gingerly. With her crystal blue eyes shining, she said, "If I had not been so deep in the drama with Rob, I might have been willing to experiment with you." That surprised me, so she explained that she also fantasized about women, and, in fact, she had just recently told her husband that at some point she would *have* to be with a woman. She said that she did make out with a woman once, and it was incredible, with such a "softness."

I told her about my current attraction and she empathized with my plight. She encouraged me to make peace with myself. She said, "Rita, you are a remarkable woman. You are intense. You put it all out there – you are like a lion!"

Eliza was no tame kitty herself. Although my intense feelings for her had long since dissolved, I still felt a lingering excitement when I gazed in her eyes. I secretly wondered if she and I might one day meet between the sheets.

Before Eliza left, after only one hour, I shared that I never wanted our visit to end. I rationalized that my pattern of separation anxiety went back to childhood. She said softly, "You are hard to leave, too," and off she went.

After she left, I took a long walk in the unusually warm and breezy day, gathered a few brightly colored leaves for the table, and finished cooking the stuffing and the fig compote. Filled with awe, I met Bryan and the boys at our friends' house for Thanksgiving dinner.

After dinner, Bryan took the boys to another party, and I stayed to talk more with my friend Dana. The party dwindled down, and I found myself at the table with only Dana, her husband Marc, and their friend Maya. Turns out, Maya had just moved to town from Santa Barbara to get away from a woman whom she had been in love with for five years.

Like me, Maya had been unhappily married and had fallen in love with a woman. Eventually, she divorced her husband and confessed her love to the woman. The woman told her to get lost. She was totally heartbroken.

I took another sip of wine, and spilled out my truth to the three of them. Maya encouraged me to just keep telling the story until I could let it go. Marc reminded me that his first wife had fallen in love with a woman and that's why they had divorced. We all wondered if women were falling in love with women because really they wanted to reclaim the juicy parts of *themselves*. Maybe it was easier to see how incredible another woman was than to see our own amazing strengths.

Maya said that while she admired the other woman so much, she finally realized that the strong attraction was to a mirror of how she wants to be herself. She found that the whole process was about releasing into herself.

As I went to sleep alone that Thanksgiving night, I gave thanks for the people who had listened to my story that day. I felt blessed to have rung the bells of honesty. And, although it would still be many months before I would be free of the fantasies about Anastasie, I at least felt more supported in the journey.

Chapter 4 – A work in progress

That Fall I suddenly felt very drawn to anything from India – the food, the art, the gods, the prayers, the dance. At my Indian dance class, I agreed to participate in a performance. Before the show began, we dressed in colorful saris and adorned ourselves with gold jewelry and rich makeup. Then we sat in a circle with our teacher, Julianna, and she guided us to meditate on the dance we were about to offer the community. She asked us each to feel the answers to the questions:

> *To whom do you bow?*
> *What will you offer?*

I bowed to God, to Shiva. I hoped to offer Beauty coming through the Divine. I asked that the dance would flow through me as the vessel – that the Source of Life would dance *through* me.

After the show, I invited Luna, Basil, and Julianna to my house for tea and leftover chocolate pumpkin pie. With the new year only one month away, I got out my new *Bhagavad Gita* engagement calendar (Mandala Publishing) to show them the splendid art of Lord Krishna throughout its pages. I did not really know who Krishna was at that time. All I knew was that he was an incarnation of Lord Vishnu who had given much wisdom to his warrior friend Arjuna on the battlefield. That advice given to Arjuna is the *Bhagavad Gita*, which means the Song of the Lord.

When I got so excited about my new calendar, Basil encouraged me to take all that energy in my throat chakra down to my second chakra, and as soon as I did that, I felt my belly get really warm. He said that my destiny was through *letters* and that I should find a Hebrew letter to meditate on and let that fire in my belly burn away all the negativity from the relationship with Bryan. He said to let myself feel that warm fire throughout my whole body – to let myself become a flaming letter. In seeing my whole self as a burning letter, he saw my wisdom coming down, but he said that I still had many layers to burn through.

Later that night, I wrote in my journal, "I am a work in progress! The exciting thing is that I finally *feel* progress. Spiritual growth is happening – layers *are* burning away. I feel spiritually grounded in a whole new way."

At that time, reading quotes from the *Bhagavad Gita* helped me tremendously. The following quote strengthened me the most – in Chapter 2, Verse 40, Krishna tells Arjuna:

> *No effort on the yoga path is ever lost, nor can any obstacle ever hold one back forever. Just a little progress on this path can protect one from the greatest fear.*

I recalled how my deeply entrenched fear of being home alone at night had suddenly evaporated the day Bryan moved out. I honored the changes in me, and I kept walking forward, one step at a time.

Chapter 5 – A time of great learning

On the Winter Solstice, I was still grieving over Bryan moving out. Sometimes when I was alone with Benjamin and Joshua, who were only three and six at the time, I felt utterly vulnerable, like I was standing at the edge of a cliff, where the wind was blowing hard.

Joshua's kindergarten teacher, Grace, taught me a lot. She was attracted to the gypsy in me, and I was attracted to her seemingly infinite wisdom. She advised that with each mistake, I should just affirm what I would do the *next time*, and then move on. She reminded me that my only place of control was in my response. I could learn to dance through the joys and the sorrows, like a flamenco dancer.

That month I could not indulge in my dancing and writing because I got terribly sick with a flu. Luna brought a pot of steaming hot soup. Basil rubbed some acupuncture points on my aching body. Then he played his guitar and they sang healing chants for me.

Joshua and Benjamin also caught the flu, and on Christmas Eve the three of us lay in bed together, feeling chilled to the bone while burning hot with fevers. We read stories and Bryan brought us herbs and soups. I felt grateful for his support.

On New Year's Day, I picked an angel card for the year. (*Angel cards* by Kathy Tyler and Joy Drake.) The year before I had picked *Release*. This time I picked *Freedom*. How appropriate. With Bryan living in another house, and Benjamin suddenly deciding to wean from breastfeeding, freedom was definitely looming on my horizon.

A few weeks into the year, I felt anxiety over my life changing so much. Grief and depression overwhelmed my system. One morning, with a painful migraine, I called Luna to ask her to 'hold' me that day. She was out, so I asked Basil if he would hold me. He said, "We can do more than that," and he gave me a mini healing session for eight minutes over the phone.

Basil asked me to put my attention in different parts of my head. Once I found a calm place above the top of my head, he asked me to take my attention down to the chakra at my solar plexus. Immediately it felt glowing warm! He said to let that warmth grow… and then to bring the calm energy from the top of the head down to the warm place… and then to let it calm and warm my whole body. It did.

Before that healing moment, I had been freaking out about everything: the boys, the housework, the impending divorce... Basil said that I was blocking the Light. He told me to remember all of the resources *in my body*. He explained, "Rita, if you calm yourself from the inside, then all of those outer things won't be so cantankerous."

After that phone call, I found a prayer (on Krishna Das' website, www.krishnadas.com) by Ramana Maharshi (1879-1950), a beautiful saint from India. Reciting this prayer daily gave me the strength to let some Light in:

> *Place your burden*
> *at the feet of the Lord of the Universe*
> *who accomplishes everything.*
> *Remain all the time steadfast in the heart*
> *in the Transcendental Absolute.*
> *God knows the past, present, and future*
> *He will determine the future for you*
> *and accomplish the work.*
> *What is to be done will be done*
> *at the proper time. Don't worry.*
> *Abide in the heart and surrender your acts*
> *to the divine.*

I said that prayer so often that I memorized it. Each time I said it, I watched my system calm down.

At that time I met Anastasie's partner, Sina. She was so freshly adorable! Her bright eyes, cheery smile, and fun spirit melted my heart. This was a woman I would never want to hurt. Meeting her was yet another confirmation of my intention to act with integrity. I kept praying to be released of the attraction to Anastasie.

I recommitted myself to focusing on my own healing as well as my mothering and career paths. Bryan said that he didn't see my writing a novel as a career move. I ignored him and kept writing. Julianna read a rough draft of the novel, and she said confidently, "I have no doubt that opening yourself to receive and transmit this story is a big piece for you – regardless of what happens with it externally. Don't doubt yourself."

I was learning to let God accomplish the work. I was learning that I did not have to do it all myself. I was learning about spiritual freedom. Thankfully I did not know about all of the lessons which were still to come. If I had known how many layers I still had to burn through, I might not have had the strength to go on. As it was, ignorance was a bit of bliss. I celebrated the progress I was making on the spiritual journey. I felt more connected to the Source of all Life.

Chapter 6 – Finding Heart

That January, the center of my chest was feeling pretty tight. In hopes of loosening the constriction, I went to see an energy healer. During the session, he kept asking "Who are you?" until I finally gave the right answer: "I am Love."

The healer talked with me about shifting my awareness from the worries of my mind down to the feelings of my heart. He brought forth a large ocean wave of truth in me when he said, "The mind cannot tell you who you are – when it tries, thank it and love it, but go into the Heart. The Heart is always right."

I told him that I felt in crisis, but he did not agree that I was in crisis. He said, "It is an emergency, in the sense that something is *emerging* through you – you are in the process of spiritual growth and you are growing up." Then he laughed as he explained that I shouldn't take that the wrong way – he thinks people grow up at about fifty years old! (I was thirty-four years old at the time.)

When I told him what Basil had said about my attraction to Anastasie being very seductive, he advised me to take the word "seductive" out of it, because to him that word implied bad intent, and he did not see bad intent in my heart. He reminded me, "Just keep coming back to Heart and sending the healing prayers out. Take all of your worries down into your Heart Space and the Heart will manifest all that you need."

A few days later I went to see another healer who rubbed myrhh oil on my heart and kidney points. Then she held my head while I focused on surrendering to the integrity of the heart's energy. She said that it was important for me to bring my heart into my mind so that I could act from there. Then she shared what she saw happening in me:

"There's a dragon inside you who is hiding your treasure. You need to tell the dragon that it is okay to let the treasure out. You've been letting your shadow or your unconscious run things, and now you need to tap into your resources and let the inner guidance of your higher self run things. You are afraid that you can't handle it alone – BUT YOU CAN HANDLE THINGS.

"You need to recognize that you have a resource deep within that will help you. You are looking for a way to Unity and to wholeness of self. You have a deeply ingrained archetype of the Dao, an image of the state of balance between male and female, but your male and female parts are off-balance right now, probably because of the marriage collapsing."

Her words certainly resonated with me as truth.

The attraction to Anastasie continued. One afternoon I actually fell to my knees, praying for release. Envious of the serene life of the cat in our backyard, I took out my journal and wrote:

15

Cat soaks in sunshine
she knows where the next meal will be
Cat looks serene
she cares not what happens next
i am impatient
running around
in this cool winter house
juggling many balls
not knowing when comfort will come
i need to soak in sunshine
to relax
to trust Spirit –
all is divine.
and these rippling chills
must mean something.
Where are you?
When will you come?
Could we soak in sunshine
side by side,
our bodies touching?

Meanwhile, on Valentine's Day I received an email from my high school sweetheart, Danny. I felt so touched by the sweetness of his letter that I cried and cried from a very deep place. I felt such a sense of *home* in my heart. At the end of the letter he had written, "Take care of yourself and remember to breathe… life is good and will take care of you."

I felt soothed by Danny's words, and, I recognized that my longing for physical touch and heart connection was intense.

On the one-year anniversary of my attraction to Anastasie, I paused to reflect and to celebrate all of the changes within myself. Although I was still thinking of her, I was also falling in love with *myself…* and finding much love in my heart.

Chapter 7 – Releasing her finally!

After living separately for more than four months, Bryan and I had settled into a comfortable schedule with the boys. We each had them for half of the weeknights, and we took turns having them for the weekends, which meant that I had every other weekend completely free.

One weekend in March I followed my interest in midwifery and traveled to Oregon for a doula training. On the drive there, I felt a cry coming, but I tried to stay happy. Then the lyrics to a Van Morrison song overwhelmed me: *"Come in the garden and just look at these flowers – we could just sit and talk for hours and hours."* I wanted to sit in the garden with Anastasie for hours and hours! I wanted her so badly. The tears began to flow uncontrollably. I could hardly drive. I cried a long, deep, loud cry, with burning waves of pain throughout my whole body.

After that big cry, I wondered how many people throughout history had suffered deeply over loving someone whom they could not be with.

Inspired by the doula training, I felt excited while driving back home. I remembered that I had picked the angel card *Birth* for that week. That was appropriate, given my attraction to working with birth, and it was also perfect on an emotional level. I reflected that during that primal wail over Anastasie – the object of my desire – I had actually felt like a woman in labor. It felt as if I was birthing a new me, and, as with childbirth, the process was both painful and exciting.

The following week I was surprised to see that the desire for her was gone. Gone. The attraction was *gone*. I felt so much gratitude. It was as if, during that big cry, God finally felt the sincerity of my intention to release her. Without that Grace, I might still be projecting my desires onto her!

At that time I still did not understand what "projection" really meant. I think that if I had truly understood what it meant, I might have been able to release her and then just be content with myself and my connection with All. As it was, I didn't really *get it*. I didn't learn the lesson.

So, even as I was releasing her, I was already developing a fantasy about Danny…

Chapter 8 – Projecting onto Danny

Less than one week after I finally released the attraction to Anastasie, my attention shifted to my high school sweetie, Danny. I started focusing on our email correspondences and thinking about him much of the time. I felt a little heart ripple pulling me toward him.

Although I recognized that Danny might still be capable of breaking my heart, I was intrigued by the maturity I could hear in his written 'voice.' I started fantasizing about the next time I would visit my family in Wisconsin – maybe he and I would fall in love all over again? I recognized that the love I felt for him all those years ago *still* lived in my heart.

A few weeks later, I wrote a long letter to Danny, and he didn't reply right away. When he did reply, he was short on words and he signed it, "I'll write ya when I write ya." I didn't understand why he pulled away, but I took it as a sign to stop thinking about him and to focus on myself.

And there was plenty to focus on in myself! Bryan wanted to know when I would be ready to proceed with the legal and financial aspects of separation. Those aspects filled me with fear and dread, but once I let go of the fantasies of Anastasie and Danny, I felt more space in my heart to face Bryan and our separation.

I told Bryan that if we first worked with a counselor for a while, then I would be ready to confront the realities of divorce. At that stage, I still cringed at the sound of the word 'divorce.' I felt scared and conflicted about getting a divorce with two young children involved.

In my heart, I knew that it was time to clean things up with Bryan. It was time to do the work with him. I could no longer distract myself with fantasies – it was time to face the truth, and all the pain within it. A strong desire for wholeness and wellness stirred within me.

Chapter 9 – Pain, Processing, and Planning

Even though we had gone to many different counselors over the years, Bryan agreed to go to the counseling sessions with me, because the new counselor planned to guide us through a closure process.

The counselor gave us an assignment to write out lists of all that we would miss and all that we would not miss about the relationship. In the following sessions, she facilitated as we shared our lists with each other. Then we made and shared lists of how we each envisioned the future form of our relationship.

The process took several weeks, during which time I was in excruciating pain. In most moments I knew that our marriage was definitely over, but in some moments, I wondered if we should try again. It seemed to me that with young children involved – Joshua was almost seven and Benjamin was four at the time – it was important to turn over every stone. I did not feel certain that we had turned over every stone.

It was a confusing time for me. When the pain hit my threshold, sometimes I would revert back into fantasies of Danny. Other times I would focus on my own healing. I continued journaling each day, which helped me enormously. I wrote about the separation process as well as ordinary life reflections, such as this one:

"Friday night I was sweeping the floors and I thought 'here I am sweeping on a Friday night,' and then I thought about how funny it is that after being an at-home Mama for seven years, I still think that Friday night means something – as if Friday is different from any other day, and as if night is different from day! When you take care of a home and children, the reality of time changes. Days and nights slip into laundry folded, meals served, baths given, stories read, and… years pass!"

Writing eased the waves of mental anguish. I wrote quite a bit about my image of the ideal lover… and about how I would feel when I was with him.

In addition to writing, I pampered myself whenever possible. I was determined to heal myself naturally – I did *not* want to numb myself with an antidepressant medication. One day I went to get a massage and the massage therapist said that the muscles in my back were "gripping." She told me that I needed to focus on consciously letting go.

I was trying to let go, to relax, to trust, to surrender, even as the fear and anxiety threatened to consume me. It was as if I lived most of my life in the primitive, fight-or-flight part of my brain. All of that stress resulted in continuing headaches and incredible fatigue.

I called my Grandma in Wisconsin and told her how tired I was feeling. She said, "Be encouraged. You will revive when your boys get older, and maybe you will even be stronger than you were before having children."

She said that I always sounded so cheerful and she always thought of me as "peppy."

I sure wasn't feeling peppy. My worries were growing over how I would support myself financially after the divorce. I struggled to find the energy to focus on career goals, and I started planning to attend a midwifery workshop in San Diego that spring.

After registering for the workshop, I panicked over the reality of leaving the boys and actually traveling alone. Bryan assured me that he would be fine with the boys for a week, and he strongly advised that I fly because he thought that I was too exhausted to make a long drive by myself. I knew that he was right, but ever since 9-11, I had felt especially afraid of flying. I was afraid that the plane would crash and I would die, and I didn't feel ready to die. However, I knew that I needed to fly, so I went to a few healers to see if I could work through my fears.

The first healer encouraged me to follow my purpose in this life even if I had fears. He said that I needed to let myself be as big as I was supposed to be – to let my light shine. He also saw that I was ready to stop identifying so much with the contents of my mind. I grew up with very black-and-white thinking, but he saw that I was now ready to see all the colors.

He gave me a couple of suggestions: 1. When I feel a headache coming on, take the earth energy up through my feet and bring the heavenly energy down through my crown and cycle those energies around in my body, and 2. Be open to the trees, plants, creatures, stones, and elements, and experience how they offer more energies and communications than what we see.

Next I visited my friend Paulina, who was a homeopathic doctor. She encouraged me to say positive affirmations while walking. She told me about a book called *The Molecules of Emotion*, by Candace B. Pert, Ph.D., and about a new film called *What the Bleep Do We Know?* Paulina said that my fear of flying was a part of the old identity that was still in my brain. The nerves needed new wiring to build up a new identity in my brain. Saying positive affirmations while walking would help the nerves wire in a new way.

I knew that I needed to go to the midwifery workshop, and yet I still felt anxious about flying. I called a Native American intuitive woman. We met and she said strongly, "This trip to San Diego is very important for you. You should not cancel this trip under any circumstances." Somehow I knew she was right. With the amethyst stone she gave me sparkling in the sunlight on my desk, I called the airline and booked the flights.

Chapter 10 – Rejection, Purifications, and Curiosity

As Bryan and I continued the closure work with the counselor, I found myself still questioning our separation. One night I called him and shared openly how unresolved I felt in my heart. He asked if my confusion was coming from fear, and I said that I honestly did not know.

At our next counseling session, I shared that I felt open to going out on a date with him. I wondered what it would be like to try again. I thought that he would be open to that too, so I felt crushed when he appeared to be closed to my suggestion. By the end of the session, he changed his tune, saying that he would be willing to go on a date, but I still felt very rejected.

That evening I was crying so hard that I was almost hyperventilating. I was definitely at the threshold of how much pain I could handle, so I called my friend Julianna and sobbed to her about how many times Bryan had broken my heart. She offered a good perspective: "It isn't just about Bryan and you and your marriage breaking up. If you think about families of origin and karmic patterns, who knows what is breaking apart through you and your process. Remember that God is working through you both. Hold onto that Rumi quote which says something like *God keeps breaking our hearts until they stay open.*"

Later that night, with my breath still catching in my throat and my puffy red eyes still burning, I wrote in my journal that I felt wildly open and strangely calm. I reflected on what Bryan and I had decided – that we would go out on a date after my trip to San Diego, and then we would 'process' the date at our next counseling session – and I couldn't put my finger on why, but it felt really yucky and weird to me. I got in bed and cried almost all night.

The next day Joshua's kindergarten teacher held me and I could almost hear her crooning, "there, there." Grace sensed that my desire to try again with Bryan was an important part of the process, and she recognized that it *really* hurt. She remembered that pain from her own divorce when her sons were young.

A few days later Bryan shared that he had been crying – actually sobbing – the night before. I couldn't believe it. I wrote in my journal, "So Bryan is crying now. I feel oddly satisfied – almost like victorious or triumphant, but not quite. Of course I don't want anyone to suffer, but I *do* want Bryan to let his heart open. Even if he is resolved to end our marriage, I still wish an open heart for him."

My heart was also softening. The stone walls of anger and resentment around my heart were beginning to crumble. Bryan looked calm and sparkly to me, and I wondered what it would be like to have a heart connection with the father of my children.

So, even though he was saying that he felt resolved, the next full moon I gave him a note with an invitation for a massage under the cedar tree. I left it open, that he could show up or not. I felt good about offering that gift to him, because I felt genuine sorrow that I did not *want* to give him massages for so many years.

I waited for Bryan that moonlit night, but he did not come. I cried myself to sleep. The next day he said, "Thank you for the note." That was it.

I called the homeopathic doctor and told her about my grief over Bryan and my tendency to start fantasizing about Danny to escape the grief. She said that my heart was opening and I wanted to let someone in, but I needed to just be with myself – to be whole and happy by myself. She prescribed the homeopathic chocolate remedy, which she said would help fulfill my need to be mothered and nourished.

Joshua's kindergarten teacher came to the rescue again. Grace saw clearly that I was going through some necessary purifications so that I could begin to trust my life. She told me to take responsibility for my feelings of rejection, and to trust the story of my life. Over hot spiced tea, she sweetly reminded me that the story was written with me in mind. She said, "The book is already written, and now you get to read it!"

Throughout all the rejections and purifications, my heart was indeed opening.

In the month preceding my trip to San Diego, I tried in vain to reconnect with friends I had known when I lived there after college. Then I remembered that Basil led workshops in San Diego. At that time Luna and Basil were in Tuscany for a month, so I sent Basil an email to find out if he had any friends with whom I might stay during my workshop.

Basil replied:
Rita,
I will be emailing Karl (my San Diego friend) today…
I will have him email you directly...
Italy is wonderful, restful and inspiring. Village life is good.
love,
Basil

Next, I received the following message:
Dear Rita,
Basil sent a note saying that you need a place to stay in May.
What days will you be in the San Diego area? I have a couple options to check out depending upon when and where you need to be.
Let me know and I will see what I can manifest for you.
Namaste ~ Om Shanti
Karl Sanford

When I read that message, I felt my breath catch in my throat. 'Karl Sanford,' I kept thinking. What was it about that name which produced such a strong feeling in me? Later that night, I wrote in my journal, "Curious about Karl Sanford. Love that name."

In the weeks that followed, Karl and I corresponded by email and he arranged for me to stay with his friend, Eric Flynn. Karl and I talked on the phone a few times, and the week before the trip he left me the following phone message: "Dear Rita, I send lots of positive, loving, warm energy your way to spark this week on your great journey."

That week I bought some new clothes and got a fun new haircut. I felt much curiosity about Karl and about the new Rita who I felt emerging from within me.

Chapter 11 – Meeting Karl and Eric

A few nights before the San Diego trip, Karl introduced me to Eric through a conference call. As he was setting up the call, before he got Eric on the line, I was surprised at the effect that his voice was having on me. We were just talking about the weather, but there was something about the sound of Karl's voice that had a very calming effect on me – it felt like a soothing balm on my soul.

During the conference call, Eric sounded like a pleasant guy. He said that his yard would be nice for studying and he had a bicycle I could use while I was there. I asked about the weather and such things for packing, and they invited me to go out to dinner with them on my first night in San Diego. Karl explained that night would be best for him because his wife would be in Detroit on business that night.

'His wife.' Those two words rang in my ears as I packed my suitcase. 'So, he is married,' I kept thinking. I had a sense that an interesting story was just beginning. I felt some apprehension about going through with the trip, but I remembered the words of the Native American intuitive woman, "You should not cancel this trip under any circumstances."

On the morning of my flight, before I left my house, I sipped a cup of bancha tea and gazed out at Mt. Shasta. Suddenly, a crazy thought flashed through my mind. I imagined Karl and I having sex that very afternoon! 'What was that?' I wondered. I was not by any means a sexually loose woman. I had only had sex with my husband for the past ten years, and before that I only had a couple of lovers.

'So why would I have that thought now?' I kept asking myself as the morning progressed. 'And why would I have that thought about a man who I have never met? Especially a married man.'

The flight went smoothly. I got my rental car and called Karl on his cell phone, as we had planned. We met in a restaurant parking lot a few miles beyond the airport.

We shook hands and exchanged a few words, and then got in our cars to drive across the city to Eric's house. I turned on my Snatam Kaur *Prem* CD and sang along while I cried many tears. At first I thought that I was crying because this was my first trip alone in seven years, and there I was, back in San Diego, the city where I had moved after college graduation.

As I continued crying, though, I became aware that there was something deeper happening within me. Karl was driving in front of me, and as I drove, I was watching him, and I was feeling a very deep heart connection between us. The sensation was like nothing I had ever experienced.

When we arrived at Eric's house, we still had a few hours until Eric came home from work. Karl relaxed in the living room, reading and meditating, while I got settled and lay down for a little rest. After a while he made us some hot tea, and we went out in the garden together.

We sat in the grass, sipping our tea, and talking about religion and spirituality. Since we both attended workshops with Basil, we spoke a similar language. We talked at great length about the interesting process of finding one's purpose here on earth.

Karl told me a story from his childhood, and, as I listened and looked in his eyes, I could feel and 'see' the beauty of his spirit. I said, "You have such a beautiful heart," and after that, we kept talking, but I wasn't listening anymore with my mind. I was gazing into his eyes, and through his eyes, my heart was feeling his heart, and my soul was feeling his soul.

Soon Eric arrived home from work and we three went out to an upscale vegetarian restaurant. I felt immediately comfortable with both men, as if I had known them for a long time. We laughed and conversed easily over dinner, but I admit that I was having difficulty focusing on the conversation. The pull to keep looking in Karl's eyes was intense. I tried to look at Eric also, but it took real effort to take my gaze away from Karl's eyes.

I kept thinking, '*What am I going to do?*' I thought, 'There is going to be no way out, but through, so just keep going. Trust your life – trust your story.' Halfway through the meal, I realized that I was falling deeply and hopelessly in love with this man, and I suddenly could not take one more bite. In that moment, I completely lost my appetite, and the desire for food did not return for many months.

The midwifery workshop was excellent. I enjoyed attending the sessions each day and studying each evening. Eric and I found that we had a lot in common, and we took turns cooking meals for each other. As housemates, we were very compatible.

On Friday night, Eric and I went to see *What The Bleep Do We Know?* It was opening night in San Diego and the filmmakers were there answering questions after the film. Back at home, Eric and I talked for two hours. The healing journey of the film's protagonist reminded me of my own journey, and I inwardly celebrated how much better I was doing in my life.

The next day Karl joined Eric and me for a hike. Before we started down the trail leading to the beach, Karl handed me an envelope. Inside was a card with a mandala on the cover. In the card, I read the following note and poems:

Beloved Rita,
You are the most lovely woman with such an open warm heart, eyes that reach right to the soul, and a smile so beautiful. You take my breath away every time I gaze upon your face – that portal to the Infinite.
May your journey that calls compellingly be one full of joy, happiness, and great service to others.
I shall always hold you in my heart as my Goddess of Passages.
Love always,
Karl

Haiku just for You!

With just one short gaze
Into the depths of your soul
I knew all was lost.

Your beguiling eyes
Were too irresistible
To not look upon.

It was then I knew
I'd fallen in Love with You –
The Beloved One.

When all evening long
Your eyes kept returning back
To soul gaze with me

Twas there I witnessed
Great beauty fringed with sadness
Within you and me.

For eternity
I am yours in Heart and soul –
Be gentle with me!

Now I must confess
Whenever the Beloved
Shows Herself to me

I'm helpless you see.
My Heart is lost to the One
Through your soul's beauty.

And a bonus poem in the Japanese tradition of Tanka –

Rita
God's deepest dream is beauty
Beauty's deepest dream is You
The beauty of your Soul's becoming
The yearning that is within

After I read that card, I could not find the words to describe how I felt, and besides, Eric was with us, so I simply pointed to his words and said quietly to Karl, "I feel the same way."

26

When we arrived at the water, we found a spot in the sand where we could sit and perform a ritual. Eric was really struggling to let go of a past girlfriend, and he had asked for our help in creating a ritual space in which to burn some of her cards and photos.

I remembered doing a similar ritual on a beach in San Diego many years back. After four years in an intense relationship with Michael, the man I had followed there from the Midwest, I finally moved away from that city. Just before I left, a friend took me to the beach and we burned his letters and photos. She burned sage around me and expressed her wishes that I would soon heal from the loss of him.

I felt honored to be a witness at Eric's ritual. Karl and I led him in the process, and I felt enchanted by how naturally Karl and I worked together. That very morning, Karl had received an email 'Thought for the Day' from John MacEnulty, and he read it to us as we began the ritual. It was about letting the waves of life flow through us, staying present in our true nature, and seeing the sacred in everything.

We sat in silence, watching the waves, each of us digesting the words that Karl had just read. It was the perfect passage for all three of us. In the months to come, I would repeatedly hear the words that spoke to me the most: *"we are spiritually unharmed by anything."*

After Eric burned some things, we smudged him and ourselves with burning sage. As we hiked back up to the car, the flowers looked even more vibrant. When we returned to Eric's house, Karl retrieved his computer which he had hidden under the bed for safekeeping, said goodbye to Eric, and asked me to walk him out to his car.

We embraced and he kissed me three different times on the lips. I was shaking and could barely speak, let alone think about kissing. I asked, "Why is there so much sadness between us?" And then I said, "I feel as though I could sit and weep with you for hours." He said, "We'll do that sometime." And then we said "goodbye."

A few days later I returned to my home by the mountain, feeling more in love than I have ever felt in my life. I was completely out of my head and unable to function in my usual ways. I called my teacher Basil for support, and he advised me to bake chocolate chip cookies.

Basil said to pay close attention to how the cookies bake from the inside out. He reminded me that I was creating my reality from the inside out, and not the other way around. He said to focus on the intent to bake the cookies, to follow the recipe scrupulously, and then to see the form.

I got out the ingredients, and that night I served chocolate chip cookies for dinner! The boys loved that, although, Joshua, forever the practical one, suggested that we have peanut butter crackers and carrot sticks with our cookies. 'Right!' I thought, 'protein and vegetables – good thinking!'

And then the correspondence began. The day after I returned home, a flurry of emails passed back and forth between us. In one of my letters, I told Karl that instead of going on a date with my husband Bryan, I had asked Bryan if he would be willing to sit and look in each other's eyes for a while to see if we had any heart and soul connection left. Bryan had reluctantly agreed. Karl responded positively, saying that he fully supported me and trusted the process.

Chapter 12 – Roses, Poems, and Release Letters

Bryan and I decided to sit together at my house that Saturday night after the boys went to sleep. On Saturday afternoon, I received a card in the mail with Karl's second handwritten letter and poem. I cried as I read the following:

Beloved Rita,
I cannot find ordinary words to describe our union ~ reunion. But I did find that I was moved, no, compelled to write ecstatic poetry from the Heart, from the One. I was compelled by first our time together one week ago now and I shared that with you when we met again Saturday morning. Yet that was just a trickle compared to what flooded out Sunday morning over a blissful two hours that flew by. So for your return to Mt. Shasta – where I will see you next most likely – I give you the first of the poems created for You as a most exquisite soul of the Beloved. The form is the traditional five line, thirty-one syllable Japanese poem which, in its purest offerings, is the vessel for expressing love to a beloved and to The Beloved. Know that I will always love you as much as we both felt in our parting embrace last Saturday afternoon.
Namaste ~ Om Shanti ~ Love,
Karl

With All Six Senses

With all six senses
I look into your eyes
And I can see
Your beautiful soul's unique essence
Emerging exquisitely.

I feel the pain
You endured for so long
As you struggled to find
The path through the labyrinth
To your Heart and to your Calling.

I hold you close in embrace
Now that you have found your way
To who you are becoming
And your calmness and stillness
Reign supreme.

I breathe in the scent
Of wild roses

29

Which perfumes your whole being
Now that the Divine Mother peeks out
With joy from within you.

And I taste the dew
Of the primordial morning
When, with utmost tenderness
I kiss the Beloved
Shining through You.

I savored the line, "I breathe in the scent of wild roses which perfumes your whole being." Just the day before, when I suggested to Bryan that we get a red rose for our sitting ritual, he said that I could get one if I wanted to, but he thought roses were "so Hallmark."

Needless to say, that evening when Bryan and I looked in each other's eyes for almost an hour, we did not feel any romance. There simply was not a heart and soul connection between us.

The next day I spoke with Karl on the phone, and I tried to explain how I was feeling about integrity, but I felt stuck inside and I could not find the right words. After we hung up the phone, a wave of anger rushed through me, and I realized that I could not continue corresponding with him while I was feeling such a lack of integrity with regard to his wife, Martha.

That night I began composing a difficult letter. The next day, as I finished typing the letter, I received another handwritten card in the mail from Karl. It was absolutely heart wrenching to read his letter and poem, as I already knew that I had to end that love affair. Here is what I read through many tears:

Beloved Rita,

   One Week Later

   I have never been so struck in awareness than when we embraced that Saturday of affirmation. Your whole being changed – and did so immediately. Your breath became utterly calm, utterly deep, utterly rhythmic, utterly soft, and utterly strong. The whole moment slowed down to fit in the eternal embrace re-found in this lifetime – and you did this through your breath. It was like a deep yogic trance and I was so mesmerized by it all, I joined you. And in that moment – for just an instant – a circle was closed and the Beloved in me was fully present gazing upon the Beloved in you without us intervening. God smiling upon God and falling in Love again and again and again.

   This prose comes easy now that I processed all this through the poetry I am compelled to write, the poetry that flows effortlessly from our

embrace. *So I offer this Tanka (the traditional five line Japanese poem) with*
pure Love from me, from the One.
Namaste ~ Om Shanti ~ Love,
Karl

<u>No One's Breath is Like Yours</u>

When I hold you, the Beloved
In these arms which are your arms
Seeking union, reunion
The prana of life
Is transcended.

For an eternity in this moment
You take my breath away
And with it gone
I am Witness
To the miracle of You!

For you bring life breath to me
Through how your breath is transfigured
By the Beloved that is you
In this moment
Of our embrace.

I feel at once your breath
Change unto me
Becoming ever so deep and slow rhythmically
Infinitely strong
Soft and Present

With your breathing so deep
Your center expands into mine
Then contracts with mine pursuing
Creating breath without breath
For me

And I hear a profound change
In the sound of your breath
A most primal sound
From the core of Being
Like Om in a low key

With this sound of your breath
In my ears so sweet
I sense the One, the Beloved

Birthing new galaxies, new Love
In Ecstasy

Then I gaze upon your face
And see the shadows part
To reveal
The most exquisitely beautiful soul
Looking back on me

With just one look
We find the completion we seek
In the jeweled hearts of each other
The Inner Chambers
Of the Beloved

I put the card away with the others, and cried myself to sleep. The next morning I sent Karl the first of three release letters. In one, I wrote, "I do not want to live on the razor's edge where a man I love deeply is gushing unavailable love all over me. I will not "covet another woman's husband" – I do not want a love of turmoil and constant struggle. I choose the painful path of right action."

Karl replied with his own attempt at release. The pain was almost unbearable. I wrote in my journal, "I am a lovely Rose unfolding, and sometimes I get hurt on my thorns!"

Meanwhile, the sitting ritual with Bryan had instilled a new sense of clarity in me. We agreed that it was time to end the marriage. We decided that I would move out of the house that we had lived in for almost eight years, and he would move back in. He would give me the financial value of half of the house, and that money would enable me to stay home with the boys a while longer – as well as give me time to heal and find the right career.

Later that month, as I prepared to move, I sent an email to Karl and Eric, letting them know my new address. I thanked them both for correctly holding the Divine Masculine within themselves while they were with me, because it had helped me to drop further into the Divine Feminine within myself.

Karl replied with blessings for my new home, and at the end of his letter he put the following two passages:

... To a little band of sowers has been given a handful of living grain. Faithfully it must be sown; surely, it will be reaped; and the harvest shall be for the sustenance of all... Hazrat Inayat Khan

... This rose, which from the Friend may come,
Produces a joy that often from God in my heart may come. Ever and anon, therefore, I consider it as a companion of The Beloved, So that

32

from the color of its appearance the scent of Someone may come...
Hafiz

I felt so confused by those passages. Why did he send them to me? Was there a hidden message contained within them? Was he trying to tell me that someday we would be together? I alternated between feeling hope and feeling despair.

Chapter 13 – Longing and Learning

That summer I only allowed myself a few brief contacts with Karl. In July I moved into a sweet little cottage, attended some beautiful births, and lived with an almost unbearable sadness. My longing for Karl was intense, and my dear friends supported me through it as best they could.

One night I took Anastasie and Sina out to see *What the Bleep Do We Know?* After the film they treated me to red wine at an Italian restaurant, and I told them the whole story about Karl. I told them that acting with integrity was very important to me. They did not know (at least not consciously) that I had played out a similar story with them just a few months before when I had felt so attracted to Anastasie, but still, I felt a strong sense that telling them the story of Karl and Martha brought healing to us all.

Another night I went to see *What the Bleep Do We Know?* with Dana. After seeing it for the third time, I could more clearly see my addiction to the emotional states of fantasy and grief. I thought of an Abraham Lincoln quote: "*Most folks are about as happy as they make up their minds to be.*" I continued saying positive affirmations and setting the intention to change my addictive patterns.

I attended some workshops with Basil, and he taught me that wherever I put my attention, the energy follows. He said, "Rita, focus your attention *inside*, on the stream of Light which is flowing through you." Luna echoed him, "Rita, you are getting juicy!"

At that time, Basil began offering small, intimate Thursday evening groups in people's homes for further chanting, meditation, and spiritual inquiry. One evening I arrived early and he had a mischievous gleam in his eyes. He said, "I talked to Karl today – he's endlessly curious about you, and slightly mortified."

I told Basil that I just wanted to sit with Karl on a mountain and figure out what it was that had happened between us. Basil said, "You *know* what it was. Rita, just because two people have a deep heart and soul connection doesn't mean that they have to live together, and sometimes it's better if they don't. Still, it's going to be difficult for you two to release each other – you will need to get clear on integrity."

After we chanted to Shiva, Basil guided us through a process to find the roots of our desires. First he explained that the antidote to every desire actually lives inside us. The work is to see the desire arising and then instead of trying to satisfy it externally or mentally, to actually drop back to where it can fulfill you from the inside.

He asked each of us to tune in to a spiritual expectation that we have of ourselves. My expectation was that I would be calm. Next he said to find the desire in the heart which was behind the expectation. My desire was for utter peace. Then he said to look under the desire in the heart for the root of the desire, which he said was actually the root of the desire's fulfillment.

I couldn't find the root, and when I told him so, he tracked what was happening in me, and then he laughed, saying, "Rita, you have vital Kali energy, and you will only find utter calm and peace by letting go and going *into* your power, and on the other side of your power, your peace will come. But you have to go into your power, and not be afraid of it. Do not squelch it out of fear of being situationally inappropriate."

That night I felt so expanded. I felt wildly awesome to have manifested such a perfect teacher and support system. I felt at *Home* with the group of beautiful beings who surrounded Basil.

I wrote an email to Karl, telling him about the evening with Basil, and asking him to share how he felt toward me. A few days later he replied, "I reflected on your feelings question, and was gifted with recognition that the best answer from an integrity perspective – working well now on healing my relationship with my wife – is to just quote the great mystic Julian of Norwich: "*All shall be well, all shall be well, and all manner of things shall be well.*" I hope you will understand as a woman of great integrity yourself."

I felt disappointed that Karl did not share his feelings toward me, so I worked on finding the root of my desire. I tracked that behind my expectation of him sharing his feelings was my desire for union with a beloved and The Beloved. Under that desire was the root of its fulfillment: my own union with my own divinity and with The Divine.

Later I wrote in my journal, "I am losing my grip on reality – on what I *thought* was reality – I am feeling utterly wild and unable to settle. Go into it and don't be afraid of it, Kali!" I wrote many pages about integrity and release, and I tried hard to ground myself in the reality of my life as a mother and as the Goddess of Laundry!

At the next one-day workshop with Basil, he told the following story for me:

> *A long, long, long time ago, a starseed transmission was given to some farmers by the Mediterranean Sea. The transmission contained all of the information about the Cosmos, and once they received that information they had to migrate. They infused their daughters with an inquisitiveness, so that they would want to know everything about the universe, but every seven generations there would be a "gap girl" who could see into higher realms and understand that the mind doesn't know everything.*
>
> *So, one of these gap girls went on a trip and met a prince. Now, this prince didn't completely have his life together, but he had enough Light and the right soul frequency, so that when they met, the higher connection and the right sexual essence closed the gap for a time. It was at just the right time, at just the perfect moment in her opening... But then our gap girl got into trouble, because she tried to figure it out with her mind. And now, after she lets go of her mind and embraces the wonder of life, there will be stars shining in her belly.*

Basil explained that the gap between the embodied soul and the Great Soul produces pain and suffering, but in reality it is not an either-or situation. Rather, it is a dynamic, interdependent *Field* in which the universal and the particular hold each other. He said that true faith – that we are Held by Something Greater – is born of experience. The alchemy of one's own experience – that there *is* a greater holding – has a maturity to it.

At the lunch break I asked Basil if he had anything to tell me, since he had just led a workshop in San Diego the weekend before. He smiled and said, "You and the prince have already achieved a high connection, and now it's driving you both crazy. It doesn't mean that you need to manifest any particular form together, but the connection needs to be authenticated."

During the afternoon session someone asked about the correct alignment of masculine and feminine energies. Basil said that the feminine should hold an energetic field of presence for the masculine to rest in. When he explained that the male and female together is rhythmically more complete in both beings, he looked at me and saw the intensity of my longing. He said compassionately, "Rita, for the 'perfect man syndrome,' let all men fully blossom in your heart."

Before the last chant, he said, "All actions bear fruit. All that longing is noticed by the Universe. Negotiations with the Universe never work. We have to cultivate a spilling-over of gratitude and noble intent behind our actions. And remember, what's going to show up is infinitely better than our constructs."

At the next evening group, Basil said that I had been too dependent on my vision – that I was using sixteen scans all the time in an attempt to see a depth that I expected to see. He said that I energetically tracked people on sixteen different tracks, trying to extract their essence. I said that I was not aware of doing that, and I wondered how I could stop doing it. He said that it was not bad that I did that, it was just intense, and that was why some people gave me weird feedback. He explained that it was just me looking for the depth that I really wanted in myself. He said, "Allow yourself to be 1/16th imperfect, and the other 15/16ths can be perfect!"

Later that night, Basil described the most powerful state as the *inaction* of a surrendered being. He said that once we surrender to cosmic forces, then we don't have to *do* – then it's just being done, and we are in Bliss. He talked about how in psychology there is this illusion that we can make ourselves better – that we can control reality – but the truth is that at a certain point we have to let go of *doer*-ship. Purposeful will is not enough. The impulse to let go of our conditioned states starts the process, but deep surrender then has to happen. And, because this is a conscious Universe which listens, once true surrender happens, the whole thing then unfolds from the inside out.

That rang so true in my heart. In fact, just the day before I had thought of an idea for a film sequel to *What the Bleep Do We Know?* The title for the film would be *Held By Something Greater*, and it would focus on the Heart. At that point in my process of opening, I had become acutely aware that we *can* change our realities with our minds, but that kind of change is very limited and reveals a lack of deeper faith. When we relax into the true essence of our hearts, we then get changed by That which is holding us.

At the next evening group, Basil offered me another tool for closing the gap: fusing the perceiver and the perceived. He instructed me to first feel the room very crisply, and then to feel Rita, and then finally to feel both the room and Rita at the same time. I practiced that for a few minutes, but then he launched into another story for me:

> *Once a young woman went down to San Diego, and she cast her net, which she had been making for a long time, and she caught a silver fish. The fish was attractive and wise. She came home and said to her friends, "Look! I caught a fish," but there was nothing there. For eleven nights she practiced: open. close. grasp. let go... and then she figured out (and six of her women friends confirmed this to be true based on their experiences with men) that she needed to give him some space...*
>
> *On the twelfth night, she cast her net, reached in, and felt something. She knew that since it was magic, she could not look at it, so she asked her eldest son to look and tell her what it was. He said, "It's a little **prince**! He is two inches high! Can we play with him?"*
>
> *She wanted to look and she even thought of maybe holding up a mirror, but then she thought that would be cheating. So she put him on the shiny polished desk without looking, and she went to bed. What else could she do?*
>
> *Sleep was always interesting for this woman, and in the morning she awoke to find that she could not move. She couldn't talk or call for help. Then she realized that she was **inside** the Prince! He had grown so big, since she wasn't watching him, that now she was inside him. She couldn't move.*
>
> *Then finally she figured out a new thing to try which she hadn't thought of before. She went into the most tender place in her heart and she felt the pure love – the true love – for him, with no grasping and no attachment. This tickled his tummy and he laughed until she was laughed up and out of him.*
>
> *She turned around to look at him, since she figured that now that she had been inside of his belly, she could look at him. She turned around... and she saw... a shimmering reflection of herself.*

Tears streamed down my face as Basil finished the story. He smiled and said, "Rita, you *are* too much, so you can just relax about that. You are a being which is meant to expand. Once you close the gap, you won't be too much for people. People receive mixed signals from you because they feel your intensity but then they feel you putting a lid on it. They will love your intensity when you learn to be fully in it without putting a lid on it."

As I was leaving that night, Basil said, "Sixteen times, Rita." And I said, "Just now? There's nothing to do about it?" He said, "Just be aware of it, and when you understand all of the dimensions which exist within you, your journey will be over."

In the days that followed, the truth of the fish/prince story settled into my being, and I was able to find the most tender place of love in my heart for Karl. Luna stopped by for tea and she brought a cute little picture of a prince that Basil had drawn for me. At the top, he had written, "Rita's Own Prince."

Luna offered me her own bit of wisdom: "Rita, if it wasn't Karl, it would be someone else, like Anastasie. He is just fuel for your fire." I thanked her for that, even though I didn't quite believe her at the time.

That night, I called Basil in tears over Karl. He said tenderly, "Rita, don't fret. It's going to be okay. Sometimes you just have to let it go through you, without sixteen-layer-analysis."

The next night I held a gathering at my new cottage. My girlfriends brought food, flowers, and blessings, and Basil arrived at the end of the evening to lead a chant. We all sat in a circle on the grass in my backyard, and Basil strummed his guitar as I introduced him to those who did not already know him. I said that I felt like the Universe was smiling upon me – like I had done something right to have met such a wonderful teacher and friend.

Basil smiled, and then he told this housewarming story for me:

> There was once a girl in a village who had sixteen shoes. Only she didn't know she had them. Each day when she put on two shoes, at least one of them was on backwards, and as she left her house, there was an eggbeater in the front door which spun her around and then she spun out into the world, looking like a forward-going girl.
>
> Then, one day, when she woke up, she felt so much excitement and exuberance for the day, that she bumped her head. Then she looked down and saw the sixteen shoes. 'Well, what is this?' she thought. She put on some shoes, with both of them pointing forward, and when she got up, since she wasn't used to having both shoes on forward, she tripped.
>
> When she went out into the world, instead of looking like a forward-going girl, like usual, she looked disheveled. But now, instead of going out into the world trying so hard to be what she wasn't, now she could go out into the world and be exactly who she was.

I was breathing in deep gratitude for that story when Basil said to the circle, "The way Rita energetically goes in on people with sixteen tracks has a jewel-like quality to it. When she goes in on you, she organizes you, and then you feel bliss rising within yourself. She does this, but she is not aware that she does this." As he said that, I *was* aware of it, and I felt very honored by him.

As we prepared to chant *"Om Tara, Tutara, Ture, Svaha,"* Basil explained that calling on Tara, the Tibetan Goddess of Compassion, helps the day flow with delight rather than with drudgery. Therefore, this was a good chant for a home-holder with two children.

Several people, including Basil, left after the chanting, but Luna, Anastasie, and Sina stayed for a while longer. We lit candles all over the cottage, and I burned sage, smudging all the corners, while they played bells and drums in all the corners. Luna chanted, "Out with the old! In with the new!"

I felt so blessed and expanded after that night of blessings, but unfortunately the next contraction arrived by the end of the week. The longing for Karl returned with intensity. The pain felt seering, and the worst part was that my four closest friends were out of town. In a moment of desperation, I called a woman named Ari, who I had met in Basil's circle, and she came over for tea the very next morning.

After listening to the Karl story, Ari encouraged me to take the experience and pull it in and use it for finding my own wholeness. She said that the integrity or wholeness in myself would be to really go into it and feel it and not waste the gift. She asked, "How can you hold it and use it to benefit yourself?" Then she announced gleefully, "You get YOU – you get to *be* the Rose, to find wholeness in yourself first, and then later you will find it in another."

She told me about a Rumi passage in which he says *if we need to burn, then burn, but don't fuel the fire with more logs... and then God will come with the refreshing cup of water.* I reflected that that was exactly what had happened with Anastasie, and I hoped that the same thing would happen soon with Karl.

Ari suggested that I ponder questions about Love. Could I open my lens about what I thought love was? Could I have the patience to wait and not know which lifetime we might be together? Could I realize that maybe we are meant to fall in love with many souls?

She also advised that I hold Karl and Martha's marriage of twenty-four years – that I offer service to their relationship by holding it with love. She encouraged me to be loyal to Martha first, as a woman and as a sister. She said, "Twenty-four years – that's a lot of living. Rita, have respect for *time*."

As she left, Ari said, "This is a high spiritual calling – and a difficult one. I'm glad it's not me!"

In the following days I began lighting candles for Karl and Martha, and I found myself saying again and again, *"Om Shanti, dear Karl, Om Shanti, dear Martha."* At the same time, I continued longing for him and trying to release him. I wrote in my journal, "It's not up to me. It's not up to Karl. It's not up to Martha. We are all being Held by Something Greater. We are being orchestrated. Cultivate patience, trust, and surrender."

I wanted to communicate with him, but I was navigating my way through a sticky labyrinth, trying to get to the integrity in the center, so I somehow restrained my longing for contact. Again and again, I worked through the grief, and continued to focus my attention on the rest of my glorious life.

Julianna nurtured me with her endless beauty. One day she brought me a Rumi poem which said "*Joke with torment brought by the Friend.*" It also said, "*the moment we accept the troubles we've been given, the door opens.*" The poem ended with this phrase: "*the sweetness that comes after grief.*" (Excerpted from *The Illuminated Rumi*, by Jalal Al-Din Rumi (Author), Michael Green (Illustrator), Coleman Barks (Translator), Broadway Books.)

The intense waves of grief weakened my lungs. Despite the strength of the summer sun, I got terribly sick for several weeks. During that time my high school sweetie, Danny, appeared in my dreams. I sent him an email to share that he was in my dreams, and he wrote back, "Are you coming to town soon?"

I started planning a trip to Wisconsin for my Grandma's upcoming 90th birthday in November. Fantasizing about having a good heart connection with Danny eased the pain and grief over Karl's absence, but the longing for Karl continued.

Chapter 14 – Longing and Releasing

It felt as though that summer would never end – it was like one long burning night of the soul for me. By day I studied midwifery and carried on with the work of motherhood, but by night I moved through intense layers of emotional and spiritual content. I wrote many letters to Karl, letters that I did not send.

I did, however, keep in touch with Karl's friend, Eric. Through emails and phone conversations, we continued to nourish our sweet connection. At first I talked with him about Karl, but then I realized that it was not fair to put him in the middle, so I told him that I would refrain from talking about Karl with him. He appreciated that.

In August I flew down to Los Angeles for a weekend workshop about water births. Some turbulence shook the plane during the flight, and I was surprised that I did not feel my usual fear of crashing. Rather, I felt myself expand into Love, with the understanding that nothing – not even death – could spiritually harm me.

While driving along the freeway, I saw an advertisement for a blackberry dessert on a billboard. The sign read *"How quickly we forget the thorns."* I thought, 'Isn't that the truth in love?'

After the workshop ended, I spent an afternoon at the ocean. The salt water and palm trees filled me with peace, and I returned home feeling a bit stronger. However, after just one exhausting day with my boys, I slipped back into my old patterns and the longing for Karl swelled again. In an effort to work the grief through, I wrote many poems. I wanted to reply to his last message, but I could not think of anything to say, and I feared that even the act of writing to him lacked integrity.

The cool breezes of September finally arrived. As the summer flowers dropped their seeds, I breathed in the scent of release. With deep hope that it was indeed time to release Karl, I wrote the following statement:

Closing Statement! – I bow to what is.
I sincerely hope that Karl is healing. I pray that he can heal his wound of sadness and find joy. I hope that he and Martha find what they need to find and that they unfold just exactly as they need to unfold. May they be unharmed by all of the energy which I sent his way. May they feel only peace and goodness from me. May he and I be free of the pain. May our falling in love be authenticated in time and space and may it be for a blessing, for the greatest good of all. May we let each other go now. It was what it was. No regrets, only gratitude. And now, going-forward energy. I go forward with gusto and excitement for the mystery and unknown of this next chapter of

my life. I close that last chapter with him. He may close it, too, now.
With a pure heart full of love...
Rita

Then I wrote this prayer:

"Dear God, I am so grateful for this settled feeling. In this cottage which holds me, I am finding the calm, the healing, the bliss I seek... in this simplicity I open more fully to the Divine Mother within... spreading shells around me, opening and inviting others to come... here in this space I have arms to hold, ears to listen, and a heart so open... I long to hold others and serve them..."

I endeavored to focus on myself, my children, my life. I prayed for the strength of mind to keep myself energetically out of Karl's energy field.

Chapter 15 – Meeting Krishna and Radha

In the following weeks I kept happening upon Lord Krishna, an incarnation of the Hindu god Vishnu. At nearly every turn of my path, there was Krishna, so I delved into him. I studied about his life, chanted to him, and taught my boys the stories of his mischievous youth. Joshua and Benjamin loved hearing about the little boy Krishna stealing the butter and fighting off the demons. They pretended to be the divine brothers, Balarama and Krishna. I delighted in their play, even as I myself pretended that Karl was Krishna and I was Radha.

Krishna lived in India about 5,000 years ago. Thousands of young cowherd girls called "gopis" adored Krishna; they rushed to be near him whenever he played his divine flute. Krishna especially fell in love with a cowherdess named Radha. The love they shared was divine and they bowed to each other, even though life pulled them apart and they could not be together.

Just as I was really feeling my way into the Krishna-Radha story, I attended a weekend workshop with Basil. The first night he told a story in which Krishna was tucked in the middle, as if just for me. I learned that Krishna was a *blue* being who wore a peacock feather in his hair. That really struck me because I had experienced the love with Karl as being "sparkling blue light."

The next day Basil explained that our higher Self is actually doing it all, and we are unfolding more than we know. Then he looked at me and said, "You are a creative writer, and once the writing finds a place to land, it will make it easier for you to talk with others socially, because then there won't be so much needing to get out."

At the morning break, Basil told me to really *feel* all the beings in the room – to feel each being's heart with my heart. He predicted that many layers of grief would wash through me that day, and he was right. It was definitely a day of purification for me. I cried during most of the chants, as the waves of grief swelled in me.

When I got home that night I felt a bit depressed. I lay on the couch thinking that if Luna or Eric would call, then I would take that as a sign from the universe that everything was all right. Within five minutes, Luna called! After we chatted, she put Basil on the phone. Even though I was not planning to attend the next day of the workshop, he encouraged me to go. Basil said, "Even a couple of hours would be good, to help you ground all that purification you did today." As we hung up, he said, "Good work, Rita." I felt such gratitude for Luna and Basil being in my life.

The next morning I realized that he was right – I needed to go for the afternoon. I brought a basket of chocolates and ginger cookies, which were well received, and settled into the chant and meditation.

Basil then guided us in a recapitulation of this lifetime. While lightly strumming his guitar, he said softly: *"What is building you? Feel back to the moment of your conception. Then feel yourself growing in your mother's womb – feel the cells differentiating, the limbs forming, the organs differentiating, the heart beating... feel your mother's emotions... now feel the contractions and feel yourself going down the birth canal and being born. Now feel your childhood and adolescence and adult life up until now – let the images come from your life. All throughout keep asking yourself, 'What is building me?' and notice how we are not building ourselves, but rather, we are being built."*

As I relaxed into that recapitulation process, my mental chatter faded away, and, I could feel the intensity of the Love between my parents at the moment of my conception. I could also feel my mother's intense excitement during the pregnancy and birth. Now I finally understood where all of my excitement came from! My Mom's excitement got imprinted on my cells and it washes through my structure and through my life. During that process, I also sensed my own excitement – I could feel that I really *wanted* to come here.

Next Basil talked about how the mind becomes that which it dwells upon. He described a good yoga practice in which you turn your attention to where the *Shakti* is working in you, by asking if it is in your heart, mind, or emotions, or is it in your subtle body or in your life situation? He said to first tune in to the breath and heartbeat, and then feel where the life force is acting. I shared that for me it felt like it was in lots of places at once and way out there. He agreed that was true.

Basil said that the Shakti, the Divine Feminine Energy, has tremendous intelligence and It holds an incredible desire to protect its beings. He said, "When a being turns its attention away from its own content and realizes that it is *not* creating its own reality, in that moment of turning around, the being gets protection, and then instead of eating its karma, its karma starts to burn."

Before leaving that day, I asked Basil about the meaning of a passage from the *Bhagavad Gita*. Chapter 2, Verse 11, reads:

> *The Blessed Lord said:*
> *You are mourning when there is no cause to lament,*
> *And yet you speak words that seem to be wise.*
> *The truly wise lament neither for the living nor the dead.*

Basil said, "He was talking to yogis who had already burned through and were living in advanced states of consciousness. The rest of us have to go through the purifications until our vehicles are ready to break through. Rita, you are purifying. Let the waves of grief wash through you, and at the same time, anchor to Something Deeper."

In the following days, I practiced anchoring to Something Deeper as the grief and anger cycled through me. I focused on cultivating patience and respecting time. On my daily walk, I practiced feeling people's energies and vibrations. I delighted in the wooshes and swooshes and other sensations that I experienced in my body when I tuned in to other people's energies.

I felt a lot stronger in myself after that weekend workshop. One day I met Julianna, Luna, and Basil for lunch. Basil kept saying how cute I was, and Julianna said, "Yes, she is off the scale of brightness."

Even with all that strength and brightness, within only a few days the desire to contact Karl resurfaced. I again asked Basil for guidance. He suggested that whenever I thought of Karl, to feel the love of our connection in my heart, and then let Karl's physical form dissolve into Krishna. I tried that technique, but the grief and anger were too strong. I just wanted to know what Karl was feeling so that I could know *what* I was grieving. I thought that if I knew his heart, my process could be clean and complete.

A painful migraine topped off the contraction I was already feeling. I put my feet into a basin of hot salt water and sipped a cup of hot tea. The Yogi Tea bag read, "*A plant can't live without roots. Your soul is your root.*" I turned on a Krishna Das CD and sang along. Those chanting CDs were one of the few places I could find solace, although the grief was always there.

I wished I was dead... but not really, because I knew that if I died I would just carry on with the same issue into my next life – that there wouldn't really be any relief in death. What I actually wanted was for my suffering to die. I wanted to burn through and be free of the suffering of the human condition. I felt pissed off and highly agitated about the contraction I was in.

Basil sent an email in which he wrote, "Focus on your own empowerment. Place your longing in the true container of the Self. Turn inward. Use your breath to stabilize your mood. Anger and grief are endless. They loop through the limbic system like a hurricane that will not abate as long as the soul is not emerging into its purpose. Stay creative."

I called Basil and we talked further about my desire to contact Karl. Even though Basil said that I liked to "spin out on this," and he advised me to "own my projection into the feelings and intensity," I still thought that I needed some contact with Karl in order to feel completion. I felt increasingly bold and fiesty. A new perspective on the integrity issue was rising in me. I suddenly decided that I also mattered in the story, not just Karl and his wife.

Three months had passed since Karl had sent me those passages by Hazrat Inayat Khan and Hafiz, but I was still churning over them, and I desperately yearned for some resolution. So I sent an email that kicked off a short little round of correspondence.

Finally Karl shared his feelings. He wrote, "The truth in my Heart is that what I experienced in our souls' gaze is Love of The Divine, love of your divine soul, love of you. That is unchanging, unchangeable. And, though it pains me beyond words, my heart tells me that we cannot be together in the physical realm. I bless you and release you. And, I will continue to send you prayers for the bliss of divine physical union and reconnection to the Love you experienced without reference. I sense the veils are ever so thin for you, just waiting to part for good. You are so amazing!"

I cried as I read his P.S. which was in response to me asking if I was just another 'gopi' in his life. He wrote, "You are Radha, you are not just one of the many gopis. Manifest Her in this world – as you already have begun –

45

so that you may transcend the grief, so that the world may transcend the grief of too much loss."

In my reply, I wrote, "Thank you very much, from the depths of my heart, for that note. Of course the Universe is listening, as I am going to Berkeley this weekend with my dear friend Julianna. We are planning a pilgrimage to the Krishna temple! I will offer flowers of gratitude that I am Radha."

The trip to Berkeley filled me with delight. Julianna and I had such fun visiting the Indian sari shops, tasting the delicious South Indian cuisine, and chanting Hare Krishna at the temple. During that worship I felt such life and fire and vibrance.

While Julianna worked on her Indian dances, I spent time writing at coffee shops. One afternoon, over a strong pot of tea, Julianna's dance teacher offered a bit of wisdom which really struck a chord in me: "*Keep your mind on God. If your mind is on God, it doesn't matter what circumstances are in your life.*"

I returned to my lovely cottage near the sacred mountain feeling calm and centered. I felt ready to face the next chapter of my life in Mt. Shasta. I did not anticipate that the next chapter would begin the very next day with an email note from Karl. I thought that we were 'done' and that the grief was behind me. I was wrong. Here is the message I received:

Subject: Flowers of Gratitude for Radha – Sorry for the need to ask
Dear Rita of Radha Becoming,

My apologies for writing just now, but you were in my thoughts and prayers this weekend while I was out in the wilderness on a personal retreat. I returned home last night with the sense I should check in.

Was your pilgrimage to the Krishna temple as valuable as I sense it to be?

No need to write back until you are ready if and when that time comes.
Blessings to the greater You emerging.
Namaste~Om Shanti~Love Always,
Karl

I wept deeply after I read that note. I realized that I *had* to find the strength to stop that love affair with a married man. I did not reply. For nearly three more months I rode the waves of grief and longing.

I continued the study of Krishna and Radha, and I took solace in the absolute totality of their Divine Love.

Chapter 16 – Support and Teachings

The boys and I settled into the rhythms of autumn, and I studied with Basil whenever possible. One evening, Basil gave a lecture about guru tests. He said, "You can tell that you are being tested by a Guru – within or without – when there are signs that you are being both tested *and* supported at the same time." Then he looked at me and said, "Rita, integrity is strong in your line of ancestors. At the time of Self-Realization, you may get to know *why* you are being tested about integrity."

Next he explained that all of our thoughts, feelings, and states are being witnessed. He laughed as he advised, "Remember that, when you are in twitdom and feeling contracted and isolated!" And again he reminded us that when we surrender, the Force Greater than us (which is actually intelligent) *listens*.

Later, I wrote in my journal, "I am being tested by Something Greater to bring forth a capacity in me... empower myself... let my soul merge with its purpose... focus on myself, my children, my career, my Krishna!"

A few nights later, I slipped into a little contraction in which I was longing and burning for heart and soul connection with a man. I created a fantasy in which Karl was buying me wild jewelry and colorful costumes, and we were sharing a beautiful, artistic life together. I cried over his absence. Just then the phone rang. When I heard Eric's voice on the line, my whole being relaxed. It was so lovely to connect with him again, and I felt that his call was proof that I was being supported even as I was being tested.

The next evening group with Basil fulfilled me deeply. When I first arrived, I told Basil how tired I was feeling, and he said, "When you say that you are tired of feeling tired and that you have felt tired all of your life, it's a script, and it isn't helpful. Sweep through your being and find where you are connected." I did that and I melted into Love and good energy. Suddenly I did not feel tired at all.

During the first chant, I felt an opening in my crown chakra, and then that opening cascaded down through my chakras, and I felt a clean, spacious feeling throughout my being – like a flooding of Shakti in my light body.

Throughout the evening Basil kept calling me a "love puddle." That made me laugh, but then when he talked about how the mind always seeks confirmation of its state, I felt sad. I thought of the difficult pattern with my boys. I shared: "When I get overwhelmed with the boys, I shut down and then I can't connect with them, and then they act badly, which confirms the negative thoughts I'm having, such as 'See, I'm a bad mother. I should not have had kids. See, I'm too tired. See, I can't handle this.' And then it's a downward spiral from there."

Basil looked at me with such compassion. He said, "Their whining and fighting *does* have an effect on you, and you have to reconnect within

47

yourself and with God to the same degree that you get disconnected. You have to rest each afternoon and you have to do your practices."

The next day my crown chakra still felt very open, but my body felt heavy and tired, and my mind felt scattered. I had a sense that I was busy – in my sixteen-layered being – integrating all the teachings from the night before. I felt discombobulated. And, I felt pain around the issue of men not *seeing* me. I wrote, "I think I have always been too much for men. The ones who *have* seen me (somewhat) were not able to *meet* me. They did not have the capacity to be with my power and not be afraid of it. However, I think Karl would be able to meet me without fear."

Even as I longed for Karl, the integrity issue caused me to push him away. As a distraction, I fantasized about Danny. I wrote letters to Danny in my journal, and I looked forward to seeing him the next month during my visit to the Midwest.

Danny also seemed interested in me. In an email message he wrote that he was looking forward to seeing me again, now that eleven years had passed since we had talked and kissed at our last class reunion. I felt open to a heart connection with him, even as I wondered if I was just manifesting yet another magnetism to yet another person. Maybe I was just needing to eat through that particular flavor of karma?

Luna's Mom came to visit on Basil's birthday, and we all went to dinner at a Thai restaurant in a nearby town. I ended up sitting next to Basil, and so the whole dinner experience turned into an opportunity for the mentor to guide the student. He pointed to the large fish tank beside our table and said, "Rita, the secret to your relationship with men is embedded in that sea coral."

At first I felt a bit annoyed with him for giving me a teaching in that moment, but then I told myself to be strong and hold the assignment. I stared at the coral, but I couldn't get anything with my mind. Luna's Mom said, "The coral is firmly planted and receptive, like the feminine, with little tickles fluttering at the top, saying, 'come here,' but not going out to "get" the masculine."

Basil nodded and advised me to *embody* the coral, so I just looked at it and let it in without using my mind, and then my heart chakra got all gushy. I told Basil that, and he said, "That's better." Then he kept telling Luna that I was "insufferably cute." Luna laughed and said that *he* was insufferably cute the way he said that.

On the way home that night I told Basil about my fantasy of being with Danny. I told him that I just wanted to be held in Danny's strong arms. He reacted to that, saying that I wanted to *use* Danny. I felt defensive, so I explained that I really did feel Danny's heart and essence, but then I bit my tongue and listened to the rest of his advice.

Basil talked to me a bit sternly, but with gentleness in the undertones. He said, "Rita, you create a psycho-romantic-creative-sexual construct about the person (Anastasie, Karl, Danny), and then when they can't live up to that creation, you deflate them. You are a potent being and you actually do deflate them. With Danny, given his track record of repeatedly breaking your heart, it would only be thirty percent of what a good relationship could be.

"You would have to dim your light to be with him. You are not the woman to change him, and even if you did change him, you would get pretty pissy in the process. It would not be good for either of you. You could do it, and it wouldn't necessarily be a mistake, but it would be choosing a longer way and it would cause you pain."

Basil explained that since the construct with Danny was the same as with the others, I needed to pull back the construct. I thanked Basil for his insights. That night I lay in bed wondering how to pull the construct back in.

Throughout the night, I dreamt of writing. I took that to be the 'answer' for how to pull back the construct. In the coming weeks, I spent much time alone, writing poetry.

Chapter 17 – Poems to Karl

Each day when I sat down to write poetry, I lit a candle and prayed to the Hindu Goddess of Knowledge, Saraswati. I prayed for the writing to flow through me as the vessel.

Here is the first poem that I wrote to Karl during that time:

Out in the vast vibrating universe,
a spark spun through the twirling layers
of Kali's belly,
broke free
and,
spiraling through stardust tunnels,
resonated with an intense excitement
within a deep love,
and,
piercing into a moment in time
landed
rooting itself in the splendor
of a cell.

The cell divided
and divided again –
embryo to fetus,
contractions to birth.
This birth so different
than previous ones.
Evening, but not dark –
Bright lights,
machines,
nausea.
Where is my mother?
An eternity in that night
of waiting –
Strange women in white,
plastic nipples,
cowmilk tweeked,
nausea.
Where is my mother?

Morning.
Mother,
breastmilk.
Relief.

Love.
Father.
Cornfields,
cows,
Is this home?
Big family,
Love,
Catholic Church.
Devotion,
prayer,
I know God.
Sense of purpose,
deep feeling of mission on Earth.

Hunger for the masculine began early.
At nine years old,
overcome with desire
for Chuck Jones,
star of Senior Play,
Charlie Brown.
At fourteen,
Danny –
I see you,
you don't see me.
Confusion growing. Clear purpose fading.
At nineteen,
Michael is home.
Four years later,
three thousand miles from cornfield birth,
"I can't be your friend."
Ah, you don't see me either.
Grief swollen for a whole year,
tears soaking the streets of the Southern City.

Finding my ground again in a mountain village,
then a karmic dance
with Bryan –
marriage, two sons,
deep struggle,
lightening flashing danger signals in brain,
trapped in dream of planet,
nausea.

Ten times past the harvest moon,
reality cracked,
trails of release and freedom opened,

healing began,
the path turned from confusion
back to purpose.

Following calling
to workshop in the Southern City,
I see you,
and,
you see me.
I know God.
Back in the mountain village,
the grief swells in waves.

One bright day,
I walk past my altar of devotion,
then turn back quickly
my eyes drawn to a photo on the wall
a woman sits between two men
in a vegetarian café
a painting of bright red poppies
drapes their shoulders.
The three beings appear happy
but I know their pain
and I see vividly
that the woman and the man to her left are deeply in love.
They cannot be together –
the beauty and sadness sparkles around them
in blue light.
I want to cradle them both
in the warm embrace of the Divine Mother
within me,
saying, "There, there. God will hold this love."
The woman, who is me,
lives life with gusto, gratitude, and grief.
In my journey toward healing and wholeness,
I offer this collection of poems,
these letters to my beloved,
*who is not **my** beloved,*
as a prayer for all beings
to find themselves
free
and full of bliss
in moments of time.

Dear Karl,
I bow to what is.

I wash my hands clean, wash my spirit clean,
of the love with you.
I sincerely do not want to cause pain
to anyone,
especially you and your wife.
I wish you all the best.
I accept your truth now,
I trust you now,
but I did not always feel this way,
and I share with you now
a collection of letters
stained with my tears
and perfumed with the rose petals of my garden...

****

I wrote many of these poems by candlelight in my cottage while sipping warm milk with ghee, honey, and spices. As I wrote, I studied the images of Hindu gods and goddesses on my colorful walls, and I allowed the passion within to merge with the pen and paper.

Dear Karl,
You sit under a Canadian sky tonight
with my dear friends
surely you are well
I feel as though
I am burning up
going crazy
my being ripping open
and scattering
to the four directions
there I lie
like seed corn
dry
and thirsty
for you
will you gather me up
and fill me
with drink?
such a feeling of discontent
I have never known –
an entirely new feeling
of wanting to expand out
into the whole
and be free of this contracted existence –

53

is that why we were called to meet?
so that I could begin to feel my way
into finding expansion
within the contraction that is being
in this body?
my longing for you is intense.
I have a continuous urge to bow down on the ground
begging for mercy from God.
I am burning,
Rita

****

Dear Karl,
tangerines bursting
and sandalwood scent
come to mind tonight
when I think of you.

I am alone
on a sandy desert
the wind is blowing
sand in my eyes
I am choking
on my tears
the air is sultry.

I have been
waiting for you to come
but alas
you are not coming
again
this has happened
before
do you remember?
we've had broken promises
and impossible appointments
before
and I'm only just
tasting a glimpse of them now

not that they matter
anymore
the longing is the same
only the scenery changes

the ocean breeze
greeted my tears
with recognition
but the desert wind
fights my tears
with rage

here in this place
surrender is wicked
I fight God
I fight myself
I fight you,
the you of my dreams.
The you I remember
and long to forget.

I am choking on sand –
thirsty for you –
for the endless beauty
of your blue ocean eyes,
for your tenderness,
and now the pain
of its withdrawal

I spin in the chaos,
waiting and wondering,
Rita

       ****

Dear Karl,
Integrity means wholeness.
When we are still connecting on many levels,
is holding back on communicating really helpful?
Or is it merely the perception of integrity?
What is the right action here?
For myself,
for my journey toward wholeness,
I feel the need to name what is happening in me.
I am struggling.
I am holding back a bold river with my bare hands.
It is at once altogether new territory, and completely familiar terrain.
In this letter, I let a trickle of those waters seep through these fingers.
I offer you my truth –

I offer you flowers of gladness
rivers of joy and sorrow
and a love so deep
that the tenderness of that love
is oh so painful.
The panic comes in waves
as does the burning...
then, by the grace of God
I find myself
holding you and your wife Martha
in peace.
May you find peace with your path,
Rita

****

Dear Karl,
Someday I will give you a book of these letters.
I will press roses on the pages which will be wet with my tears.
I have seen us in a vision
and it makes me crazy
to not know,
to not trust my intuition.
I miss you so much –
such burning
such longing
I must be crazy!
Somehow I march forward,
with enthusiasm and gratitude,
doing the work,
living the Beauty,
holding the sorrow.
Oh, how I miss your voice and eyes.
I love you,
as ever,
Rita

****

After writing so much poetry, I did feel new healing energy stirring within, but I could not deny that I still felt grief over Karl, curiosity over Danny, and a growing connection with Eric.

Chapter 18 – A journey home and willful releasing

As I prepared for my trip home to Wisconsin, Eric and I started talking on the phone more often. He said, "Talking with you expands my mind." As he told me about the anxiety he was feeling in his life, I longed to hold his pain in the warm embrace of the Divine Mother within me. In my heart I felt such a tenderness toward him. He told me that I sounded "unencumbered." I was indeed feeling lighter.

On Halloween, I went to see an artsy film called *I Heart Huckabees*. It felt good to laugh out loud. I came away from the film asking myself one of its central questions: "*How am I not myself?*" I reflected that I felt most my juicy, happy self when I was writing and when I was chanting to Lord Shiva. I felt Held by Something Greater in the spiritual sense, but in the physical sense I still longed for touch. I felt lonely and I longed for the calm strength of masculine support. I longed to be held by a man.

The next day when I went out on my walk, I passed two men digging in the dirt. They smiled and spoke with me, and it felt nice, but as soon as I passed them, I burst into tears. I thought, 'They are so beautiful. The masculine is so beautiful. Oh, I am so lonely. I wish I could stop wanting Karl. Before I met him, I didn't know that he was possible, but now that I know, how can I stop wanting him? Can I find a way to feel held by my own masculine energy so I won't hunger for it so strongly out in the world?'

Later I wrote in my journal, "I am in a deep winter cave of longing and sorrow. When will the spring bird sing release in my heart?"

The week before my trip home, Bryan and I signed the papers of marriage dissolution at his attorney's office. I felt glad to be one step closer to divorce. I no longer felt afraid of the word divorce.

Although Bryan had offered for both boys to stay with him, at the last minute I panicked and took Benjamin with me. He actually turned out to be a fun little side-kick and I was glad that I brought him along.

We stayed at my parent's house for a week and I basked in the glow of family love. One afternoon while Benjamin played with his grandparents, I treated my three younger brothers to a movie. It was my fourth time to see *What the Bleep Do We Know?* That time I felt such compassion for the protagonist, Amanda, and I cried deeply when they said that there would be no God waiting to punish us.

When I heard that there would be no God waiting to punish us, I felt relieved. Suddenly I understood that I was not a sinner for falling in love with a married man – God guided us to meet, and, difficult though it was, I was learning to let God hold the love.

At my Grandma's 90th birthday party, I delighted in her beauty. At the dinner table, surrounded by our loving family, I whispered in Benjamin's ear, "Take in this moment and remember it for all of your life. Look at the candles burning brightly in the center, look at your Great Grandma's eyes sparkling with laughter, look at your uncles and great aunts and cousins and grandparents. Look at that seven-week-old baby girl sleeping in her papa's arms. Feel all the love in this room and remember this family."

The next day Danny (my high school sweetie) picked up Benjamin and me to go for a little hike in a woodsy park. It was a beautiful autumn day and we talked as we pushed Benjamin's stroller along the leafy trail. Then we went inside a warm coffee shop for mugs of hot cider. Benjamin and Danny colored pictures together while we talked.

There was one moment, when Danny and I were looking into each other's eyes, that I felt the love of his heart, but most of the afternoon I sensed that we did not have a very deep connection. He did say that I was cute a few times, and we did flirt around a little, but mostly I realized that we were not meant to be together again.

That night I lay beside Benjamin and cried quietly. I felt such sadness over being so cute and yet so alone. I wondered why was I so cute? What purpose did being so cute serve?

The next day I felt gratitude for the connection with Danny. I felt a sense of completion with him.

On the day of our flights back West, I really enjoyed watching all the people in the airports and on the airplanes. As I tuned in to the love of all the hearts, I felt incredible love in my being.

Julianna picked us up from the airport and made us dinner. I told her about how I had been crying over being too cute and asking why was I "insufferably cute." She said wisely, "Rita, go ask a flower. Go ask a wild rose out in the forest who no one ever talks to... well, except the insects and butterflies talk to it..."

Once I settled back into our little life by the silent healing mountain, some powerful energy states started moving through me. First I felt intense anger that I was *still* thinking about Karl. As I delighted in the anger, it transformed into a gnarly good Kali state of bliss, laughter, and crazy energy flowing through me. Joshua and Benjamin loved it. When I first let my wildness out, Benjamin dove into it – literally, he dove into me! We fell on the kitchen floor together, and both boys swam like little frogs in the river of my ecstasy! I felt so free.

I pulled down Karl's photo and ripped it into little pieces which I then burned in the kitchen sink. I said, "I release you, and I am sorry that it is with anger." I prayed to an evening star that I would be free of him when I woke up the next morning.

Before bed I wrote, "My soul is in danger if I keep swimming in that grief soup over Karl. I release him with my will, and I pray that my heart and spirit will soon follow."

The next day, Julianna and I went out to brunch and then hiked in the woods. I spread the remains of Karl's photo in a manzanita grove. Then with a static wild energy, I ran down the trail, yelling and laughing and chanting to Kali. I felt free of Karl.

That night when a few memories of Karl flashed before my eyes, the tears came quickly. I felt stuck in a painful place in which I could no longer feel the blissful freedom from the afternoon hike, and yet I was unwilling to let a wave of grief wash through. I felt so crazy. Then I felt as though Karl was standing behind me and I heard him ask "How could you just let me go like that?" I wondered if I had imagined it, or was it possible that he was somehow resisting my release of him?

I picked an angel card for the week: *Release.* How perfect. I sent Basil an email and asked him if it was just my stuff, or was Karl somehow holding me back from letting him go?

Basil replied, "Rita, true connection manifests as a descending grace that soothes the system, brings balance, and aligns one's heart... these are useful criteria to apply when considering whether this kriya with Karl is fundamental or projected drama... love, Basil"

What did he mean by *that*? I felt so dense and ashamed, like I wanted to run away from life. I reflected on the brief time that Karl and I had spent together: while I was with him I had felt descending grace and balance, but in our separation – with the confusion around the integrity issue, the worry over falling from grace, and the grief over not being in contact for long stretches – I felt out of control. I did not feel soothed.

I prayed earnestly to Lord Shiva to help me release all of my stuff around the situation so that I could feel the truth. I knew that in order to really discern the Truth, I would have to get out of the way.

Chapter 19 – A Thanksgiving that burned with the fire of true release

Even though we were almost officially divorced, Bryan and I were still friendly with each other. We decided to go together with our boys to Dana and Marc's for our annual tradition of Thanksgiving dinner with them.

I gave Dana a card in which I wrote, "I am most grateful for our friendship. It is wonderful to share this journey of mothering with you – with all its mystical and mundane aspects." Over the years, Dana and I had laughed heartily about our phone conversations – often we would be discussing some deep metaphysical idea when suddenly one of us would need to wipe a child's bottom or add the right spices to a soup!

After dinner Bryan and the boys left for another party, and I headed up to Julianna's cabin for pie and stories with Luna and Basil and a few other friends. Basil took one look at me and said, "32! – no, now it's 64!" He saw that I was tracking on many more levels than my usual sixteen. He loved to tease me about those sixteen tracks! I laughed so hard that my nervous system began buzzing, so I asked him if 64 was too many for me? He raised his eyebrows and said, "108 – *soon.*"

Next Basil told a beautiful story for Luna in which she was a jaguar in a forest. The last line of the story was: "*and then all the tasks of living and all the prayers of the heart were the same.*" Seeing the tears in my eyes, he said, "Rita, your process is so volatile – you are like hot water on a really hot griddle which keeps bubbling up and sizzling.

"You have 64 petals in your heart and under the 63rd petal there is a ladybug. But the problem with ladybugs is that they have very small wings and they fly a short distance and then land on the wall… and then they fly a short distance… and then they look up and see an eagle flying and they feel like *uhhhhh!*"

Later I asked Basil what the purpose of being insufferably cute was, and he said, "It's an invitation to maturation. Once you mature you won't be *insufferably* cute, but you will still be cute – you will always be cute."

I told Basil that I was really tired of feeling so immature, and he said, "Forward. Go forward with patience and dignity. Play with your rascal self more dynamically rather than trying so hard to pull it back."

Basil then talked to the group about the western romantic notion of pouring all of ourselves into one other being and then expecting that being to fulfill all of our needs. This notion is ingrained in the United States, but it actually doesn't make sense and most of the world finds it peculiar that we believe that way.

But then, Basil also said that eventually we have to turn ourselves over to something, and most people find it easiest to turn themselves over to another being. He added that the being we surrender to is not necessarily our life partner or lover. I wondered if he said that for me regarding Karl?

60

That full moon night I stayed in Julianna's temple. She slept upstairs with her cat, and I slept downstairs surrounded by exquisite images of Sri Krishna. The next day she and I enjoyed long hours of connection over hot tea and delicious food. We took a refreshing hike in the misty woods and later gave each other massages by candlelight. While I was touching her back, she relaxed deeply, and I joked, "I could probably have my way with you right now," and she purred back, "you probably could!"

As darkness approached, Luna and Basil arrived to have dinner with us before the evening group began. While Luna and Julianna heated the food, Basil kept calling out different words in English and in Sanskrit and asking me to do little movement phrases to express their vibrations. It was so much fun!

The first word he called out was "eternity." Basil said, "Rita, define eternity for us as you dance it." As I danced, I said, "*Eternity is the coming and going, backwards and forwards, until it comes together in a circle.*" Basil smiled at that definition.

After I performed each little dance he would tell me what the Sanskrit word meant, and it was surprising how correct my movements were, just from feeling the vibrations of the words. Basil said, "This is going to be a good night."

When the group got settled that evening, Basil announced, "Welcome to Julianna's parlor. We're going to continue a parlor game we've been playing. I will say something and then Rita will feel the vibration and put it into movement."

He then proceeded to call out phrases for each of the beings present. I danced the purity of one woman's intent, the inferiority of another woman's ancestral voice, the culmination of another woman's longing, and the capacity of another woman's heart to melt into love.

Basil explained: "All states exist as vibration, but they become action and motion. In the ancient healing temples, the temple dancers helped the people to release things by correctly manifesting vibrations through movements. This is what Rita has done here tonight."

I looked around the room and smiled at each of the sweet beings. I felt so much love there. Basil smiled, saying that those movement phrases were a way for me to let my rascal out with dignity!

Next he explained that when our fixation on our personality loosens, the emanation of the Self brings out our true purpose. It is this emanation of the Self which supports the fixation on the personality while we work through our karma. Then eventually our *essence* begins to shine through.

As usual, I was writing down every word he said. The room got quiet, so I looked up at Basil. He was looking right at me. He said, "Look at Rita, streaming essential Grace. She is almost to maturity." Then he told me to watch the movie *Gandhi*, paying close attention to how Gandhi held his energy and commanded leadership through quiet strength.

Finally we took a break for pie and tea. A woman named Diana approached me and told me that she had recently talked with Karl. She had met him on Basil's Canadian retreat. She said that Karl was having a hard time; that he was not a perfectly enlightened being. She wondered if I even knew who I was in love with? I did not understand why she said those things to me, and I got flustered by her comments.

When Diana went to get pie, I sat down and started crying. At first the cry was about Karl, but then, the longer I cried, there was no content. I wasn't thinking about anything at all. I just felt like a container which a huge swell of energy was moving through. Burning currents rushed throughout my body. Luna sat with me while I wept loudly.

Finally the cry turned into a laugh, and I laughed until I was shaking. By then, the others had finished their pumpkin pie, the break was ending, and Diana brought me a cup of steaming hot tea. We all chanted *Om Namah Shivaya* to Basil's sweet guitar notes, and I felt such grace and peace.

As Basil left that night, he put several coins into my slippers and he said playfully, "Rita's going to Bali! Rita's going to Bali!" Basil really wanted me to go with them on the Bali retreat that February. I told him that I would think about it.

It snowed up there in the woods that night, and as I drove back down into town the next morning, I didn't realize yet how changed I was. It took a few cloudy-minded days and a migraine headache, before I realized the transformation which had occurred in me. The grief over Karl's absence was transformed into pure love.

I felt in awe of that transformation. I wrote him a letter to let him know that I had felt the burning fire of true release. I wrote, "I am now holding the love which we experienced in our souls' gaze – I am holding it tenderly, yet with strength and power, and it is causing me no pain. This change is astounding to me."

I continued, "My sense is that we are in ever-present union in another realm. I continually see many shells about us… and the ocean. The past lifetimes together, the present union in an ethereal realm, and the future visions of us, all exist in one endless wave. And I do not need to act now, nor do I need to know the future. I have deep gratitude for our meeting. What a sparkling treasure. What a healing elixir."

Karl replied, "I have also just recently released you. We both know deep down that we have experienced release – and, true to our energetic union that you note, we did so simultaneously in agreement. We both know we will come together again whenever needed to do the work of God. Thank you for the gift of you. There is so much to say, but words cannot do."

That same week, the judge stamped my divorce final. I felt such relief. I felt like celebrating! I was officially divorced from Bryan and I had finally released Karl. I felt happy and free.

As I was falling asleep one night, I had the sense that once ____ ____ ____ happened, then I would have plenty of energy and I would go-go-go and I would write many things and accomplish much work. The next morning I couldn't remember what words were in those blanks!

Chapter 20 – Release one and the next one comes!

Six nights after Karl and I released each other, Eric called and we talked on the phone for over two hours. We flirted around, and I felt our connection going deeper. In bed that night I felt like I was falling in love with him and I wondered if I was creating yet another construct of psycho-romantic fantasy?

Even though Eric and I had a lot in common, he was working through some intense anxieties, and I wondered if we would make each other anxious. I knew that I needed to be with someone who was really calm and grounded – someone who would melt me in my heart and soul – someone who would get me out of my head!

I did feel calm while talking to him on the phone that night. We each relaxed into a very sweet space, and I wondered what would arise next.

The day after we talked, Eric went on a business trip for a week. I felt restless and intensely curious all week, but I did not call and leave a message on his machine because I wanted to see if he was as curious as I was.

By the time Eric returned from his trip, I was feeling quite a heart flutter and a longing to be in his arms. When he called, I shared that in our last conversation I had felt an energy shift. To my delight, he said that he had also felt something go deeper between us.

We started talking on the phone more often and we planned a weekend when he would come up to visit. We wanted to see how it would feel to spend some time together.

Eric shared about his longing for union with a woman, and I understood it as my own longing for union with a man. I felt a growing desire to be alone with Eric in time and space... and to let the whole world fall away.

I wrote Basil an email and told him about the release of Karl and the connection with Eric. I imagine Basil was laughing as he wrote the following back: "It is clear that you are wired to fall in love!" Then he gave me three pieces of advice: 1. Only think of Eric when thinking of him. 2. Bake bread daily. 3. Get a guinea pig.

I began baking bread, but I decided that I could not handle the added responsibility of a pet at that time, so I did not get a guinea pig.

While I practiced only thinking of Eric when thinking of him, I sent an email to Karl on Christmas Eve to let him know that Eric was planning to visit me in January. Karl replied, "I send you and Eric blessings as you explore great potentials together. Know that both of you are in my prayers just as both of you have been for so long."

I thanked Karl for his blessings and I stated confidently that I felt relieved that he and I were done. Just as I typed the words, "I feel like celebrating," the phone rang. It was Basil, calling from New York. He said "a little bird" told him to call. I told him about how Karl and I were done, and he said, "Rita, put your elbows together in front of your body and breathe into their union... that's good. Now, if you don't think about Karl for three days, you're done. If you think about him, you're not done." Just then we got disconnected and he did not call back. That rascal!

I felt convinced that Karl and I were done, even though I *did* have thoughts of him during those three days. Still, I was feeling so strong in myself. I felt in love with both Eric and with myself, and I rejoiced that as the year was coming to a close, I was embodying the *Freedom* of the angel card I had chosen for that year.

That night I had a dream in which Basil excitedly said to me, "You have some healing *mangas* inside of you. You will do healing work with others." In the morning I called Julianna to find out if "mangas" meant something in Sanskrit.

She did not find the word "mangas" in her dictionary, but she found that "manga" means auspicious and "mangalam" is the time at the end of a performance when the dancers thank their teachers and the gods.

I spent much of New Year's Day chanting to Hindu gods and goddesses. I had bought Krishna Das' CD, *Greatest Hits of the Kali Yuga*, for myself for the holidays, and as I sang with that CD, I could feel myself diving deeper into the Hindu Ocean.

Inside the CD jacket cover, I read this quote by a fifteenth century poet named Tulsidas: *"The Name repeated with either good or evil intentions, in an angry mood or even while yawning, diffuses joy in all the ten directions."*

As I chanted along, I felt that the veil was so thin for me; that I was so deeply with, of, and for God. I cried as I relaxed into a deeper union with the Beloved. I fell in love with Hanuman, Ram, Sita, and Durga, while still feeling in love with Krishna, Radha, Shiva, and Kali. I suddenly understood how they were all connected to each other and how they were all inside of me and outside of me.

I found my new understanding echoed in a little book called *Hindu Gods and Goddesses* by Swami Harshananda. He explains that the various Hindu gods and goddesses are like the waves of the infinite Ocean that is the One Supreme God. We ordinary human beings are like bubbles, and it is only when we bubbles get attached to the waves that we then become aware of our Unity with the Ocean.

I prayed to Shiva, the Auspicious Lord, to help me remember my unity with the Ocean – to help me remember that the True Teacher is within and without. Again and again, I offered myself to the Light and Peace of the Lord.

I picked an angel card for the New Year 2005: *Beauty*. I smiled as I prepared a beautiful pot of black-eyed-pea soup. I sipped hot tea and relaxed as I wrote in my beautiful new Rumi engagement calendar. I had a good feeling about 2005.

Chapter 21 – Connection,
Rejection, and Celebration

As the weekend of Eric's visit approached, I felt both excited and nervous. At times I thought that I was crazy for falling in love with Karl's friend. Was it really possible that I had fallen in love with both men? Was this really my life, or was I now acting in a soap opera? The connection with Karl and Eric felt very intertwined with my deep love of myself and of God. Our brief time together had been quite a Meeting, quite a joining of three souls.

Luna wrote in an email, "Knowing your deep capacity to love being in love, I hold you in the capacity of your true wisdom... may this connection with your self and with Eric be with eyes awake and streams of friendship... you deserve nothing but delightful being."

I continued baking bread, and one night Benjamin said, "This bread is yumming me out!" I shared that with Basil in an email, and he replied, "Yumming me out is a good clue that Mom might be grounding."

Eric's visit finally arrived. He brought me many gifts and we enjoyed a wonderful weekend together. We talked, we kissed, we touched, but we did not have sex. Although we were both longing for union, Something held us back.

On Saturday afternoon, I lay resting in my bed, while Eric meditated in the living room. I wrote this little poem in my journal:

Dear Eric,
You sit still on green pillow
on sea of emerald green
What do you hear?
I hear a hundred thousand
bells
ringing throughout my being
each with its own tone
some happy
some sad.
All wanting
to merge
with you.

Monday morning I drove Eric to the airport. It was a sad goodbye. On the way home I pulled the car over and had a good cry. Eric called that evening and we shared that we were missing each other.

I felt so in love and I thought that Eric felt in love too. I invited him to come up for another visit on my birthday weekend which was just two weeks away. The next day he called to say that he had thought about my invitation, and while he really wanted to see me again and to celebrate my birthday with me, he was feeling resistance to engaging in a long-distance relationship. He said he would want to date me if we lived in the same town.

I felt so crushed. Through many tears over his rejection, I made an appointment to get my hair cut. I intended to get my hair cut short, but not as short as the stylist actually cut it. I cried over my lost hair. I couldn't believe I had lost both Eric and my hair right before my birthday.

The day before my 35th birthday, I had a vedic astrology reading over the phone. The astrologer said that meeting Karl and Eric had been very good for me; that it was a dignifying experience for me. He thought that even though Eric and I did not have sex, the shakti experience with him had been good for me. He also thought that the haircut was a good move for me, that it was like getting rid of accessories – like what nuns do.

The astrologer confirmed my intuition that I should wear an emerald ring on my left middle finger. He said that wearing an emerald would help with my mothering and with my writing. With the emerald, people would start taking my writing more seriously. He also saw that wearing an emerald would help me in counseling others. He asked if I had ever considered becoming a counselor.

I couldn't believe my ears! I told him that for more than a decade I had wanted to become a counselor, but the timing had not yet been right for me to pursue graduate school.

I felt happy with the astrologer's response to that. He said, "Rita, you are a natural-born counselor. Whether or not you ever go to graduate school, you *are* a counselor. You are already a counselor – you are just uneducated and unpaid." I tucked that information away somewhere inside me, and continued obsessing over Eric.

I talked with Eric that night, and he reiterated that he did not want to pursue a relationship with me. He said, "I'm not in love with you. There is some disparity in the way we feel." *Ouch.*

When I was enduring the pain over Karl, I began a daily chanting practice. I chanted along with a five-minute *Om Namah Shivaya* chant (on Basil's CD) each morning and each night, and that chant sustained me through all the grief. With the grief over Eric, I knew that I needed more than just ten minutes of chanting each day, so I began a regular meditation practice after my evening chanting.

On my birthday, I celebrated my growth on the spiritual path. Even though I was filled with intense pain over Eric, I somehow held myself together externally. Dana and I joined Luna and Basil for a chanting concert led by a radiant Sikh woman, Snatam Kaur. Her voice soothed my soul like honey dissolving in warm tea.

After the concert, Basil looked into my grief and said, "Rita, your first lover has to be the creative descent. You should show up for it every day, and then whoever comes will not be polarized by the intensity in you."

In celebration of myself, I ordered the emerald. That night I wrote, "The more broken I become, the more whole I feel. I am holding so many opposites. And, as Basil's birthday collage for me reads, *I quench my longing in Brahma*."

Chapter 22 – Hitting the wall
and pulling the projections back in

The grief over Eric's rejection soon consumed me so totally that the Light felt utterly blocked from my soul. In that state of darkness, I wrote, "Dear Eric, with the taste of your love still fresh on my tongue, I am filled with sorrow. My dear one, I am yours, but you are not mine."

Karl sent an email checking on me. He wrote that he and I were linked as twin flames. I didn't know why he said that, but I was too depressed to even write him back.

I struggled every hour to hold life together with the boys. Joshua and Benjamin energetically soaked in my negativity, and they fought with each other a lot more than usual. Their fighting stressed me out and I yelled at them more often than I would like to admit.

I called Basil and told him that I felt as though I was unraveling. He said, "Yes, you are certifiably unraveling. The moral of this story is *Thou shalt not place false images before Me*. Rita, men are magnetic for you – you need a demagnetizer, not a haircut! But, don't worry, haircuts are good for burning old karma. You are doing great, Rita."

Later I sent Basil an email and asked him where I could get a demagnetizer. He replied, "Your demagnetizer is living right there within your creative capacity. Honor it as a gift of the gods and be disciplined in its expression each day. Treat it like a faithful lover and show up for it every day."

The next night the pain hit a most excruciating peak. I even felt suicidal. In utter despair I called Basil again for guidance. First he said to close my eyes and listen. Then he said strongly, "Rita. Belly. Rita. Heart. Rita. Throat." I breathed in the strength of my name and focused on my belly, heart, and throat. Still, the pain was so acute that I felt as though I could not take one more breath.

Basil explained what he saw happening in me: "Things that are based in projected need will fall back on themselves. The fall-back is painful. It is time for a man (and woman) fast. You have a tear in your psycho-emotional body, and you can't keep picking at the wound, or it's not going to heal. You still haven't completely healed from Karl, and now you are suffering over the loss of Eric, but *why* are you suffering? You've lost the object of your fixation, but you haven't lost the connections. You still have good connections with both Karl and Eric, but the illusion that you have lost them keeps you in a suffering state. You keep putting your energy into the wound instead of into *life*."

At that point I was crying so hard that I could hardly hear what Basil was saying, so he said loudly, "Rita, you've hit the wall! You've done well – you've hit the wall early. The weight of your projected material coming back at you is very painful. Your suffering is acute enough now to break the ego fixation, so you are now a lot closer to realizing the bigger Unity. It's like a joke – you are so close, and you don't realize it.

"I know this is painful, but this is actually the most useful stage I've seen you in. A good pain reliever right now would be for you to contemplate the deep connection you still have with the beings you've been involved with. Contemplate where the connection is living."

I told Basil that I did not know how I could heal the wound. He advised me to pick up every relationship in which I had fallen into my addictive pattern of misplaced longing, and pull back all of the projected psycho-sexual energies. He reassured me that I would feel where the connections still existed after I pulled back the projected energies.

When I had first called Basil, my boys were acting crazy, but at the end of our conversation, they were playing happily in the next room. Basil said that he could tell that I was doing better since the environment around me had settled down. He said, "The two bubbling beings in front of you are confirmation of your true nature. Rita, slow down to half of your normal speed, and feed them dinner as serving life and men. Break your personal suffering and serve them."

I thanked Basil for being there for me, and he said, "This will take time to integrate. It would be hard for you to get into another projection from this place. You will have to become really at home with yourself so that you can integrate this and start over."

That night, after Joshua and Benjamin faded off to sleep, I got out photographs of the people with whom I had played out the addictive pattern of projecting my needs. As I looked at each of the beings, I focused on pulling back all of the misplaced longing which I had put onto them.

Surprisingly, I felt the most energy coming back from Michael, the man I had followed to San Diego after college. I thought that I had released him many years before, but apparently I still needed to pull the energy back from him.

The next morning when I found myself crying over Eric again, I wrote in my journal, "Maybe now I'll learn how *not* to play with fire…"

Just then Basil called and asked if I could come to the workshop that day. I explained that I had the boys, but he said that I really needed sadhana. I knew he was right, but I felt overwhelmed by going that day. Again he said it was important that I come, if even for a few hours.

Somehow I pushed through the depression and called my dear friend Paulina. She agreed to watch my boys for a few hours that afternoon.

When I arrived at the workshop, Basil asked me to do a few movement phrases in front of the group. About thirty-five people watched as he called out some Sanskrit words and I danced to them. It felt good to move the vibrations I sensed in the words. The last word was *Saraswati*, and I was so delighted to hear *Her* name that at first I could only laugh. After I danced for that Hindu goddess of knowledge and learning, Basil said, "Rita, tonight invoke Saraswati. You are a highly sensitive psychic being, and you have to be very careful what you put your attention on."

Then he said to everyone, "The point is to wake up and pay attention to the portal of awakening. The echo of the human heart bounces off the Source of Creation. The secret in the echo is that it is all echo – everything is a reverberation of a vibration coming back from someplace. The purer you become, the more you can read the echo, and then you can see where it's coming from – it's all coming from yourself. So, follow the current of your awakening, which is uniquely known to you – you have always known it, but it may take you there differently than the way you thought."

During the tea break I told Basil about my process with pulling back the projections. I asked him if the tear in my emotional body came from my college boyfriend, Michael. Basil looked into me deeply and said, "No, the tear did not come from Michael. You came into this lifetime with the destabilization. It's from a past life in which you performed tantric sadhana and you ran too much sexual energy through form. Tantrics use the form world to become enlightened, but this is very dangerous. You were very powerful and sexy, and you got way out there with it, so you have to be careful with that energy now."

When we all sat down together again, Basil said, "You have to train your perception – I can't underline this enough. You have to have the discipline and the integrity to keep looking until you see what you see. What we place our attention on determines the driving nature of our energy. The most difficult bottle to wean ourselves from is the bottle of personal problems – they are so compelling. But once we stop seeking problems, the higher energies rebalance our beings. If you can see the matrix in which your problems are arising, then you can float your experiences in a wider context."

Someone asked Basil to define "*sadhana*" and he said, "Sadhana is the path of action which results in the realization of the Self. This is happening all the time to everyone, but you can make it cycle quicker with skillful means and skillful actions."

Julianna asked Basil to talk about attractions and aversions. He said that attractions and aversions are the fastest ways to clean our vehicles. They can be very useful to us if we go into them and let the space around them open. However, he noted that beyond attractions and aversions there lies tremendous heart in cultivating a radiant respect for the unfolding of each and every being.

Basil continued, "All significant partners in life are completely predestined, so you don't even have to worry about attractions! You can watch your dreams – the material in the dream state will show you the direction of your true motion since you can't manipulate it."

In closing, Basil explained that unconscious constellations of energy are always coming, and how we deal with them determines if we speed up or slow down our sadhana. I shared my fear of failure – I felt afraid of what I might do in the next month to sabotage the heart opening I was feeling there at the workshop.

Basil smiled at me and said, "The residual constellations of energy keep coming to all of us. Rita, you need to lighten up – the fact that you are suffering about it is proof of the integrity of your intent."

70

Next he said that the last chant would be my name. I couldn't believe it. Basil asked everyone to focus on my good qualities of power and beauty as they sang my name. He strummed the guitar and a whole room full of beautiful beings sang *"Rita"* over and over. Burning currents pulsed throughout my body and I felt as though I came home to myself. What a powerful experience.

I thanked everyone and I bowed to Basil before leaving. When I got home, I told the boys that we would make pizza to celebrate "Mama coming home to herself." I lit a candle next to an image of Saraswati and we enjoyed making pizza together. It was the most connected I had felt with my boys in a very long time.

The next day Basil called to check up on me. I told him that I was doing much better, and he said, "When you need a man to focus on, pull up Ramana Maharshi. Ramana is your new boyfriend!" I wondered aloud if I would still need a man to focus on, and he said, "Oh, you will need him because of your wiring, so go get yourself a picture of your new boyfriend!"

My "new boyfriend" was a wrinkled Indian saint in a loincloth who left his body in 1950. This was going to be interesting.

I went to the bookstore and bought *The Essential Teachings of Ramana Maharshi: A Visual Journey* (edited by Matthew Greenblatt, InnerDirections Publishing), in which I read the following quote by Sri Ramana Maharshi:

We think that there is something hiding Reality and that it must be destroyed before the truth is gained. This is clearly ridiculous. A day will dawn when you will laugh at your past efforts. What you realize on the day you laugh is also here and now.

I liked this new boyfriend! I sent Basil an email and thanked him for Ramana. I wrote, "After the experience with Eric, I'm not moving on – I'm moving *in*."

For a few days I felt strong inside myself, but then the pain over Eric rose up again. I started craving Karl's support, so I sent him an email asking him to hold me in his prayers. When Basil heard about that, he told me sternly, "Rita, the most important thing is to engage your new boyfriend, Ramana. Karl's energy is so close to yours and when you two connect, you spin out together like velcro, and then you both get very buzzy. Be careful with him – it's playing with fire."

I asked Basil about the visions I had seen of Karl and me together. He said, "If it's meant to happen, there's nothing you can do, so there's no need to worry about it. However, your tantric background makes you prone to projected visions. Tantrics create psycho-sexual visions and then the visions happen. A tantric really has to know what they are doing or there can be really bad outcomes."

Basil sighed and continued, "Relax, Rita. Stop obsessing. When you get that buzzy feeling, that means you are losing your juice into the process with Karl. It's okay for you to have contact with him if you can let it go, but keep your attention focused on Ramana!"

In the following days I endeavored to study the teachings of Ramana Maharshi. The teachings were simple, yet hard to comprehend. I felt dense, like I couldn't understand them, but I continued absorbing them because I really wanted to transcend the pain and suffering over Eric's rejection.

Chapter 23 – Support from Karl and my new boyfriend, Ramana

While I studied the teachings of Ramana Maharshi, Karl and I began an email dialogue. My intention in communicating with him again was pure – or so I thought. I simply needed support in the heartbreak over Eric.

Karl addressed me as Beloved Rita of Radha incarnating. He assured me that he was holding me in his prayers.

In my reply to Karl, I wrote, "You call me Radha, but now I actually look more like Frida Kahlo... when she cut off her hair to look like a man! I'm off to bake bread..." He replied, "I love Frida, her work, her soul's essence, so your appearance is still Divine, and you are still Radha incarnating. May your kneading ground you fully to the depths of your true divinity."

Even though I sensed that the renewal of contact with Karl might be dangerous, I continued writing him and sharing about my process. I felt like he understood me better than anyone else. In one of his messages, he wrote:

"Beloved Rita, I continue to be filled with awe by the courage and strength you show in your inner work – I can feel it whenever I connect. The old soul that you are is breaking through.

"You have been Radha before long ago and you are on the path to becoming Her fully again. I just want you to know that your Divinity is a most beautiful jewel of Light. The painful work you are doing is making such a difference within and without in this time. Trust and know you will break through to the ground of your True Self."

I thanked Karl for his support and I shared about the overwhelming depression I felt, especially during the ovulation phase of my hormonal cycles. As I was becoming evermore sensitive, I could almost feel the moment when the shift occurred – I could almost feel the hormones altering my brain chemistry.

Karl wrote, "I am reminded of a Basil story that reflects the rememberings of the Tlinglit and Salish people: *Creation is a dance on the edge of chaos; on the one side the infinite potential that may be manifest, on the other side emptiness tinged with the potential for insanity in the act of creation.*

"Because you are so sensitive and becoming evermore so, the moment of potential for creation within your womb as a woman may be what shifts you to that edge where the dance of potentials occurs. Right now, that dance feels depressing, yet it is also great joy peeking out as recognition of your divine ability to create life."

After a few more emails, Karl asked if we might talk on the phone, so that we could share our processes more at length. I felt a little confused by that. Suddenly I did not know whether or not we had truly released our attachment to each other. I wrote Karl and explained that I was not sure if I was ready to talk on the phone because I feared that talking might be a test that we were not yet ready for. What if something shifted energetically? I told him that the issue of integrity was coming up for me again.

I wrote, "If we explore a friendship and try to discern and live out how we are meant to serve each other, and in the future that exploration turns into the visions I have seen, then, upon looking back, I'm not sure if I would feel integrity with respect to Martha."

We decided to sit with our intentions for a while and to wait on talking on the phone, but we did continue the email dialogue. Somehow it felt safe to write letters.

On the Chinese New Year of the Rooster, Karl wrote, "It is interesting that it is the year of the rooster THIS year, since we were both born in years of the rooster. Another 'coincidence.' What it might mean, I know not."

I replied, "On this Chinese New Year, I am embracing my new boyfriend – Ramana Maharshi – given to me by Basil, even though I am still feeling grief over the loss of Eric."

Karl responded compassionately: "Dear Eric has inner healing work yet to do. He knows this and is working very hard on that. Past relationships, as you know, have left deep psychic scars. My sense is he knows what he must do within himself before he can engage in that way in the world again.

"I honor his strength, given not only the amazing soul that you Are, but the extraordinary physical beauty (another sign of Radha incarnating) everyone tells me you exude. It is funny in a way, but I was so struck gazing into your soul through the window of your eyes while we were together, that I barely noticed anything else about you physically! But, since several people have remarked on this aspect of you, I know it to be. So Eric's strength must be indeed superhuman!

"Ramana is a worthy 'boyfriend' for you. Basil had to choose carefully, given the scarcity of souls capable of holding you with no attachment. I am drawn to Ramana as well – no surprise."

Even as I felt supported by Ramana and Karl and Basil, I still felt very vulnerable and stressed with my boys. I shared the following with Karl: "When I am working with pregnant women or writing or interacting in the groups with Basil, I feel so whole, so connected. But when I am with my boys, in my mothering role, I feel lonely and disconnected. I really want to connect with them, but I can't. It's very painful and frustrating.

"After the last workshop with Basil, I made pizza with the boys, and I was totally present with them. I really connected with them in a way that I don't usually. I have had that experience of really connecting with them such a small percentage of the time. I know what it feels like, but usually I can't force myself to do it. It's like I just shut down."

Karl's reply surprised me. He wrote, "We share in the fact that our great gifts just now are in our work to the world and that we are most challenged in this moment on the home front. I know that we will both find the hidden pathway through, and when we do find the path through, our gifts will shine evermore brightly and purely for The Beloved and this world. I think the key for both of us (in our challenges) is the same in some sense."

That night while I lay between the boys as they fell asleep, Joshua said, "Mama, I feel sad, and I don't know why." I explained that we don't always know why we feel sad; that sadness comes in waves like the ocean waves. It comes and goes. And then I lay there crying quietly while they were falling asleep.

I wondered if integrity existed in the correspondences between Karl and me. I thought of him writing that he felt challenged on the home front. Since he and Martha did not have any children, I assumed he meant that he was challenged in his relationship with his wife. I wondered if I should just cut off the contact again. I did not want to cause a marriage dissolution.

I did not sleep very well that night, but I was gifted with an amazing experience. I'm not sure if it was an out-of-body experience or what, but it felt like much more than just a dream:

> *There was this grid which filled my room – it was all squares, and there was a bright light in the center of each square – and I have a sense that there were maybe little round peacock feathers about, like the ones Krishna wore on his head – and I went into the grid with all of my being, and Karl was in the grid of lights also, and it was a feeling of union, and of indescribable bliss, joy, love, and light...*

I shared the experience with Karl and he replied, "Your dream feels extremely powerful. My last transformationally important dream which was not a dream was very similar. It was several months ago that I experienced it:

"No one was in it and yet all of the Cosmos was at the same time. Amidst an all-encompassing midnight turquoise sky (there was no ground so 'sky' isn't really right, rather it was as if I was suspended in the middle of the Cosmos and the Cosmos was in me), soft creamy yellow points of light were everywhere and they were alive and pulsating gently. They were filling me with love, awe, and wonder. About this point I realized that I was not dreaming and still it went on. Finally, I felt the bed under me and bid farewell to the vision."

Karl continued, "Rita, remember the feeling of union, bliss, and joy that YOU were so profoundly gifted with this morning. It is The Beloved, through Krishna, reminding you that you Are that in your essential nature, you always have been that. That is in fact what I 'saw' and experienced when I gazed into your eyes and found your stunningly beautiful soul created by Shiva-Shakti."

I continually felt grateful for Karl's support.

After much contemplation, I decided not to go on the Bali retreat with Basil and Luna. I did not want to travel so far from my boys... And, I knew I needed to focus my attention on finding the path to a more fulfilling mothering journey.

It seemed that the biggest obstacle to a more fulfilling mothering journey was my intense desire for union with a man. One night I sat crying while chanting with a Krishna Das CD. I put *Kaashi Vishwaanaata Gange* on repeat and as I sat singing that chant over and over, burning sensations pulsed throughout my entire body.

The next day I wrote to Karl, "Last night I sat chanting with a song on Krishna Das' *One Track Heart* CD. I cried a deep burning cry, and AFTER that, I read in the CD booklet what it meant. I'll transcribe it for you here, because it felt so powerful to me:

> *Hara Hara Mahaadeva Shaambho*
> *Kaashi Vishwaanaata Gange*

> *In the ancient city of Kashi (Benares), on the banks of the Ganges river, Shiva is worshipped as Lord of the Universe by naked, ash-covered yogis, who sit all night at Manikarnaka – the burning ghat where fire consumes the earthly bodies of those who have come to Kashi to die – and chant this mantra until dawn. Boatmen row on the holy river with Shiva's name on their lips. Sadhus light their chillums calling Shiva's name. The old and sick wander the streets, waiting for the moment when Shiva Himself will come and whisper the Divine Name **RAM!** in their ears as they take their last breath, assuring them birth in heaven.*

"Karl, in many moments I wish I could just leave everything and go sit by that river! Or check myself into an ashram. I often find myself thinking, 'I wish I was dead,' and it's not a suicidal thought in the literal sense. It's more like, 'I wish this struggle within me would die.' I am no longer comforted by the thought of really dying, because I understand now that I would just pick up where I left off anyway! With that new understanding, I am reaching a bit of a crisis point in which I am realizing that there is no way out of this struggle within me, but THROUGH. I can't escape myself any longer!"

Karl replied, "Rita, you know your 'work' is not to be found in the isolation of an ashram. Visit you will; stay, I sense not. You *Will* break through. It is awe inspiring to know that you feel you cannot escape your Self any longer. And when you enter your Self, you will find what I glimpsed through your eyes – a divinely inspired Goddess whose soul is so stunningly brilliant in the lightness and peacefulness of Being, so strikingly lovely, that your breath will be taken away. So remember to Breathe!"

I appreciated Karl's encouragement, although I still felt stuck in my own drama. In my reply to him I wrote, "In studying Ramana and Krishna, and in absorbing what Basil tracks, I am struggling because I understand it all intellectually, but then, when a wave of sadness over Eric comes, if I give in to the suffering over that, then I feel like I'm failing at the spiritual work.

"In the beautiful copy of the *Bhagavad Gita* which Eric gave me (translated by Eknath Easwaran, Shambhala Publications), it says:

Not dependent on any external support, they realize the joy of spiritual awareness. With consciousness unified through meditation, they live in abiding joy. Pleasures conceived in the world of the senses have a beginning and an end and give birth to misery, Arjuna. The wise do not look for happiness in them. But those who overcome the impulses of lust and anger which arise in the body are made whole and live in joy. They find their joy, their rest, and their light completely within themselves. United with the Lord, they attain nirvana in Brahman.

"Oh Karl, I so want to be free of my desires! I am so frustrated with that aspect of my being. Basil says I am close, and I see glimpses, but mostly I still feel a lot of desire. I really want to find my joy, rest, and light completely within myself, and if I could do that, then I could use all that extra energy to pursue the life I really want."

That night I wrote many pages in my journal about integrity. I wondered if Karl and I should be corresponding so closely. The contact with him didn't feel quite right, but cutting off contact didn't feel right, either. Strangely, I did not feel as though I had any control in the matter.

I studied Ramana Maharshi's view of destiny. When his mother requested that he return home with her, this was his reply:

The Ordainer controls the fate of souls in accordance with their destiny (prarabdha karma). Whatever is destined not to happen will not happen, try as you may. Whatever is destined to happen will happen, do what you may to prevent it. This is certain. The best course, therefore, is to remain silent.

(*The Essential Teachings of Ramana Maharshi: A Visual Journey*, edited by Matthew Greenblatt, InnerDirections Publishing.)

Chapter 24 – Letters

Rather than remaining silent, over the next couple of weeks, Karl and I wrote each other many long letters. I felt really wild inside. I wondered *how* I could go into my vital Kali nature – *how* could I discharge my passions without feeding new desires? I felt in crisis, like I was splitting and fragmenting in many directions.

I knew that if I focused on my true Self, I would go beyond the desires and crises of my little self. At that point I felt so tired of crying and grieving. I thought, 'I can't feel sorry for myself and certainly no one else should.'

I really wanted to transcend the cycles of depression, so I took out a card and wrote down some key points from the words of my beloved teachers – Basil, Lord Krishna, and Sri Ramana Maharshi:

> *Devotion to the Lord of the Universe.*
> *Concentration on the Self – Who Am I? – Atman~Soul~Spirit.*
> *Remembrance of "I am not the doer."*
> *Path of selfless service.*
> *Radiant respect for the unfolding of each being.*
> *What is destined to happen will happen.*
> *Patience with the process. Purifications.*
> *The Heart is the only Reality.*
> *To remain as one's Self is to enter the Heart.*

I carried the card around with me and set it beside my bed at night. I read it anytime I felt a cry coming. Again and again I read it, and slowly the teachings seeped into my soul.

Meanwhile, I found a book at the library called *In Days of Great Peace: The Highest Yoga As Lived*, by Mouni Sadhu, a European man who lived in Ramana Maharshi's ashram in India just months before Ramana left his body. Although Mouni Sadhu published the book in 1952, I found the information to be extremely useful to me here in 2005.

As I delved deeper into my true Self, I could feel the desires melting away, but my heart still felt a little stuck. In that gap, I felt a little empty and bored. I was used to the excitement of the emotional ups and downs of all my juicy problems! I wondered, 'How long must I wait until I reach the blissful juice of an open heart... the juice of my Realized Self?'

Then Karl sent a belated birthday card in which he wrote, "Two tanka poems: one for Radha, one for Rita – one poem in truth." Here are the two poems he crafted for my birthday:

Resplendent wild rose
Awakens our every sense
Divinely Inspired.
Heralding New Spring, new hope
Amidst the winter's grey.

Revealed Divinity
Intensely Courageous.
Through her inner work
A most painful heart opening.

I felt touched by how Karl was 'seeing' me, and yet the question of integrity still surfaced in me. I sent him a message to clarify my feelings (of pure, unattached love for him), and to ask if he felt that our contact had integrity with respect to his wife Martha.

He replied, "Rita, I am actually feeling blessed by our contact. Let me explain why. A very large part of my 'work' in the world is to manifest a morphic groove that helps restore the balance of the Divine Masculine and Divine Feminine.

"The specific path, the way, the vibration, I am compelled (by God I truly believe) to try to establish is one of deep intimacy between the masculine and feminine that is not grounded in sex. Rather, the intimacy is heart to heart, spiritual, nourishing, and pure. Well, I am not quite pure by any means, but thanks to the test our two souls agreed to take as I was working on my calling, I have come to a new level of being where carnal attachments are more like embers to the almost all-consuming flames we fanned last spring. Mindfulness on the embers is still needed on occasion as the metaphor is sound.

"I feel blessed that since we passed our test and did not give in to carnal attachment last year, and both of us hold a purity of love for one another, we actually came through with a deep intimate friendship – what I am called to do! If that isn't amazing, I don't know what is! It was my test on integrity on my path to help create this vibration in the world (especially in the West); it was your test, in part at least, to rise above the patterns of your past lives towards the purity of Love in Radha's Heart.

"You can see just how missing intimacy like this (between men and women) is in our world. So much pain, so much suffering, so much grief, so much hate just now to dissolve with pure Love.

"I have not talked with Martha about our re-connection at this new level of being, because she is struggling with how much I have changed in the past year. As I move ever faster towards my essential Self, she questions who I am becoming, and I feel that I cannot share what is happening within me because she gets too upset.

"I have intimate friendships with many women – the ones you call my 'gopis' – and I do not relate all the details to Martha (though they are ethical and do not cross boundaries reserved for marriage), because she does not understand my calling. When I do try to tell her, she says, "Stop, you are just reminding me that you are changing, and I don't want to go there." With you, I do not feel any attachment to you, and so I feel that our contact is okay.

"My sense is that surviving the burning of our intense attached love and evolving into supportive friendship was part of the grand plan towards healing the Earth; invoking and rebalancing the Divine Feminine and Divine Masculine. We are human (thank God!) and others down this path will occasionally fall into attached love and I see right now that we have shown that there is a path back to pure Love and friendship – regardless of outcome downstream. This is the truth that I sense within and trust."

In my reply to Karl, I wrote, "I 'thought' that I was 'done,' that I had released the attachment (to you in the form world), but then as I read your letter, I found myself still wanting to be Radha – to know that I am not "just" another dear soul who you work with; to know that our heart to heart, pure love is somehow special. Herein I find the embers of my attachment. There is no painful longing associated with the love I feel for you, so that is encouraging to me.

"So now, I continue (alone with myself) this test, this journey to the purity of Love in Radha's Heart."

I also shared with Karl that I understood how hard it was to not be able to share about the spiritual life with your partner – I had lived through the same problem with Bryan. In my husband, I had felt an underlying current of irreverence, which, in the end, I could not tolerate for one more minute. He and I just did not speak the same spiritual language.

Even after the divorce, I still struggled with how to communicate better with Bryan. I knew that I needed to stop sharing anything personal with him, because I rarely liked how he responded. I sat with the question, 'How can I best serve Bryan?'

Finally it came to me, when reading a chapter on karma in the *Bhagavad Gita*. As I read about the karma that builds up each time you get angry, suddenly all of the anger which I had felt toward Bryan over so many years appeared in my mind's eye, and I understood what a debt of karma I must have accumulated with him.

I realized that the way to serve Bryan was also the way to burn my karma and to dissolve the threads of anger still knotted between us… the way was simply to pray for him. I began sending Bryan blessings and healings, and I envisioned him surrounded with goodness.

I wrote to Karl, "I want to say that old cliché, "You deserve better than that," but that doesn't really fit with my new understanding of Karma. You are where you are, experiencing what your soul is destined to experience. My deepest prayer is that you find your way through to a peaceful, supportive, and pain-free home life – whatever that needs to be in the manifest realm will surely happen in its time.

"As it unfolds, know that I hold a vision for whatever healing needs to happen – for you, for Martha, for the whole. I truly believe that whatever karma needs to burn will burn, for as long as it needs to burn, and you might not even know the extent to which that burning will ripple out and affect the whole."

Karl thanked me for my support. In response to my remaining attachment, he wrote, "It is interesting – and not coincidental – that the one thing you still found yourself wanting, though attachments were released, was to be Radha, to know that you are not "just" another dear soul who I work with. Those same embers are with me. Of course we would be in the same space!

"As for your Integrity 'thing' as you call it, Basil has said that integrity is a defining element for you, and I honor that in you. I shall endeavor to keep my intentions at a level of purity which is worthy of your friendship and trust."

Karl's letter was very long. Our letters were getting to be so long that we jokingly called them novels and novellas. Even though we shared about our remaining embers, I temporarily felt better about the integrity of our contact, and I relished in the strength of the support that Karl continually offered me.

Chapter 25 – A novel Novel idea... *Karl-Rita*!

After a while, I began to wonder if the way Karl and I were jokingly calling our letters 'novels' was mere coincidence, or perhaps a sign? Then one night, while doing some yoga stretches with my favorite Krishna chant playing, I was singing *Hare Krishna* and looking up at the stunning Krishna-Radha print which I had bought at the Berkeley temple, and suddenly an idea for the novel of our story came pouring through me with the burning sensation of creative fire.

The next morning I wrote a letter to Karl with this subject line: "A novel Novel idea... *Karl-Rita*!" I shared this idea for a book:

"I would compile all of our email letters, changing the names and places of course, into a book which would address this human dilemma – what to do with attractions, attached loves, and sexual energies when we feel them towards someone who we cannot be with physically.

"People are falling in love all the time, and if one or both are married, that is often disregarded and vows are quickly broken, without too much questioning. All that karma! This story offers another way – the way of the Heart, the way of pure love, not grounded in sex. A healing story for our time. A modern day Krishna-Radha divine love story."

Karl replied immediately. He wrote, "Start now. This is absolutely fabulous – it must be from God/Krishna for it resonates so deeply and supports our emergent vibration of divine love while spreading that vibration out into the world. When I said back in December "Now we have work to do," I could not know this unfolding. Basil says you are a gifted writer. I know you are from our correspondence. Begin now, Rita.

"This shows the hand of God as it has aspects that mirror our work, my calling, your calling, while at the same time spreading the fragrance to the world for healing and a path of integrity. What clinches the fact that it is from the hand of God is that it also is a container for reinforcing the purity of our Love. If we were to 'fail' the novel would be useless. So its constant reinforcement for us is a gift in the form of 'golden handcuffs' until such time or life when integrity is ever-present. Who else could have come up with such a clever idea with a hook on both of us?

"I am here to support this work of God through Rita/Radha any way you want or need."

In my reply, I shared with Karl that I felt confused about my career path and I wasn't sure if it was the 'right' time to write the novel. I just couldn't figure out what I should be doing.

I wasn't sure about the midwifery path, and I really wanted to pursue the counseling path. I had felt drawn to become a counselor since my early twenties. I wondered if I should go to graduate school or if I should write a book first. I kept making all these grand plans with goals, but the new me didn't like to follow plans! The new me would make a plan and then toss it aside. I asked Karl for his insight.

He replied, "If you re-read your 'novel' to me, Rita, you will find that it SCREAMS OUT the answer to the question you ask me. But to be clear, I will reaffirm my answer:

"Begin now…

"… actually this is a beginning, you have already begun. Your questioning, societal influenced mind just hasn't caught up to the Truth you have splashed vividly across the pages to me. If you don't believe me, then re-read it and make a simple mark on a slate for every time you say you want to write vs. every time you say otherwise. Once you are done, then begin.

"The pressure you mention only comes from within, but it is not your soul's doing. Bryan was perfectly right when he said that he did not see your writing a novel as a career move. What you are called to do never shows up as a career move. If you follow your Bliss (borrowing from Joseph Campbell), YOU will move the career, not vice versa. You are Blessed here because you are expected to write, just as you 'admit' Basil divined.

"BEGIN NOW, Rita. Accept the gift from Shiva."

I decided to stop making plans and to let Radha guide my being. As Karl advised and Radha confirmed, it was time to begin writing the novel.

Karl found a book called *The Divine Consort: Radha and the Goddesses of India*, and he wrote to me, "The parallels between your energy and Radha's archetype are uncanny. And, what shook me to my core, were the parallels in my energy and how I manifest in the world with that of the Krishna archetype, along with all that we have been experiencing and working through together."

Delight filled my being as I wrote our story. In my journal, I wrote, "Let Gratitude be my food and Grace my drink. I bow to what Is – again and again." My emerald arrived in the mail, and as I waited for the jeweler to set it, I thought of what the vedic astrologer had told me – *that the emerald would help with having my writing taken seriously*. I wasn't even wearing the ring yet, and the forecast was already coming true.

As I wrote, I focused on allowing the writing to simply flow through me as the vessel. I offered the writing for the healing of the Whole, and I prayed that the novel would be a way for me to serve others.

One morning while chanting, I asked, 'Where is the Shakti working in me now?' I sensed that it was in my essential soul field directly straight out from my heart, and I immediately felt my heart open a little. I felt like I was on the edge of indescribable bliss, and I wanted to go there, but my heart was just not open enough yet. Some tears streamed down my face – even getting close to that Bliss felt overwhelming.

Meanwhile, the depression which came with ovulation intensified. I watched my pattern of going from a state of excitement and happiness to a state of depression and blocked light to a state of spinning out and over-thinking and then back to excitement and happiness.

When I was in the depression, I felt self-loathing. I would stare at Ramana's photo and feel ashamed. I wondered if I was pure enough for the Path?

I wondered how much of that pattern was biochemical and hormonal, and how much of it was my personality and ego trying to hold on and not be shed? I remembered Basil saying that a lot of great beings lived lives that did not look very neat because they were what we call "manic-depressive" in the way they opened and closed. I was not a great being, but I certainly opened and closed intensely.

Karl offered support for the depression which at times consumed me. He wrote, "You Know that you are so much greater than the depression and grief you feel, just as the manifest realm, our world, is so much greater than the grief and sadness that She bears just now. Hold onto this.

"Hold onto your inner work for Self and the world. And, to borrow the last line from a Pueblo blessing: *"Hold onto my hand... even though I am away from you."* Rita, I shall hold the Light for you. I am here whenever you need me."

I thanked Karl for his support and I shared the following with him:

"This afternoon I was thinking about how I don't read the news because I get too upset... but, since I am so sensitive, I must be absorbing what's going on in the world without knowing about it consciously.

"Then! I was lying with the boys tonight while they fell asleep, and Joshua said – seemingly out of the blue, but he must have been picking up on what I described above – "The way that they could end the war would be to not have countries anymore. When they made the new maps, they could make them with no words, no lines, no boundaries – nothin' – and then they wouldn't know where Iraq was and so then they couldn't attack." Then he said, "There wouldn't be any more signs saying 'you've entered such and such place...'"

"I was laughing and crying at the same time and he asked why and I said, "That was such a beautiful vision, Joshua. Thank you for sharing it."

"Wow! How brilliant is that? If we could all just BE beings on the earth, without boundaries, then we could have peace. If only it could be as simple as my seven-year-old son envisions it."

Karl replied, "It IS as simple as your son envisions. That IS where we all are heading, though we are in dark hours just now. But the dark heralds the dawn of precisely what your son's vision is. That knowing is found in many traditions.

"I see you are already doing so much to not take on the world with your great sensitivity. Ultimately you will pass through it into Bliss amidst the horror and hold it all compassionately and in service without it attaching to you."

On Karl's birthday, I sent him a card in which I wrote, "Happy Rooster Year Birthday to my fellow Rooster! I celebrate your 48 journeys around the Sun. I am so glad you were born. Since I was born in the rooster cycle behind yours, on the day you were born, I was just a 'twinkle in my father's eyes' as the saying goes. Literally, though, I'm sure I was smiling from some distant star! I wish you many blessings for joy, bliss, and peace this year and always. Gladness and friendship, Rita Ann."

At that point, for some reason Karl and I had some difficulties with emailing. I sent a few letters which he never received. He suggested that we try talking on the phone. I agreed that I was ready to test the new level of purity we were both feeling.

So, on March 12th, exactly ten months after the day we had met in person in San Diego, Karl called and it was the first time we had heard each other's voices for over nine months.

Karl was surprised at how 'vibrant' my voice sounded, because he remembered my voice as being 'soft.' I had forgotten how quietly and slowly he talks – I had to slow myself way down to meet him energetically.

I brought up the issue of integrity again, and he not only heard my concern, he voiced his own concerns about it. That was such a relief to me. I shared that I finally felt caring about Martha as a sister – rather than feeling like I *should* care about her, I now felt genuine concern for her. He said that he also felt concerned for her.

I told Karl that Julianna had advised me to cut off contact as a blessing for him and Martha. Julianna thought that the highest path would be for us to let each other go for a while.

Despite her advice, Karl and I agreed that it did not feel right to cut off contact entirely. However, we did decide that it was best for us to slow down. For a while, we would only have contact when needed.

That night, I laughed out loud as I wrote in my journal, "Nothing has to be as complicated as I've been making it." I remembered something Basil had once said, "The antidote to the fog of self-absorption is service."

I kept focusing on the Path toward the Light. I *so* wanted to lose my ego and be able to serve others.

One night, I awoke and 'heard': *There is a group of people in this country who will soon be going very quickly to the Light, and you can be one of them if you want.'* Oh, did I ever *want* to be one of them!

The next day I focused on holding a steady field of attention for my boys. I endeavored to put their needs before my own.

My brother came to visit and we went to the jeweler to pick up my emerald ring. As we were walking back to my car, a 'crazy' old guy said the following as I passed him, "There's a woman walking who looks like she knows what she's doing and where she's going."

I hoped he was right.

Chapter 26 – Falling back into the strength of my Self

One night as I was falling asleep, I felt a *purity* in my whole being. It was a blissful feeling, but it only lasted for a minute. Then, in the middle of the night, I opened my eyes and I sensed that if I just kept looking, *Something* was going to visit me from another realm. But then everything in the room got very buzzy, like there were billions of beings trying to get to me at once. I closed my eyes and went back to sleep!

The next day I received an email from Karl in which he thanked me for our phone conversation. He wrote, "I realized after we talked that the embers of desire were gone, the embers that remained after we released each other from the fire in December.

"What remains is a great and grand Love of unfathomable depth, beauty, and purity with you; it is a vibration we must hold for the world; it is a vibration for eternity, for healing, for wholeness in a divided world, a divided divinity. This weekend was transformational for me – breakthroughs that are now manifesting for work and with Martha. Our conversation was one of the keys to unlocking that door through. Thank you."

I replied that I felt relieved to hear that he did not feel any embers of attached love desires. I did not feel any either. I did, however, feel concerned about our contact over the previous month, and I shared that I was questioning if we were holding integrity at all times.

Karl replied, "I sat with the integrity issue this week, after knowing that all remaining embers of desire and attachment for you had dropped away as I found the next level of Being foundationally, a new 'quantum level' of purity in my work of holding this vibration for pure intimacy between the Divine Masculine and Divine Feminine.

"It is done! This warrants a celebration – at least in the subtle realm. On Sunday, it came to me that a major section of the novel has been completed with our discourse over the last couple months. I believe this was intended and necessary, despite recognition for me that, in retrospect, there were impurities and subtle attachments on my part. I am sorry for that though I did not see them clearly in the midst of it all. Thank you again for this full release!"

I did not respond to Karl's letter. At that point I was doing another internal search over the integrity (or lack thereof) of our recent contact. Also, I was trying to understand why I did not feel like celebrating.

The following week Karl wrote again. His message read:
Dear Radha of Rita Ann,
Know that I hold you in Light as you work within the stillness in this time.
Love~Namaste~Om Shanti, Karl

I called Basil and he said what he most often said, "Rita, it's not about Karl. It's about you. You pour your devotion into the man, and then it is too intense for him, and so he cannot hold his form. When you stabilize your being and pour your devotion and wonder into the One, then the masculine will be able to stand *beside* you and wonder *with* you."

I knew he was right. Why was he always right? I decided to surrender to the truth he spoke. I focused on letting go of Karl.

That night I had a beautifully exquisite dream:

> *I was looking at a book, which I was very excited about. The book was truly amazing, with photos of bright flowers – golden light was shining through exquisite petals of reds, oranges, hot pinks... and the people of India could see a sacred white cow out on the horizon. It was as if the book's landscape was ALIVE... in living color...*

On St. Patrick's Day, before heading to the evening group with Basil, I wrote in my journal, "Ramana Is ever as He Is, and I'm not quite pure enough to join Him where He Is, so it is a challenging relationship with this boyfriend! I know that I am being Held by Something Greater, and I also know that I AM that Something Greater which is holding me. Still, I am not pure enough to sustain that knowing."

That evening Basil told me that the multi-dimensional levels that I track in my being are all offerings. He suggested that I cultivate a sense of *wonder* as an antidote to all of the buzzy static that surged through me.

With the kindest tone of voice, he said, "Rita, you have gotten so good at tracking the levels, that you are *so close* to dissolving the ego, but the irony is that the more you track them, the more they lock down, and it is a struggle which is driving you crazy... but once you let go, a magnificence will come through you which will be good for the people around you."

During the break, Luna asked Basil, "How many levels is Rita tracking?" Basil answered, "Twelve. But they're solid." Next Basil looked at me and said, "You've been alone too long." Julianna asked him what I could do about being alone, since I didn't have a partner, and he said, "She has to just keep deepening. She's going to do a lot of teaching."

After we all chanted *"Om Shanti, Shanti Om,"* Basil told a story for me:

> *Once a young woman went to be an apprentice with a potter in the center of a village. She landed in a pot on her bottom and he said, "I like your spunk!" He took some earth and put it on the wheel, and she watched very closely, and she was so awe struck that she fell into many shards on the floor.*
>
> *She tried hard to pull herself back together. Pots held food and water and they also held all the changes...*

At that point, I could hardly see Basil's face anymore and I felt as though I might pass out. I couldn't hear his words for a while – the story was so intense for me. I heard him say something about God's will, and then suddenly he said, *"into Nothingness."* He stopped the story abruptly there. Maybe he could tell that I really was about to explode into many shards on the floor!

The next evening, when I was longing for a man, Basil called. When I started telling him that my third and fourth chakras felt stuck, like a thick grey mass surrounded them, Basil started to say something, but then there was all this static on my phone.

I said, "I can't hear you because of the static." He said, "That's an accurate metaphor!" He continued, "Rita, you ground in the masculine, and through the man you feel your own shakti. You have to pull your energy back from the masculine, and fall back into your Self and figure out how to ground in yourself – in your whole Being, not just in your heart. Fall back into yourself, not looking out to Ramana or Krishna, even.

"Fall back into your Self. That's your practice. And, be in the company of other seekers, as they correctly mirror your own longing. This longing is not for a man. Understand the structure in you that grounds through the man, and stop using the grief to ground yourself. *Fall back into your Self.*"

I practiced falling back into my whole Self by focusing on the energies moving throughout my being. Just placing my attention on those energies released sensations of profound relief in my entire system.

A few days later I attended a day workshop with Basil, and I felt calmer than usual. I completely understood when he said, "All experience is being absorbed into Being, and once you see that, then you see that everyone is taking themselves too seriously." I sure could relate to taking myself too seriously!

Basil offered another definition for *sadhana*, which I really liked: "*Sadhana* is the unraveling of the layers of your being, which results in Consciousness, Bliss, and Truth... and then your own form of service gets purified, and then you feel better."

He then explained about karma and purifying all the layers of our beings: "Any time you do something to deepen and expand, the karma rises to the surface and then it unravels. You have to have the courage to hold your form as you purify.

"The nature of Spiritual Awakening is bi-polar: your system rises up to an ecstatic level of consciousness and then it comes back down and purifies. If you can let go, it will purify through.

"A week before the Buddha became enlightened, he went through a recapitulation of hundreds of thousands of lifetimes – all of the experiences – until he understood all the structures and he understood how he came to be the present form."

At the morning break I asked Basil about my cycles of depression. He said that I needed to structure my life so that I could have times for nothingness because I needed more down-time to integrate all of the openings and expansions.

Next I asked him about my relationship to the masculine. He said, "Because of your tantric past lives, you run sexual energy through the male form. You're doing it with me right now. You need to become aware of it and notice why you like being around the masculine so much – how does it affect you? Does your heart open? What happens in you?"

I thought about that, and, although I didn't really understand it yet, I sensed the truth of his words. I *did* like being around the masculine – I felt more feminine in the presence of men.

After the break, we chanted *Sante Maria Di Deo ~ St. Mary of God*. Basil explained, "Mother of God is the most stable light body – it is far out in your energetic field, and when you tune in to it, it is a container of vibration that allows all other vibrations to be experienced. If you stabilize at that vibration of Light, you will feel the Bliss of the Mother's Love for all creation."

As we finished singing Sante Maria, I felt Basil looking into me. He said softly, "Rita, let that vibration just BE in your heart. Align your heart with the field about six to eight inches above your head, and feel the fullness in the deep structure of the Heart. Let it be there – you don't need to run out and act on it all – you don't need to express it all. Just let it BE."

Basil then talked about surrender. He said that true surrender arises out of the ripening of one's conditions. Every drama we have ever experienced is trying to move us toward surrendering. The central question, he asked while looking right at me, is *"Can you live a surrendered life or not?"*

Next he told a funny story about Neem Karoli Baba, the guru of Ram Dass and Krishna Das. I felt so excited when Basil concluded, "Neem Karoli Baba went around completing karma for people all over the place – very high beings have fun doing these things." I thought to myself, 'I want to have fun completing karma for people too!'

At that point, Basil looked at me and laughed. He said, "Rita, you're going to take Shiva out on a date! Your investment in the masculine needs to move up a notch on the levels. You have all this longing in your heart to pour a surrendered sense of being into a relationship – this longing can only be met by Shiva.

"You need to learn about *Bhakti*, the path of devotion, in which you pour your adoration into the Divine. It is different from *Tantra* – a tantrika invests in forms, so she pours her devotion into objects. This can be dangerous because you can get stuck when you anchor to lower frequencies. The siddhis – magical powers – can be seducing.

"This is why I am offering you a date with Shiva – so you can pour your devotion into a proper stream. The men floating around you right now are there largely from your will. True spiritual transformation and its power – *shakti* – are different than earthly powers gained through the will."

Basil then said that I would take Shiva out to Burger King. I said, "I am NOT going to Burger King!" Basil explained why he picked Burger King: "Tantrics go into dense places, like graveyards and sites of shootings, and use

89

the dense energy and clean it up. It will be a good experience for you to do a tantric cleansing ritual at Burger King with Shiva."

That night I called Basil with a few more questions:

R: When I feel overwhelming sexual energy, if I have an orgasm, does that slow down my sadhana or is it passion that I need to discharge in that way?
B: Good question. Use the breath to bring that energy up to the heart... then the urge won't be as strong. Orgasms keep the lower brain centers activated, so it would be good for you to avoid them right now.

R: I am confused about career – I can't discriminate or discern what I should be doing. I can't hear my inner voice of wisdom.
B: You are in between two structures right now. You've left the old world, but you haven't gotten into the new world yet, so it's like you are changing gears. Be patient, and remember that it's all held together with Love – it's like a mother holding the most tender and precious child.

R: How can I be rid of Karl?
B: Why are you in such a hurry to be rid of him?

R: Because I can't find the integrity in our connection. My friends are seeing a lack of integrity and I can't discern for myself right now. You said that he and I could use our connection to purify – how could we do that?
B: The only way to purify with Karl is for you each to continue to burn the desire into pure compassion – to give up all attachment. This takes scrupulous honesty and is difficult to achieve, but is possible. However, it is probably best to not have contact until you feel more clarity.

On the night of the next group with Basil, the pain of a migraine consumed me. While driving to Basil and Luna's home, I almost fell asleep and I welcomed that – I felt so awful that I actually wanted the car to crash. I felt so tired of doing this life. I shared that with Basil, and he said, "That is good."

He explained, "This migraine is emotionally caused. You have to get in touch with the grief." I said, "but I thought you said that the grief was 'looping' in me and I needed to let the grief go," and he replied, "Our conditions are always changing – before, the grief was looping, and now, you need to go into it. It is a deep grief."

Basil then told this story while looking in my eyes the entire time:

Once the Buddha went to climb Vulture Peak with six of his monks. On the way up he asked the shortest monk to go up and get them some water. The monk started climbing up, but on the way he tripped, and he never forgave himself, because he didn't do what his Master asked him to do.

Later Julianna and I were looking in each other's eyes, and Basil cautioned me to stop connecting through the eyes. He said not to bring so much current into my migraine head. He also 'saw' that I had turned her into a tantric object. Julianna told him that I actually felt softer to her – she didn't feel that my gaze was piercing. Basil agreed by saying "Actually, the way Rita goes in on people is quite lovely. She is making great progress."

Then he looked down at me and said, "The other side of your manic side is this – lying there on the floor in the migraine state – and now this just has to unravel for a while. You have to just let it."

A little while later he looked down at me again and said, "Look at Rita just streaming *Grace*. She's cute as she unravels. What are we going to do with this girl?"

I felt better by the break, and I thanked Basil for his wisdom. I shared that I had 'heard' not to eat meat, and I asked his opinion. He said, "I wouldn't eat it if I were you, but I'm not you, so I won't tell you what to do."

The next morning I sat in meditation with candles burning to the Goddess Saraswati, and I thought of how writing is my passion – writing IS my calling. Then I began to cry – a deep cry with no content. I cried and burned and laughed all at once.

Later I understood that the cry came out of a deep grief over how long I had denied myself the full expression of my writing gift. I grieved over how I had pushed it down, saying that it wasn't good enough.

I sent Basil an email in which I declared writing as my calling. I felt much stronger when I sat down to work on the novel that day.

The next night I dreamt:

I was talking on the phone with someone and throughout our conversation, the person kept saying over and over, "You are getting closer to realizing the Truth."

Chapter 27 – Patience

My parents visited in the spring, and one day my Mom and I bumped into Basil at the natural food store. He told my Mom, "Your daughter is a live wire."

My Mom and I had always been very close, but during the divorce with Bryan, I pulled away from her because I feared that she would judge me. During that spring visit, she and I began to reconnect and I experienced many moments of total love and heart opening to her. That felt so good.

I also felt close to my Dad. He had always been very supportive of my writing. While sipping hot tea together in the sunshine, he told me that Walker Percy wrote two novels – unpublished – and then he published his third novel at age forty-four, and it won many awards, and then he published six more novels! That inspired me to keep writing.

I did not tell my parents that I was writing a novel about the pure love Karl and I had found. I thought that they would surely judge me for being in love with a married man. Who wouldn't judge me? I was surely judging myself.

I wanted to reply to Karl's last message, but I was struggling over what to say. Also, I felt annoyed with myself because I was actually feeling some longing for him again. I wrote in my journal, "We may be together in the ethereal realm, but here in the manifest realm, I feel trapped in chains. I may not go to him. I may not gaze in his eyes. I may not sit in his presence. Such a longing – but no grief or pain, just a yearning to return to that absolute depth of Love and Light that I experienced through his eyes."

One night I had a funny dream:

> Basil told Benjamin to tell me, "You need sex, drive, energy, and depth, and the snacks will be okay." Benjamin was jumping up and down, telling me that over and over.
>
> Next, I met a man who resembled Karl, and he told Benjamin that the snacks would be difficult and dangerous. Then Benjamin went and relayed that message to Basil, and Basil said, "tell him not to approach the journey with that spectre of intensity – and tell him to enjoy the bacon!" Then I was getting ready to go visit the man I had met, and I wondered how he would receive me. I felt excited.

When I awoke, I felt some longing for Karl, and I thought, 'I am surely not holding the purest vibration here!' I didn't even know how to name what I was feeling, as I was too immersed in the absolute energetics of it, but I endeavored to somehow get back to the pure vibration I had felt with him before.

At the next retreat with Basil, within moments of being in that 'Field' with him, I knew that I was *home*. He described the process of opening our crowns and offering the lower sensations (of our bodies and psychic structures) up to the spiritual fire above our heads. He explained that when the lower sensations go up, other higher qualities come down, and then you become witness to the relaxation of the silken descent of compassion, deep understanding, profound strength, and wisdom.

I melted when Basil said, "Everything is the embrace of Consciousness. Every experience. It takes a mature heart to recognize that, because when the heart is contracted, there is shame and blame and a feeling of unworthiness. As the heart matures, it softens, and then everything that arises becomes a demonstration of this amazing Universe. There's *rasa* then – and non-duality. Remember, the unfolding of your contractions releases *your* map Home."

Next Basil talked about vocations. He said, "Our vocations choose us to purify us and they will put us through the ropes and shake us until we are pure enough to hold them, and then we will get more subtle assignments." He looked at me, laughed, and told the group, "Rita's vocation has descended – we can have a vocation descent party!

"Her vocation has descended, but her soul has to mature and when it is purified and matured, the vocation will flow. This will take time and the bodily sensations may be quite intense. Once purified, she will serve others by communicating to them that we are all connected."

At the break I rushed over to Basil and poured out my impatience. I asked him how long it would take for me to purify my writing vocation. He laughed, held out his hands, and said to one hand, "here's Consciousness vibrating over billions of years," and then he said to the other hand, "and here's Rita's writing kriya."

"Rita, your intensity is your gift – stop trying to modulate it – the intensity makes karma burn faster. You don't get to decide when or how your destiny will unfold – it's your job to purify. For you, purification will happen by going intensely into all of your emotions and not trying to dampen them down."

When we all sat down again, Basil's eyes twinkled with mischief. He looked at me with a burning gaze and said, "The real motivation behind our spiritual practices is the direct experience of the embrace we all long for. When we are ready, Reality breaks through, ignites us, and then waits patiently to see if we are patient."

Later in the day Basil talked about Muktananda and other high beings. He said, "What they say is intense and potent because it is titrated to the Truth. They watch themselves arrive wherever they go, in each moment." Then he looked at me and said, "Rita will be there soon."

At the next break I asked Basil what he meant by 'soon' – did he mean days, months, years, or lifetimes? He said, "Rita, you wouldn't want it to come any sooner because it is so intense – you have to first build the capacity to hold it." I started crying and he said, "sooner rather than later."

In the late afternoon session, Basil explained how each being opens differently. He gave several examples. For me, he said: "Rita opens through recognition. She has to feel *seen*, and once she feels seen, it's like letting one of those children's balloons go out of air! There's a lot of power in that, but she is used to receiving some negative feedback, so she has a lot of shame wrapped around her."

He then described how all true teachers have the ability to mirror correct vibrational frequencies, and he looked at me when he said, "The faster you vibrate, the more time slows down, and soon becomes now." He asked why we are in such a hurry, and then he answered his own question: "We are in a hurry because we feel so uncomfortable with the tension between our personality and our essence."

Someone asked about relationships, and Basil said that for a relationship to work, the partners have to open the same way. Tears ran down my face when he said, "Relationships are revealed from the inside out – you cannot construct them, you will discover them. If you surrender, then your lines of light will meet someone with the same lines of light and then you can unfold together within the matrix.

"A good way to tell if you have true connection with someone is to put in your chakra dipstick and make sure you feel the connection in your fourth, sixth, and crown chakras – and also above the crown." Someone asked Basil how to do that, and he said, "Check in with Rita soon."

He kept saying "soon" to me – it was driving me crazy! I knew I was in a kriya, but I didn't even really know what that word meant, so I asked him. He said, "Kriya is movement which purifies," and then he laughed and joked, "Rita, you are a walking kriya!"

Basil offered us a daily practice – to ask the question *"How am I connected to the Cosmos, to the Absolute?"* He explained that if that question is at the top of the agenda, then everything else naturally falls in under it, but if that question is not at the top, then you feel situationally miserable. When you inquire about the Truth of your existence, Consciousness leaps up because the Universe is *very* interested in the unfoldment of the Universe.

As I left that day, I felt more patient. I hugged Basil goodbye, and he teased, "Soon, Rita. *Very* soon." I laughed as I drove home.

Chapter 28 – The search for integrity continues

One warm spring afternoon, I suddenly became inspired to write Karl a letter.

I wrote the following: "I am calling upon Saraswati, Durga, and Radha to help me write this letter. I am asking Them to write through me, and to help me find: *humor* where I feel anger; *integrity* where I feel attachment; *bliss* where I feel longing; and *compassion* where I feel desire.

"Integrity. Purity. Trust. Release. These themes swirl around us, and dive into us in waves driven by the rhythms of Consciousness. I ask myself, 'How can I hold this? How can I approach this again?' For it is the same each time, and yet different.

"Karl, in writing the novel, I have learned that it was just a few days before your birthday that we began to lose our footing in the integrity labyrinth. Now I am questioning whether to keep trying to get to that integrity in the center, or whether to just turn around and run out of that spiral. I keep hearing '*you have to get out of there*,' but I don't yet know how to do that.

"In your 'celebration' letter, you recognized that there were impurities and subtle attachments on your part, and you said that you did not see them clearly in the midst of it all. I also recognized my own attachments and I am also sorry for them.

"When I read your letter, I did not feel like celebrating, because I could still feel my attachment. And when I realized that we had fallen again, I felt angry at both of us, and I wondered how I could now trust either of us to be in contact with integrity.

"I know that you are not willing to tell Martha about our friendship at this time, and to a certain extent, I understand. Or rather, I accept. And that may work for you with the other 'gopis' – you may feel that you can have those intimate connections and not share them with Martha – but it won't work for this Radha.

"For me to have intimate contact with you and feel integrity about it, Martha would have to know. It's just not clean any other way. The novel will hold us to purity to a certain extent, but within the novel, the characters are human and they are trying to find the integrity, which means they don't always succeed. That's okay in hindsight, but we can't keep doing that.

"So where we go from here, I don't know. Basil once told me that we would not be able to release each other, and I think I'm beginning to understand that more fully. My current longing for you is not painful – there's no sadness or confusion – it's different than before. Maybe the thing to do is nothing – just not be in contact for a while. You thanked me for a full release – I am sorry that I am not upholding that."

I continued, "I sent Basil a message this morning asking about my 'boyfriend.' I have found the study of Ramana to be quite useful, although frustrating. Since Basil says that I have a vital Kali nature, I am wondering if I might need Ramakrishna more than Ramana?

"I have tried to open in the way of the Direct Path described by Ramana, but it doesn't feel like the way I open. Basil makes more sense to me than Ramana, and I seem to open best when I'm not trying to! Also, I am equally in love with Shiva and Krishna, and my heart swells with Ram and Hanuman as well. I am having fun with it all, and I laughingly asked Basil if Ramana should still be my boyfriend."

Karl replied,

Rita Ann,

Thank you for opening to what is bubbling for us. I have found a new level of purity and it continues to get deeper. Much has happened for and within me since mid-March when we last conversed. I have gotten much greater clarity on where I am going with my calling, my future work.

And, after I sat with Basil two weekends ago, clarity on what I must work on next came. Then you wrote and re-affirmed it needed to be done. Finally this morning Basil called and asked about the same thing.

The first order of business is to open to Martha with love and compassion about all that is happening with me on the inner planes and how it is shaping up to manifest in the world. This includes what once was impossible to venture into – my grounding work with the Divine Feminine embodied in the 'gopis' you mentioned in your note, and in you.

This will take some time for us to process and work through. It will be good though. The old way of walking on eggshells around Martha with respect to what I am growing into vocationally and spiritually was not working. Boy that should have been obvious! Hold us in your blessings, if you would.

I am saddened that you experienced anger, attachment, longing, and desire. I sensed in my 'celebration' letter that this would be the case for you (at least that you would not yet be celebrating). I am sorry beyond words for this.

As to corresponding, I would ask that you at least write when you are in need as I may be immersed in the work with Martha and not always catch it energetically. And I would ask that I be able to do the same if needed. When I talked with Basil today, he did not say to stop all correspondence with you. However, I will honor your sense here regardless.

Keep on with the novel – you have more material now :) and it is getting intense!

I am curious what Basil said about Ramakrishna – my sense is you don't need amplification of vital Kali energy (you run that well) – you need the non-dual fullness of the emptiness of Ramana.

Love~Namaste~Om Shanti,

Karl

In my reply I thanked Karl for the grey which I 'knew' he would send. I acknowledged that life is not as black and white as I can paint it at times.

I wrote, "I am most happy to hear that you will be opening to Martha about your grounding work with the Divine Feminine. I will of course hold you both in my prayers.

"I liked what you said about Ramana – I think you are right, I do need the non-dual fullness of the emptiness of Ramana. *And*, I think I need Ramakrishna at times. Here is what Basil wrote in response to me asking about Ramana, Ramakrishna, Neem Karoli Baba, Shiva, Krishna, Ram, and Hanuman:

"always useful to have several spiritual friends (who happen to be boys)... Ramakrishna is a good and potent dance partner..."

"I laughed, because of course he was right – they *were* all boys! Basil has been working with me on paying attention to how I run sexual energy through the masculine form. He alerted me to a structure which I have, in which I find my own divinity through the masculine. I am now aware of it conceptually, but I have yet to catch it energetically, so I am still doing it. This is one of the reasons why I cannot talk with Eric again just yet. I miss talking with him, but until I feel more grounded, I sense we should not talk.

"Which brings me to the question about you and I corresponding. Because of my need to break this pattern with the masculine, and because I would like to wait until Martha knows, I think you and I should not correspond for a while. I am not proposing to cut it off completely like I did before – I like the grey of your idea... that we write if we are in need, but otherwise, let's take more space for a while. It might be worth considering doing the same with the other 'gopis' while you are doing this work with Martha – to free up your psychic space so that there is more room for her. Just a thought.

"I feel that I need to be alone for a while to really come into my power. I've been depending too much on Luna, Basil, Julianna, Dana, and you...

"So! That's my long way of saying that I need to hold to what I said yesterday, which is that I would like to wait on corresponding with you until such time as Martha knows about our connection and contact.

"But please *do* reply to this letter – let's continue corresponding here until we each feel 'done' for now. Okay?"

Karl replied immediately. The subject of his email read, "Actually the grey is rose." He wrote, "Thank you for your note. Your words resonate truth and I rest assured in them. I will call upon you if needed as you note you will do as well. I may also check in if I sense the need for you.

"Another interesting parallel – I certainly have had a pattern to ground through the Divine Feminine, though it is more emotional than sexual.

"Your knowing to let go of dependence on others is beautiful (and hard!)... I send you Love and Light for this work.

"You ARE breaking through!!!!!!!!!!!!!!!!!!!!!!!!!!!!!!!"

A few weeks passed before Karl wrote again. He sent a list of Krishna and Radha celebration days, saying that he would be present for me on Radhastami, Sri Radha's appearance day.

I sat staring at Karl's message for a long time. I felt stunned that he would write such a letter after what we had agreed to in terms of holding integrity.

After stewing for a few hours, I wrote back, "In response to what you wrote, I have a few questions. It is not important whether or not you answer these questions to me. What is important is that you have the courage to answer them to yourself and to Martha.

"Does Martha know yet about our connection and recent contact?

"Does Martha know that you see me as Radha?

"What are your intentions in honoring me as Radha?

"Does Martha know your intentions for Radha's days?

"I am 'there' as always for you Karl, and, more importantly now, I am deeply spiritually present for Martha. Om Shanti, Rita Ann."

Karl replied, "Perfect timing! We have been working through (with ups and downs) what I am called to do, how that relates to 'gopis' in my life, and more. You are next to address. Technically, I 'see' you as carrying Radha energy within your incarnate body and soul. The celebration of Radha days for me is in honor of the Radha archetype so needed now in this world. You manifest much of that archetype now. The important work just ahead is in relation to your first question – hence the timing of your note. Thank you for that nudge."

A few weeks later Karl sent a very short message, "Martha and I are working through heavy, difficult stuff right now. It is needed, it is timely, it is important, it is good."

I replied, "The work with Martha is THE most important thing right now. Indeed I feel this deeply, and thus I have been staying out of your field. Keep up the good work. You are both in my prayers."

Karl responded, "Thank You Dear Rita Ann. Much healing energy for You."

As I continued writing the novel, I felt that I was ever closer to the integrity I so wanted to hold.

Chapter 29 – Samadhi, Surprises, and Gold

At Basil's next evening group, he told this story of *samadhi* for me:

*Once, long ago, in the beginning of time, there was a being who was not quite a man or a woman. He/she lived in the support of lush green jungles with tigers. When he/she went over to the glistening water, he/she saw gold shimmering there. He/she picked it up and it **was** gold, and in that moment he/she had a brief samadhi in which he/she saw the fabric of existence. He/she was holding the gold in front of her second chakra and that stream of the samadhi went into her second chakra. This time, when she sees the fabric of existence, instead of bringing it into the second chakra, she needs to bring it into the Heart.*

During the opening chant, I felt as though the Sanskrit syllables were being chanted through me, without any effort on my part. I felt the third chakra knot in my belly dissolve, and I thought, 'Why would it hang on any longer? It's not in charge.' My heart felt so open. I kept thinking, 'I'm history,' meaning that my personality was history. I swelled with Gratitude for the transmission of that bliss.

That evening I was feeling very calm and I thought that I had released my attachment to Karl, so I was surprised when Basil suddenly asked me to look into the candle flames and see Karl's form and my form and watch them melt into each other. I was confused by this, and so he explained why he still saw an attachment to Karl:

"Rita, one of your holy truths is the interpenetration of opposites. The tension of holding that truth creates your constrictions because you take the intensity down into your lower chakras, and then you see a copulating universe in which everything wants to mate.

"When you learn to take that intensity up, by vibrating to the Truth of the interpenetration of opposites, then that intensity will just be total Love. Then you will be in love with all of life... and you will go around joining opposing forces everywhere! You will wake up chasing butterflies, and falling in love with garage doors and mailmen and your boys and carrots and onions and refrigerators and the natural food store... and you will have enough love for everybody and you will have enough energy... and your writing will be better... and your capacity to understand people and things will go way up."

So with Karl, Basil said that it was the interpenetration of opposing forces – it was, and always would be, *an opening*. But, he cautioned, I *had* to let go of my attachment to the outcome and just see our two forms melting into pure Love. Basil sternly reminded me that I was not in charge here. And he reminded me that with my tantric background, I *think* that I am creating things, but that is actually dangerous because it interferes with the Descent. He said,

"Remember, Rita, master Tantrikas create things in the form world and that interferes with the silken descent of Consciousness."

After the tea break Basil began talking about attractions to others, and he said, "Pay attention, Rita!" He explored the difference between magnetic portals and radiant openings: "Unconscious attractions flow out of content in our psyches. The content goes through magnetic portals and it is very intense when it is directed onto one individual. Once the unconscious is released of its content, the soul field radiates uniformly and then you fall in love with everyone." "And," he said looking right at me, "that's a whole lot easier on your system."

Then he said, "Rita, you will burn through every form until you let go. Every relationship, every job, your boys, Bryan… every form. Once you let go, you will be in love with everything and you won't need to lock it down onto one person. And then you won't need to burn through forms anymore."

I asked how I could let go more, and Basil said, "Rita, surrendering to experience is the fastest way through." Luna laughed and said, "That's exactly what Rita teaches women about childbirth!"

As I was leaving that night, Basil gave me an assignment: "Rita, to spread this thing out and take the pressure off, greet every human being that you meet with the intention and perception that they are the Beloved."

He also advised me to wear gold over my thymus. In my mind's eye, I immediately saw a gold lion on my chest… perhaps a symbol of the Goddess Durga's Lion?

A few days later I met with a healer who clears energetic connections. I told him of my ongoing struggle to integrate the experience of falling in love with Karl. He asked me to send Karl energy from my heart.

Next he guided me to ask Spirit to help me reframe the way I thought about Karl. During the session he sensed that something shifted energetically between Karl and me.

At the end of the session, he laughed as he gave me a bit of advice: "Enjoy this time of your life – you're a vibrant young woman who *should be* falling in and out of love. What great stories! Just don't get too identified with the content of the stories. Expand your field and be as big as you are supposed to be."

The next day I felt so much better. I felt cleanly and clearly in my own energy. The longing for Karl was gone. My way of thinking of Karl was even different. I kept thinking, 'What a great story!' I felt blessed instead of burdened.

That morning I sat down to work on the novel with fresh enthusiasm. Just then, the phone rang. It was Basil, calling to check in. He so rarely called, and when he did call it was usually because he sensed that I was in crisis… so I was perplexed as to why he was calling just then.

He said that he sensed "rising bliss and confidence" and he said, "Don't put an upper limit on your bliss!" As we hung up, he said, "Remember, every time I check in, it doesn't mean that something terrible is happening."

With great joy I returned to work on the novel. I wrote all morning until it was time to pick up Benjamin from school. He chattered away while I made lunch and listened to a Krishna Das CD. I happily put hummos, cheese, and olives on toasted naan bread with olive oil, but when I bit into that delicious combination, I burst into tears.

Before that dinner with Karl, I used to spend a lot of time and energy creating elaborate gourmet meals, but ever since that profound heart opening, I had largely lost my inspiration to cook and eat.

Basil had often worked with me on that, so I called him and asked why it was hard for me to enjoy food which tasted good. He said that it had to do with how I put an upper limit on my bliss. He said, "Rita, you are not frustration. You are not desire. You are a daughter of Creation. Get to work revising your ceiling!"

Over the next few days, I felt sick to my stomach. On the night of Basil's next group, I considered staying home because I felt so awful, but *Something* pulled me there. Later, when reading over the notes I took, I realized how perfect it was that I had gone.

The first thing Basil shared was a quote from Christ to St. Thomas from the Dead Sea Scrolls: "*If you do not bring forth that which is within you, that which is within you will destroy you.*" Basil explained that the strongest reason people don't move in the spiritual process is due to an intuitive knowing that if they really stepped into the flame of themselves, they would have to deal with *all* that is within them – the entire panoply of history, including all the greatness and all the vastness.

Then he spent half the evening talking about the strong bodily symptoms that often arise when beings are doing deep work.

Basil said that when people are in the process of letting go of personal will – and surrendering to the fact that they are actually vibrationally wider than they thought – at some point they often become fairly convinced that they have a brain tumor or cancer of the digestive tract or that they will soon have a heart attack. Of course, I had just been wondering myself (that very afternoon) about the possibility of colon cancer!

I relaxed as I listened to him talk about how the immune system's function is the differentiation of Self and other. I intuitively felt the truth of his explanation: "When you suppress your urge for enlightenment, this creates confusion and your immune system lowers because it actually *wants* to unfold your enlightenment."

Basil explained, "The purpose of the body is to transmit Consciousness, and if you resist, you will create pain. Each contraction of pain has some absolute truth embedded in it. If you stop asking, 'How can I feel better?' and start asking, 'What Truth is trying to be shown to me?' you can regain your strength."

After the tea break that evening, Basil talked about courage, discernment, and guidance. He advised: "Whatever is arising, don't cling to its phenomenon and don't hide in your strategies ('being sick all the time' is one strategy), but rather, stand firmly in your being, in the unraveling. Have the courage to BE with what is emerging, and the discernment to *know* what you are experiencing.

"In this time of dissolving form, in this declining empire, ask yourself, 'What am I called to do?' and listen to your inner guidance. There is a lot of anxiety out there in the Collective, but if you take in nourishment (friends, food, practices, prayers), and listen for guidance, then you will be able to navigate through – no matter what happens. All of the *information* in this age produces anxiety that is both contagious and crippling... As yogis and yoginis, it is our responsibility to continually calm ourselves so that we not only lessen our personal anxieties, but we also lessen the amount of anxiety that we contribute to the Collective Anxiety."

As the evening ended, Basil told a short story for me:

> *Once there was a firefly of Consciousness buzzing around inside a cupboard. She couldn't figure out how to get out – she was buzzing around lighting up motherhood, career, parents visiting... but she couldn't see the instructions. Then she closed her eyes and thought of God, and when she opened her eyes she saw the instructions: "Open Here."*

In the following days, I still felt sick to my stomach and my head also hurt, but as I contemplated the teachings from that night, I began to take courage. I started focusing my attention on surrendering to each and every experience.

Then one night Karl was in my dream, and that really rattled me. Fortunately, the next night I had an appointment with the energetic healer again. I asked him if I might've gotten energetically connected to Karl again through the dream, and he said yes.

We said a healing prayer to disconnect me from Karl energetically, and then we found that I was energetically connecting with Karl's wife, Martha. The healer guided me to ask Spirit to send the energy from my deepest Heart to hers.

Next he found that I had been leaking energy out of my eyes – I had been going out to the world through my eyes. He explained that the way I had been using my eyes was really not a correct use for them. I had been trying to use them in the way that the third eye is meant to be used, and that's why my eyes felt so fried.

After he infused the aura of my eyes with joy, he suggested that I begin an ongoing exploration in letting the world come to me. He said, "Let your eyes be relaxed – instead of connecting to others through your eyes, connect to them through the Heart Oneness."

At the end of the session, he reminded me that I was in a time of transition in my life. He said, "*Savor* this time of rebirth – wait and watch what is emerging. Pamper yourself, ask for help, take in nourishment. Take in pure, holy energy from the Universe. Sink your energetic roots down deep into the earth."

On my way home that night, I thought of how blessed I was. The universe was continually guiding me to people and events that supported my heart opening.

In meditation that night, I understood that this lifetime I was meant to *get it*. Indeed, there was nothing more important. And yet, I needed to stop trying so hard, because I was feeling so burnt-out. As I fell asleep, inside my head I chanted the names of God over and over, and it felt as though the entire Universe was spinning super fast within me.

The next morning I felt depressed and extremely fatigued. I forced myself out on my morning walk, but when I came home I did not feel like working. I stretched to a *Hare Krishna* chant, and then, instead of writing on the novel, I went to sleep all morning.

When I awoke, I glanced at a photo of Sri Ramana Maharshi, and I felt amazingly tender inside. I could finally feel the softness of his gaze. At last I felt worthy of his embrace.

That night, I wrote the following poem:

Creative springs are dry –
I need some juice.
Where can I find some?
Look inside
says the Wise One.
Why is She in hiding?
They won't kill Her this time.

Many times around the wheel
of oppression
with much pain
She doesn't trust
that this place is safe.
Look, Wise One,
eat these riches from my fingers.

Rita could fly
now.
in fact
she already soars
in that place
of One Heart
where we all soar together
on the One Path.

This flight she seeks
already flutters within.
she has only to
still herself

and she will hear
the Wild Fluttering
of every vibration
of the Universe –
there, in her own Heart.

During my meditation that night, I felt incredible love and compassion for both Karl and Martha – especially Martha. I sent love from my heart to hers. I felt a high frequency vibration of Love with her, and I felt merged with her in that place where she and I are One – where we *all* are One. I thought, 'I have to lay down my rose.'

Suddenly, vibrating to *her* essence was all that mattered to me. The next night, in meditation, I again dove deeply into the love I was feeling for Martha. Energetically, I felt as though I was merging in a union with her essence, and I felt such Beauty and Truth there. Just a slight thought of her would send me into a state of Bliss.

I later wrote a poem in celebration of my ongoing flight home to the bliss of my Self.

Rita's Flight

Ah, the Wise One was right.
Look inside for your juice.
Rita looked inside
and found Surprises delighting!
High love vibration with Martha
is the gold Integrity
at the labyrinth's Center!
This Gold illuminates the Heart of all –
sparkling rays touching
each cell of Creation –
glistening to the ten directions –
melting,
and the liquid gold
flowing warm like honey
out through the tired and worn stones
of the labyrinth
and beyond the ancient trees
and penetrating the stars of eternity,
which is like the coming and going
backwards and forwards
until it comes together
in a circle.
And Rita is there,
smiling with Martha,
and Kabir and Mirabai.

After *Rita's Flight* flowed through me, I sat in bliss for several days. I felt full and whole. I felt in love with everything and everyone, and I recognized those feelings – they were familiar to me from childhood and from calm times throughout my life.

That Friday night, after Bryan picked up the boys, I listened to some African music while cleaning the cottage. As I danced about, I noticed a slight longing for a man bubbling under the bliss. After enjoying a quiet meal alone, I did some work at my desk, took a hot bath, stretched, and sat down to chant and meditate.

Later, in bed, an intense sadness arose. After such a good meditation, I thought that I had sufficiently elevated my consciousness so that I would not slip back into longing, but I was wrong.

Even as I cried loudly and punched my pillow, my Higher Self was *laughing* and talking to my little personality self in the *vasana*, the magnetic pattern of desire. I heard my Self say, "In your Spiritual Heart, where you understand the Oneness – the greater Unity of *all* beings – there is only Love... Love for men, Love for yourself, Love for all beings. This pain you feel now is from the intoxicating wine of *maya*. It isn't Real."

As I lay crying, I suddenly became convinced that the pain was because Eric had rejected me, and I allowed myself to fall back into longing for *him*.

A few days later Basil called to check in. I told him about my hysterical cry over missing Eric. Basil said, "It's not about Eric, and it wasn't about Karl, and it wasn't about Anastasie, and it wasn't about Bryan... and so on..."

I tried to say that it felt different, and he said, "It is exactly the same pattern – same longing, same tone in your voice, same sadness. It may feel different because Eric is a different being, but it's the same pattern. And so you can rest in the wisdom of that – because it's a pattern, it isn't Real, and once you land in your own Truth, all this stuff will evaporate."

I understood intellectually but not emotionally. After I hung up the phone, I followed Basil's instructions: I wrote, "*It is exactly the same pattern*" forty-nine times and posted it on my fridge. I found the writing of that – forty-nine times – and the looking at it – to be both reassuring and painful.

I took comfort in Basil's words. At the end of our conversation he had said, "Rita, I have compassion for you – this is a very deep pattern." And so, even though it was painful, I understood the need to crack open that deep pattern. With sheer determination, I committed myself to not falling in love with anyone else – until such time as I could finally break through that pattern.

That night in meditation, I laughed as I remembered something which Basil had said during our phone conversation, "Rita, you *do* have intense connections with Karl and Eric, but that doesn't mean much, because *you* can have an intense connection with a doorknob!"

As I sat laughing, a certain new queer feeling of peace shimmered within and without my being. I felt the One Heart and there I found compassion for myself and for all beings. I understood how each being is unfolding in their own time, according to a Greater Plan. A radiant respect for All shone forth from my heart.

In that state, I glimpsed an understanding of how samadhi comes and goes; of how the content still flows through, but one doesn't cling to it – one stays firmly and courageously in the Bliss of one's Self.

Before sleeping that night, I wrote:

With immense reverence for Time,
I went out into the starry night.
Under a waning moon,
I pulled a few weeds from my vegetable garden.

With gusto and gratitude,
I embraced the whole process
of the ongoing journey home
to my Self.

With earth in my fingernails,
I bowed to what Is
as I offered this prayer
to Heaven:

*May **all** beings find themselves*
free
and full of bliss
in moments of time.
*And may all beings **know***
how truly Connected
we all Are.

Chapter 30 – A deep bow to all the men in my world

A dear neighbor friend of mine hosted the next evening group in her tastefully decorated home. I gazed at her interesting paintings as Basil gave a lecture on the metabolization of Time. He explained that everyone processes time and shows up in their own way. Then he described how each being in the room metabolizes time. For me he said, "Rita read the Cliff Notes of Consciousness and she has a discrete idea formation of how one is supposed to show up. So, she waits impatiently until the idea formation meets up with the shakti."

Next he said, "The higher the state of consciousness you live in, the more eternal the time which flows through you. As your consciousness expands, your body-mind's response to time shifts. Your body's metabolism actually changes as Consciousness changes your soul."

My favorite part of the evening was when he talked about how our cultural construct lacks stories: "We don't hear many stories in our culture, which is a shame, because when beings hear the words, "*A long, long time ago…*" their consciousness expands and they get to better understand time formations."

Basil advised that in everything that happens we should imagine "*A long, long time ago…*" because that would tune us in to the formations of streams of Being. He said, "Things make more sense with *a long, long time ago…* in front of them. With every problem you encounter, just remember that *a long, long time ago something began which is now present.*

"*A long, long time ago* widens the scope and allows you to be present in this moment. And, being very present in this moment, you actually go out to the edge of history. When conscious of Time, you become more dynamic, more spontaneous, and less predictable. Your organic timing becomes much stronger."

Then Basil told a story for me:

> *A long, long, long, long time ago there was an herbalist. She had her pots and she knew exactly how long to boil each herb. She told time by the dropping of water from a bamboo into a dish and she knew: bay, twenty-four drops; rose, forty-nine drops; peppermint, two drops…*
>
> *But then one day a frog came to the door and said "kiss me," and as she puckered up and kissed him, she lost track of time and the pots started to burn and everything got chaotic. The alchemical botanical laboratory was destabilized.*

Luna asked, "How did she get back on track?" and I said, "She didn't – that's why she came into this lifetime with the destabilization!" Basil nodded, saying, "Yes, she's working now on getting back on track."

Later Basil said that an attitude of Reverence in the face of Time can be very helpful. He looked at me, laughed, and said, "Rita, God is a frog waiting to be kissed."

At times, all of the spiritual work felt overwhelming to me. On May Day, at a beautiful children's festival, I lay on a blanket in the sunshine and breathed in first overwhelm, and then gratitude for my life.

As the giggling children ran around me, I wrote, "Earlier today I was feeling lonely, but then I remembered something I learned reading C.G. Jung's Foreword in *The Spiritual Teaching of Ramana Maharshi* (by Sri Ramanasramam and Shambhala Publications): my loneliness isn't Real – my loneliness is an insatiable hunger that comes from the Western illness of externalization."

That passage inspired me to continue the practice of turning inward rather than reaching out to others for my happiness. That night, while listening to a song called "*Raki*" by Oliver Mtukudzi, my heart opened as I listened to his voice. I could feel the depth of my soul through the music. With a grateful heart, I rested in my own being.

A few days later I finished writing the novel. I took it to the print shop, made copies, and put one in the mail for Karl. Then I went to the farmers' market and bought myself fresh flowers. I called Dana and Julianna and invited them to celebrate with me over Italian food and red wine.

Julianna questioned the integrity of writing the novel. She asked, "How can writing a novel – about your emotional affair with Karl – be in service of his wife, Martha?"

After we hung up the phone, I cried deeply, and then I wrote Julianna a long email letter explaining myself and my actions. At the end of the letter, I said that I did not feel comfortable celebrating with her while she was judging me so strongly.

In her reply, Julianna still did not accept my actions, but she did write that she honored my path. She recognized that my longing for union was a deep river.

Julianna and I talked on the phone later and we agreed to let it all sit for a while. She said that she needed some space from me because she saw that I was stuck in a pattern… and she needed a break from trying to mirror it back to me.

Even though I felt hurt by Julianna's judgment, I somehow managed to enjoy the celebration dinner with Dana.

After listening to me talk about the novel and about Karl and Eric, Dana said, "Rita, both of these men are in love with you." As we parted that evening, she remarked, "Lately you have a twinkle in your eyes – I keep thinking of you as a wood nymph!"

Meanwhile, Eric and I began corresponding again by email. I shared that I felt ready to talk on the phone again. Several months had passed since our last phone call. We set a phone date for Saturday night.

On Thursday, I sent the following email to Basil:

Dear Basil,

I hope this finds you and Luna doing well on your travels.

One night last week, I saw a reflection of light on my bathroom wall. At first I couldn't figure out where it was coming from, but then I realized that it was a reflection from the doorknob! I had a good laugh, since you had just said that I can have an intense connection with a doorknob!

Today is May 12th, exactly one year since the day I met Karl and Eric. I am celebrating and filled with gratitude for the connections and openings.

A few nights ago, I dreamt that you told me, *"Something BIG is about to happen with you, Rita, and you are going to call on me, and I'm not going to get any rest."* And then, in the dream, I told you, *"I also sense that something BIG is about to happen. Today I saw – not in images or colors, but in words – the magnitude of the Light which is about to pour through me – it was so intense."*

What sense do you have of that dream?

I am appreciating my boyfriend Ramana more each day.

Thank you, Basil, for that gift.

With ever-rising bliss,

Rita

Basil replied in less than an hour with the following:

Rita,

Thanks for the doorknob update…

and for the dream…

Probably an accurate assessment of light yet to come. To the degree you clean your relationship to the masculine, you will become a vessel for the highest light…

A deep bow to all the men in your world for holding you in this journey and reflecting all back towards you…

much love,

Basil

I read Basil's message again and again. Then I cried and laughed while dancing to African music. I offered a deep bow to Basil for being such a totally amazing teacher. He really knew when to honor me. I felt so overwhelmed with emotion that I almost couldn't take it in.

The next day, moments after I re-affirmed my desire to be in the NOW, my little guy Benjamin came up to me and asked, "Mama, what is more important, what is happening now, or what *can* happen?" I was so amazed at the timing of his question that I could hardly speak to answer him.

While the boys were at school that day, I sat sipping hot Ceylon tea and gazing at the beautiful flowers on my desk. I took in their beauty, and then I felt overwhelming joy over the little water drops on the butterfly-shaped pea sprouts on my toasted bagel. I felt calm and blissful as I realized that I was finally starting to *enjoy* the little things again.

I looked at the photo of beautiful, soft Ramana, and I asked, "Am I going to be a teacher? Am I going to be handed down some teachings?"

Saturday night came and the phone rang at the appointed time. I felt a bit nervous as I picked up the phone, but as soon as I heard Eric's voice, my whole being relaxed. I sank onto the couch and gazed into the candle burning on the table in front of me.

We talked for over two hours, and it was absolutely wonderful for me. I told him that I had committed myself to breaking out of my addictive love pattern.

Eric asked how I intended to break out of the pattern, and I told him, "By accepting your truth and being willing to be dear friends of the heart with you." I explained my intention to stop running sexual energy through the masculine and to stop reaching for a man with the expectation that he would fulfill my longing for God.

As we were hanging up the phone, I shared how great it was to talk with him again, and he asked, "Can we do it again sometime?" I said yes. Elated, I wrote in my journal until way past midnight.

I wrote, "I am still in love with Eric, and I guess it doesn't matter whether or not he feels the same toward me. I can adore him and enjoy the juice of absolute heart connection that we have over the phone." Then I wondered, '*How am I going to clean my relationship to the masculine here?*'

The next morning, the sky rained hard upon the earth. I lit a candle, and read the introduction to a sweet version of the *Ramayana* (by Ranchor Prime, Mandala Publishing). I was particularly touched by the following passage:

> *In one sense, Ravana represents the dark side in us all, that part of our psyche that tries to love by possessing, rather than releasing. In his misguided attempt to love Sita he imprisoned her, and that bound him to the path of self-destruction. This is the fate of selfish love: it harms both the lover and the beloved. The love that is material binds us, whereas the love that is spiritual sets us free. Through the fire of grief, or through voluntary sacrifice, our misplaced attachments are purified and transformed, and the pure love of the soul shines forth.*

Reading that passage reminded me that I really did love Eric purely in my heart, and I did not want to harm him (or me) with a selfish love. And suddenly, I *GOT* the pattern! The deep pattern about which Basil had instructed me to write forty-nine times was exactly the same. I suddenly could clearly see my misplaced attachments and projected needs.

And once I saw them, I found myself standing firmly in myself, *OWNING* it all – the misplaced attachments, the projected needs, the loneliness, the migraines, the struggles with the boys...

... The feeling of being the victim disappeared quite suddenly as if by a strong magic force or wind. And there was such a feeling of power and peace associated with owning my part in it all. In that state of power, I bowed deeply to the men in my world – the men who had held me through the twists and turns of the ongoing journey home to my Self.

As I relaxed more deeply into owning my own 'stuff,' I felt as though Krishna, Shiva, and Ramana all kept rushing in to fill me with Love and Light. I felt a pure love for Eric, and if I stayed in my Self feeling that Love, it was so Blissful, but any time my little ego self caught wind of the love for Eric, a longing to be near him would arise... but now I was onto that vasana!

Like a spiritual detective, I began to track all the clues surrounding the *vasanas*, the magnetic patterns encoded in my being over so many lifetimes. I began to see my loneliness as a vasana that was not Real. The loneliness was just a little break in my Deep Connection to the One.

My Deep Connection to the One began spreading and taking over. Gradually the vasanas lessened in intensity, as the illusion – of separation from God – lessened.

My little self wanted to hold on to the desire for union with a man as my ultimate purpose here on earth, but my higher Self *knew* that *God* was actually my purpose here this lifetime.

Chapter 31 – Spiritual detective falls in love again and again…

While Julianna and I sat with the rift between us, I continued to contemplate the integrity issue. I wrote in my journal:

"At the soul level and at the cellular level, there is no conception of "integrity" regarding the societal form of "marriage." Also, if we lived in Biblical times or in some places of the world today, where men have more than one wife, then it wouldn't be seen as a lack of integrity for us to be in love. Karl would simply marry me as his second wife. All the judgment on this comes from society and religion. Yet, the question of integrity here runs deep for me."

Meanwhile, more than two years had passed since I had had sex with a man. I was trying to breathe the sexual energy up into my heart, as Basil had suggested, but I was growing weak! One night I wrote, "The moon is shining half-full in all Her Glory, and I am full-to-bursting with sexual energy!"

I got in bed and pleasured myself while praying to Lord Shiva the whole time. I offered the released sexual energy out for healing anywhere it might be needed in the Whole. I asked Shiva to clean my relationship to the masculine and I prayed to be a pure vessel for Light.

The next day I felt lighter, calmer, and happier. I wondered if my offering pleased my Lord? I bowed to Lord Shiva again and again, and I focused on being married to only Him.

That evening I got an email from Karl. He said that he had read the novel and he would return it to me soon with a few edits. At the end of his message, he wrote, "The novel is stunning. Right to the very last letter, I was unsure just how you were going to finish it – suspenseful to the very end. Once I read that last letter, it was obvious and most beautiful."

It was funny, but when I read that, I felt so unattached to the writing of the novel. I did not feel any sense of pride for writing it, but rather, I felt as though the novel was written *through* me.

I still felt uneasy about having contact with Karl, so I wrote him yet another letter asking him if he had told Martha about our connection and contact. He replied, "Martha and I completed our conversation about the dialogue you and I have had over the past year. It was not as difficult as I feared (naturally). It has been healing for each of us.

"She knows about all the periods we were in contact and the 'happy ending' which is only a beginning of course. She knows the essential heart attachments we have had and how we incrementally released them into unconditional love. Thank you for the nudge."

Just as I started feeling better about the contact with Karl, I started feeling worse about the contact with Eric… because there was no contact! For a few days after our wonderful phone reunion, I felt such a pure love for him, but then, when he didn't call again, I started wondering why he wasn't calling.

Even though I really wanted to talk with Eric again, I knew better than to call him too soon. I knew that he needed time and space to process our phone call. So I waited… and waited, and finally, after two weeks, when I was just about to burst with impatience, he sent the following email:

Hi Rita,

It was good to talk with you again. I really care about you, your well being, and the courageous inner work you are doing. As I believe I've said before, it has certainly inspired me to do the same. All this inner work will continue to pay dividends (for us both) I'm sure.

After our conversation though, it became clear to me that I'm not ready to reconnect at the present time. I can't explain it much beyond a deep inner knowing that I have more personal work to do. I don't know if you felt the same on your end or not. This brings me much sadness, but I'm getting this sense that I need more time before reconnecting as dear friends of the heart – which is my sincerest heartfelt wish for us. I'm just not able to do it right now and think it's going to take a bit of time. I thought I was ready, I wanted to be, but in fact I wasn't.

Rita, this is certainly not farewell (at least as far as I'm concerned), at all, but just a "bye for now," until such time that I can come to you from a place of wholeness – something I'm unable to do right now, as I am really struggling with some of my own stuff.

My heart is very heavy over this Rita. I think it took a while for it all to catch up to me.

Know that you are in my thoughts and prayers and in my heart.

With Love,

Eric

I wrote back and explained to Eric that I knew we still had a very sweet heart connection – a connection that would endure a break in contact. I told him that I trusted his deep inner knowing, and I knew that we would reconnect when the time was right. I shared that I was feeling the peace and power associated with owning my 'stuff.'

Eric replied, "I am sincerely touched. You are amazing – all the hard work you've been doing sure seems to be paying off and I am so glad that you've reached a place of Peace and Power. I can literally feel it coming through your email. Wow! This is fantastic and makes me smile ☺ Blessings to you my Dear One and I look forward to reconnecting in the hopefully not-too-distant future."

He wasn't ready to reconnect? What a surprising twist to the story!

A few days later, I went to get a massage, and the massage therapist advised me to take baths. She said, "A bath is spiritually moisturizing." Then she gave me an affirmation to say: "*I AM letting go. On all levels.*"

Yes, I was letting go.

At that time, I met a beautiful Peruvian woman named Raya who led *kirtan* – call and response chanting – in a nearby town. I began attending

113

evenings of kirtan with her. As a Krishna devotee on the bhakti yoga path, Raya performed traditional prayers and pujas (rituals) before beginning the chants. Adorned in a colorful sari, she lit incense and tossed rose petals onto the beings in front of her. Each kirtan I took her a fresh rose, so she lovingly called me the rose gopi.

The first time I sat with Raya, during the first chant, I experienced a strong coming-home feeling. Upon hearing Radha's name, I swelled with emotion.

I felt so in love with Krishna and Radha, and I wondered if I had worshipped them in past lives... I suddenly felt as though I had lived in India before.

When I felt myself go into a deeper space, I could feel Karl there. I felt a bit of longing, and at the same time, I kept a bigger perspective of Time and Consciousness and the Greater Plan. I reaffirmed my commitment to being there for his wife, Martha, and I reminded myself, "Keep your mind on God."

When I got home that night I felt so high, but the next day I felt very depressed. The cycles of depression with ovulation were intensifying such that I began to question my resolve to *not* take an antidepressant.

I wrote, "Wait. I really don't want to numb myself with medication. Give it another year with the spiritual practices. Read about great beings and saints. Throw the depression and shame into the spiritual fire, and open to the healing path that is correct for me."

Then I read that Ramana Maharshi was most inspired by the life of Kabir and by the saints in Shiva's cult. Ramana felt an intense desire to be one of those saints. I, too, felt an intense desire to be a saint, and I remembered that I had always felt that desire – even as a little Catholic girl.

I sensed that I would not be a silent saint like Ramana – rather, I would be *out there*, putting Love and Light *OUT*, through words, both written and spoken.

I wrote Basil the following email:

Dear Basil,

Here is a progress report from a spiritual detective!

I am having more fun with the process now – delighting in all the "clues"...

My love of food is returning, especially for Italian and Mediterranean foods...

My love of LIFE is returning – I hope that I never have to go into such darkness again.

Last night I saw a documentary film, *The Wild Parrots of Telegraph Hill*. It was correct mirroring for me – I fell in love with Mark Bittner; with his saintliness.

I've done some really good release work with both Eric and Karl. I burned through the victim in me – I finally GOT the pattern... So now, the vasanas still rise to be purified, but they don't fully grip me like before.

114

I still have tender feelings with Ramana, and I'm in love with Shiva, Krishna, Radha, Rama, Sita, Hanuman, and Saraswati...

And the writing coming through me has been getting better...
I finished a novel that Karl has edited, and I feel that I am living myself into the truth of my calling.

Even with all this progress, I do still have the third chakra knot in my belly. It won't let go! I am praying, meditating, purifying (no meat, no orgasms... well, except for a few), practicing patience... I still have some depression with the hormonal shifts, which now manifests as crying for no known reason (I can't blame it on Eric or Karl now!), and I still feel really tired a lot of the time.

On a funny note, shortly after you and I corresponded about my doorknob connections, I was having dinner with the boys and Joshua wouldn't eat the soup. I urged him to just try the black bean chili. He took one bite and said, "UGG – this tastes like roasted doorknob!" (I had not told them anything about the doorknob connections – I laughed so hard when he said that!)

Overall, I am feeling more surrendered to the mothering path, and I am enjoying the boys more. I am bringing more humor and they appreciate that...

Well, that's a good report for now – there's always more... the Dance goes on... through all the ups and downs, thankfully there is more underlying calm now.

I'm looking forward to being with you and Luna again soon.
With ever-rising Gratitude for you and your teachings,
Love,
Rita

Basil replied,

Rita, thanks for the update... and the purification alert...
It's important to align with one emblem of the divine and stay in marriage to that particular one –
skittery mind makes for skittery love affairs...
watch clouds daily
eat more aduki beans
stay away from chocolate
read Kahlil Gibran
invite your boys into your playful heart more...
we are a bit tired of traveling...
love,
Basil

After I read his message, I went into many reactions over him saying that I needed to align with one emblem of the divine. I did not know how to choose only one – I felt so in love in so many directions, and besides, weren't they all One anyway?

115

Basil had said before that it was clear that I was wired to fall in love, and now he was saying that I had to choose only one? I did not understand that, and the harder I tried to choose one, the more delusional I felt with the process. I began to doubt myself as a vessel for Light.

I felt ashamed of myself, like I wasn't doing it right. In that place of shame, all kinds of vasanas surfaced: loneliness, desire for union with an earthly man, embarrassment, and thoughts of suicide. I didn't really want to end my life, but I wanted to escape the pain of the spiritual path.

I felt as though I was further away from the goal than ever. As I sat in meditation that night, a huge cry burst forth. While I cried, I was filled with self-loathing.

After I stopped crying, I took out my journal and wrote, "I *do* love myself. I am doing the best that I can. Remember to cultivate a radiant respect for the unfolding of each being, including my own unfolding. Be gentle with myself. Let go of attachments to *all* others, including all aspects of the Divine."

When I emerged from all of that, I felt calm and humbled. I wrote the following poem to Basil:

I cannot choose between the red and yellow roses

I cannot choose between my sons –
How, then, could I choose between Shiva and Krishna?

I cannot choose between my brothers –
How, then, could I choose between Sita and Radha?

I cannot choose between my parents –
How, then, could I choose between Hanuman and Rama?

I cannot choose between the sun and the moon –
both are shining always within and without.

Nothing is separate
All is One –
my nature, the greater Nature, God,
and all the emblems of the Divine.

This Oneness is always within and without –
How then, could I align with only one?

How can you ask me, great teacher,
to choose between my fingers?

How can I choose only one chamber of my heart?

With much weeping and delusion and doubt,
I tried to close down the open chambers,
but they refused to close!

My Heart dances in many directions
with enough love for All –

I fall back into my Self
and listen within

I look out at Ramana
and breathe in his gentle guidance –
to remember –
to return to stillness –

And, there, the love for Shiva and Krishna
blooms quietly
like the red and yellow roses.

When I read the words of my own poetry, I felt strong.

Chapter 32 – June retreat and love poems to God

A week before Basil and Luna were scheduled to return from their travels, I fell into a serious contraction. I felt very depressed, even numb. I wanted to ANNIHILATE my mind, ego, and personality structures. I felt like I was light years away from realizing the Greater Unity.

Yet, even in my self-loathing bubble of shame and despair, there was a tiny chard of hope that *believed* that I was actually close to the goal – so close that the ego defense was wrapping me in a heavy, thick garment of depression.

I was scared to believe in that little hope because it almost felt like an ego trick – like a delusion of grandeur.

I wrote in my journal, "Maybe I'm not going to reach the goal. Maybe the patterns are too strong to release? Maybe the mayic veils are too thick?"

By the next group with Basil, I was feeling less depressed. When I walked in, Basil said, "Rita's here in all her elegance." Then he asked how I was doing. I said, "I'm still me," and he said, "not quite."

That evening Basil explained that the correct naming of things releases them. He then described the key qualities of the Divine Mother: "She is always present, always nourishing, and always interested in our well-being." To name and release the Mother, he led us in the chant, *Om Shree Matre Namaha.*

At the end of the evening, Basil advised that we each practice seeing the world as the Rose of Existence. He said, "We all have pain and suffering, and we have to open anyway – now – and not wait until we feel better."

Later that night I wrote in my journal, "In listening to Basil talk tonight, I got such a pearl of acceptance for what I am unraveling; such a jewel of compassion for myself. I felt patience arising."

The next day on my walk, I felt such bliss. I experienced a long, sustained feeling of ecstasy, almost orgasmic. I felt so in love with Life and God and Everything and Everyone. I wondered if I could grab onto that expansion and hold it as an underlying current, even during the inevitable contractions.

That night, after the boys went to their papa's house, I lit candles and listened to Krishna Das chant to Ma Durga, the aspect of the Divine Mother who rides a lion and slays the demons with her many weapons. I lit incense, danced, and shook a little bell. Then I sat in meditation before going to sleep.

The next morning I felt purified and refreshed. As I chanted *Om Namah Shivaya*, I felt waves of gratitude. Then I got in my car to drive to a three-day retreat with Basil.

While driving and chanting to Shiva and Durga, I felt whole. I felt strong in my being and ready to greet whatever would come to me during the retreat.

The first chant of the retreat was, appropriately for me, *Om Namah Shivaya*. Within seconds of chanting, I relaxed into a deep state of ecstatic bliss with Lord Shiva. I felt Him purifying me with the Divine Ganges River flowing through me, and I also felt the goddess Durga within my being.

After the chant, Basil correctly named what I had been feeling during the chant. He said, "Rita is trying to figure out what to do with all of those currents running through her. She has power surges with tremendous passion embedded in them, but she is not just that. She is also the one who is perceiving the currents and learning how to let that energy flow in ascent to God."

Basil then advised everyone, "Take your openings extremely seriously! You are *There*, when deep states happen. But when you are in reactions, don't take them too seriously – just let them go through and release them."

Someone asked Basil how we can purify our *nadis*, the subtle vibratory channels which hold the tendencies of lifetimes of experiences. Basil said, "When we create heat – *tapas* – that raises the vibration of the tendencies. How to create more heat? Devotion, cultivation of the heart's longing, and a passionate desire for Liberation – these are triggers to move the heat. Once the heat is moving, just let the current run."

During the next chant, *Om Ma*, I felt many bodily discomforts at first, but then I felt an ecstatic Union with Lord Shiva again. I felt a burning current, like a Ganges purification, and I sensed Durga there, riding Her Lion with passionate rapture as She worked to slay the demons of our minds.

Then, in that ecstatic bliss state, I felt a profound sorrowful longing to return to the Ganges River – to be beside those holy waters, wearing long skirts and anklets with bells. I missed that Holy Place of heat and Light and I longed to return there… (Note: I have not yet physically traveled to India this lifetime.)

After the *Om Ma* chant, Basil talked about the Award of Grace. He said, "Grace is a home-free card – when you pull it, you get Home more quickly. It's mysterious why some souls pull it – it's free and you never know when it's going to hit.

"I remember when it hit Rita – I was standing by the window, and she was standing at the stove, stirring the soup. She was worrying so much about being a good mother, that she missed it. I watched as it rippled up the back of her spine.

"Once Grace hits, you can relax and enjoy the process. And then if you are Rita, you can go out and enjoy looking at some bucksome men!"

Basil laughed as I protested. I said, "That's *not* the kind of men I'm attracted to!" He explained, "Rita, when I give you the image of bucksome men, it creates distaste in your desire structure which takes that desire down a notch. This is an exercise of tantra yoga – focusing on the opposite image of your desire can neutralize that desire."

He smiled at me for a moment, and then said, "Rita, when you stabilize your connection to God, then men can come, and they will be awakened and it will be lovely."

While we waited for lunch to be served, Luna and I lounged on the couch together, and she asked how I was doing. I told her about the novel and about the more full release with Karl. Then, just as I was launching into the story about Eric cutting off the contact after our wonderful phone call, Basil joined us, and he told Luna to watch my heart. She saw that it was "prickly" and Basil said, "It's prickly because Rita was falling into her addiction to sensation and she knew that she was doing something that was not good for her heart."

Then he said to me, "Rita, it's your choice whether you want to have the apricot silken descent with deep creativity flowing out of it, or you want to have that spidery spikey web in your heart." I asked him if it was really my choice or if it was already predestined, and he said, "Oh, it's your choice, and it will take discipline. You have been working to clean your relationship to the masculine, and letting go of addiction to sensations is next. To help in letting go of that addiction, continue abstaining from chocolate."

Basil looked at me in a funny way for a long time. When I asked what he was doing, he said, "I was clearing you of content." I asked if that would be temporary and he said, "Maybe not – you never know when Grace comes."

He continued, "Rita, you have important things to write which are not your story. You need to start writing more to purify your imagination. You are running stories through your imagination because of your addiction to sensation and content, so you have to purify that vasana. Keep going into Bliss in Sadhana!"

That afternoon I looked at myself in the mirror and my beauty felt powerful to me. I knew that I had often used my looks as power, as a way to magnetize people. I did not want to do that anymore. I wrote in my journal, "I want to find that place of absolute inner connection with Lord Shiva – which I have felt so strongly today – and let that Light emanate out to others for healing."

After dinner Basil talked about how we are each being deconstructed. He explained that we should have gratitude because what is deconstructing us is also *constructing* us anew. He used me as an example: "Rita has been landing men and words with vigor. After lifetimes of using the form world to reach ecstasy, she has now found ecstasy in her own inner states. She's now in Bliss with God."

I smiled, and Basil continued with a little story for me:

And our heroine, without any content, took to canning peaches and serving strawberries with whipped cream... and she opened a food kitchen to feed those who were underprivileged... and in her spare time, because she had some now that it wasn't all filled with anxiety, she wrote beautiful love poems to God.

I felt so much joy stirring around in my being. Basil saw this, and he said, "Rita, instead of forcing content into a story, deepen into the beauty that arises, and describe *that* as love poems to God. Remember that language should be in praise of essence and of the miraculous unfolding of each being. Writing should communicate the elixir of ecstasy."

That night I prayed to become a vessel through which the goddess Saraswati could praise essence.

The next morning, after chanting, Basil gave the following lecture:

"As yogis, we have to cultivate the Witness – the ability to be behind what is happening. We have to pull back far enough to read the patterns, and to understand that the patterns of resistance are not the essence.

"When the shakti of *seeing* comes through the nervous system, it can be draining until the body is trained to run that much current. When you burn through the ego structure and the flow of prana in the subtle body becomes more smooth, then the world becomes ecstatically beautiful.

"On the Yoga Path, when the separated forces begin to unite, they create heat, and the heat is the fire which takes you home to the Self. So you are burning from the inside. In order to get to the Union, you have to see where Union is lacking. You should always be suspicious if you are reacting to the surface of things. When you are in the deeper states, you see depth everywhere.

"It is inconceivable to your ego, but you will be replaced with a better you. When you anchor to the place that is *not* you, then what *Is* emerges as a prayer. When the quality of emerging becomes your baseline, your ego starts to float – and then you don't cling to the rising pieces – and the more you let go, the more the icebergs of the ego melt. Self-effort has to be tempered with the humility of the realization that *you* cannot do it – you are not the doer – only then does your effort bear fruit. *Grace* itself is the source of the opening."

Later that morning, during a break, I wrote the following poem:

> *Have I truly chosen the red rose,*
> *O' My Lord Shiva?*
> *Does it matter if the color changes?*
> *I've chosen the Rose of Existence!*
> *With a few little strategies*
> *lingering in pockets,*
> *all the while the Rose blooms –*
> *ever-fragrant,*
> *ever-opening,*
> *taking me deep –*
> *to the current of Durga heat.*

I gave the poem to Basil and he read it, but did not comment. Later on he said, "Rita is the Queen of Content. The upside of this is that her writing has *Rasa*. The downside is that she can become rigid about her story-lines." I knew what he meant. For example, I had a tendency to complain that I was tired all the time, and I could become very rigid in that story-line.

The next morning, on the last day of the retreat, we chanted *Devatma Shakti*, and then Basil gave a "Weather Report" for the beings present. For me, he said the following: "Rita will be to the top of Jacob's Ladder of fretting by Tuesday, and there will be trouble with the youth on Wednesday evening, but by Friday she will have found a new way of embracing the inner lover."

At the morning break he gave me an assignment: "Rita, when fretting, count down from 108. Eventually you can learn the 108 Sanskrit names of the Goddess and recite them, but for now just count down from 108.

"And remember, Rita, educated seekers are articulate and skillful, and they know not to fret at the surface. They know that it is far better to surrender the surface fret and let the inner planes work them."

When I sat back down, I felt the love of all the hearts around me, and I wrote this little poem:

> *O' My Lord Shiva*
> *What a beautiful stew!*
> *I sit in gratitude*
> *boiling*
> *with Durga heat.*

That afternoon Basil talked about the strategies we use when we are trying to hold on to our attachments. He said, "In order to truly let go of attachments, you can't have any secondary games or strategies going – you have to actually truly be willing to let go, and if you do let go, then your life will fill itself."

I asked, "How can someone put down their strategies when their strategies don't want to be put down?" Basil smiled, and said, "Rita, you will transcend your tendencies through *Passion*. Instead of waking up each morning and saying how tired you are, when you awake, feel your Passionate ecstatic love for God and say, *"Wow, I am in the arms of the Beloved, and I am going to see that through this entire day."* In order to put down your strategies, you will have to become more interested in something else."

In the last hour of the retreat, Basil talked about selfless service. He explained that a subtle form of selfless service is to make others more important than yourself. He said, "If when you look at someone, your content rises more than who they really are, then you are gnawing on the bones of yourself. But when you truly put others' needs first, you see into their depth and that helps take your own heart knot away."

Then he looked at me and said, "Rita, when you're having a down day, and the boys are crabby, think of what you can do to serve the beings around you, and then do it. The ability to pick up and serve is important in helping Westerners with their feelings of isolation and separation. Ask yourself how you can serve more."

The day after that retreat, I felt disconnected, like I was in a gap between contraction and expansion, but a few days later, on the Summer Solstice, I felt more connected again. I felt such gratitude for those days at the retreat. In the sunshine by the lake with my boys, I wrote:

"O' My Lord Shiva, my heart swells with gratitude for that time in the Core. As I watch the red rose come forth, the glee spins around! I still love the yellow and pink roses – just hearing their Names, a blossoming pulses – Rama, Sita, Hanuman, Krishna, Radha! I sip hot tea with rose petals, and delight in You, My Lord Shiva, as I breathe in the current of Durga heat."

A couple of nights later I dreamt that *I was talking with a man with dark blue skin!* I felt happy when I awoke, but later that day I fell into the gap again. I wrote the following poem:

O' My Lord Shiva,
From pickles to peaches,
my life is about more
than a hot cup of tea!
My life is about more
than the stories I tell –
I see the fabric of existence
but I am not yet purified
to sustain the Light –
I am numb in the Gap,
knowing You are 'There'
and the vasanas are 'here'
and I am in the nothing
between there and here.
O' My Lord Shiva,
Please return me soon
to the current of Durga heat.

In that gap, I collapsed into a heavy contraction one night. The next morning I wrote, "Last night I opened a can of thick, black *maya* and took a big drink! Oh, Lord Shiva, please help me release all illusions and negative tendencies."

During the last week of June, Karl and I exchanged a few emails about the novel. In one email to Karl, I shared that I was thinking of shaving my head – in celebration of freedom. He replied,

"I am awed by the intensity by which you pursue your inner work of transformation and honored to know you. Must you abandon your lovely hair on your path? Or can you do something more metaphorical? As we move with intention ever further into our Essential Selves, the stirring and the purification will only continue – it will just be more subtle content. So all we can do is try to enjoy the journey (that is what I hold to).

"It appears I will be in Mt. Shasta sometime this Fall to work with Basil. More on that later along with the joy and the pain."

What? Karl would be in my town in the Fall? I wasn't sure what surprised me more – that he would be in town soon, or that he had discouraged my hair shaving. I felt agitated by his message.

On the first of July, Karl called on the phone. He told me that he and Martha were most likely moving toward a mutual separation, which was not because of me. He asked me to pray for Martha in the coming weeks, and I said that I would definitely hold her in my prayers.

As we were hanging up, he said, "If you get your hair shaved soon, it will grow some before I see you."

What? Why did Karl care what my hair looked like? I hung up the phone, feeling a certain kind of rebellious determination to get rid of my hair. I called Anastasie and Sina and invited them to shave my hair on the Fourth of July.

Chapter 33 – Rita Ann Shiva!

The night after Karl called, I wrote:

"I can relax now and find true Union with Lord Shiva... Marry my Lord... *Rita Ann Shiva!*"

One day I drove to a nearby city to do some shopping. On the freeway exit, a homeless guy stood with a cardboard sign which read "Homeless, Work or Food, Thank You." My heart cracked wide open. It was as if my heart spread out across the valley. I felt pained by this question: 'How did he get to that place?' And I asked 'Why are we not taking better care of people?'

I gave the man a package of crackers. He said, "God Bless You," and I said, "God Bless You," and I drove on, wondering, '*How can I finish my sandwich now?*'

I reflected that the homeless man and I were briefly connected as I passed the crackers to him – for that second when we were each touching a side of the package, it became a live connection, rather than just one more homeless guy on the street. That connection touched me deeply and ignited a fire in me... the fire of compassion that longs to help people in need.

The next day I felt tremendous gratitude for food, as I wrote the following poem:

> *O' My Lord Shiva,*
> *I am blissing*
> *on the elixir of ecstasy*
> *in this food I prepared!*
> *Escarole chopped thinly,*
> *fresh lemon juice,*
> *pure olive oil,*
> *sea salt and black pepper,*
> *cheddar cheese –*
> *crumbled so creamy and white,*
> *red cherry tomatoes,*
> *whole wheat naan toasted –*
> *O' Divine Lover,*
> *Play with me!*

On the Fourth of July, Anastasie and Sina arrived with the brilliant sunshine of midday. I poured glasses of red wine, lit a candle and a stick of incense, and twirled a little bell while I read the following poem:

Ode to Shiva for July 4th Hair Shaving

O' My Lord Shiva,
I am drunk on the wine of Your Love!

With this hair shaving,
I release the deep pattern

of projecting my needs and desires
onto another earthling.

With this hair shaving,
I embrace this Union with You,
Dear Shiva —
this Union of ecstatic Bliss
which is dancing me deeper
into my true Self
and spreading Joy
to the ten directions!

With this hair shaving,
I enjoy the freedom
of self-sufficiency,
I rest in the current of Durga heat,
I trust in the Mystery,
I delight in the surprises!

With this hair shaving,
I swirl in the Beauty
of the infinite Rose of Existence
which is blooming in my Heart.

I then shared the following with my dear friends:

"This hair shaving is a religious offering of sorts – it is a commitment to putting the Self first... Self being the one universal Heart of Bliss, that Place where we All are connected. This is a commitment to releasing all the strategies and patterns in me which block the Light of the Self. I am focusing on *Release – Bliss – Joy – Freedom – Beauty.*"

We drank a toast and then headed to the back steps to get rid of my hair. Rather than going all the way and actually shaving my head, I chose the number six blade on the clipper set. When they handed me the mirror, I laughed! I was buzzed in more ways than one – the wine had gone to my head, and, I had a really cute buzzcut!

That night I sent my *Ode to Shiva for July 4th Hair Shaving* poem out to several friends by email.

Ari replied:

May it be so
and may the compassion
you offer to the world
reflect back
upon you
as you hold yourself
gently
in the twists and turns
of this
wild and precious life.

Karl replied:

On Beauty – This Rita Ann

Your Beauty Within,
Beauty Without, and Around...
Your Beauty Abounds.
The Rose that you Are
Can never be concealed
By just a haircut!

Well, that haircut was such a good move for me. My head felt so light and open. I loved my buzzcut! The next night I danced around my kitchen eating crackers and then I wrote the following in my journal:

"I feel so satisfied in the now that I feel as though I could dance alone in my kitchen eating crackers for centuries and not feel lonely! I feel so satisfied with my Lord Shiva and with the Self that I am evermore sinking into and delighting in. In *There*, the ancient tides of forever hold me, and that is All I need. I am Ripe. Or, *almost* Ripe."

A few days later I sent an email to Karl asking him a few questions about the novel. He answered my questions and then he wrote,

"You are still, and always will be, a soulmate for me. My sense is that the 'big work' for this lifetime that we gifted each other with is successfully complete. I do look forward to seeing you in person again this Fall; I know it will be affirming of our transmutation of conditional love into unconditional Love for each other – pure."

I replied:

"You are also a soulmate for me. I also feel that we have transformed the attached love into a pure love. As for our 'big work' being complete, I'm not as clear about that as you are. My sense is that there is more, though I have no clear picture of what (or when) that would be."

Then my parents came to visit and I didn't correspond with Karl again for a few weeks. I went camping in the mountains with my parents and my boys. After thirty-six years of marriage, my parents were still in love. The loving affection between them filled me with longing for a man.

While the boys played games with their grandparents, I read *The Storyteller's Daughter* by Saira Shah, and as I read about the atrocities in Afghanistan, I felt embarrassed about my longing for a man. I vowed ever strongly to release that deep pattern and to seek my true Self, that I might become a vessel for Light unto this earth in pain.

Even though I felt frustrated with myself, I noticed that I was beginning to feel more patient with the process. I was not taking the pattern as seriously as I had before. I thought of Basil saying to me at that last retreat, "Chocolate and men – a while longer."

That night, by the dim flashlight's glow, I wrote in my journal:

"O' My Lord Shiva, dance through the layers of my distorted being, burn through the layers of anger and fatigue, clean through the layers of darkness and doubt, O' My Lord Shiva, I am Yours!"

The next morning, while the boys built a fire with Grandpa, I wrote:

"O' My Lord Shiva, the varied stripes of attached love – I am not much fond of them. I am Yours, Shiva – Let me ride on the wild tiger of Pure Love!"

I kept reminding myself that I had buzzed off my hair to be in Union with Shiva. I felt stronger that night as I wrote:

"O' My Lord Shiva, Gratitude rings through the bells of eternity in the ecstatic layers of my being. O' I am Yours! O' My Lord Shiva, You have gifted me beyond beyond – What can I say? I know that I am NOT my body, NOT my mind, NOT the patterns and content flowing through me. O' My Lord Shiva, when will I be purified? I so long to hold onto You, to be a vessel for Your Light – when will I be Your saint? I feel closer to Ripe – but not there yet. O' My Lord Shiva, Dance me closer to Ripe!"

Since it is my nature to open and close in a very intense way, the daily expansions and contractions continued, but with each passing day, I could feel the Ground of Being deepening beneath it all.

Then one fine July afternoon, Basil called to check in. I told him about the most recent contraction, and he said, "Rita, when you realize that you are passion becoming Itself, then you will realize that it's not your passion and then you'll stop chasing yourself. You are trying so hard to dampen down your passion – you need to make peace with the Passion within you, and then when Karl visits this Fall, you'll be fine."

I tried to remain calm as I answered, "Basil, Karl thinks that he and I are done, but when he told me that, I didn't believe him." Basil said, "I didn't believe him either. You are both making a valiant effort to be done, for which you get credit, but you are not done.

"You each tried to shut down something that wasn't organically ready to be shut down. This was honorable, but the truth is that you will not be done with each other until you resolve it to its highest component – until you resolve your feelings for each other into pure Love. And then, all of your tantric stuff will get cleaned up."

I shared that Karl was still showing up in my dreams and visions, and Basil said, "I rest my case. The fact that he's appeared in your dreams and visions means that you have a deep spiritual connection. Actually, the connection between you two is quite lovely. You're not done, but it's not what you might be thinking Rita, so you don't have to freak out – but if you want to freak out, then go put little Infinity signs all over your front porch!"

Before we hung up, Basil said, "Good work, Rita." At that point, I really needed to hear that I was doing good work. I collapsed into my bed feeling much gratitude for Basil. I felt grateful that Basil had confirmed the truth that I already *knew* – that Karl and I were not done.

For the next couple of days, I experienced really wonderful connections with all of the people around me. I actually could feel myself *being where I was* in each moment. And I really enjoyed being with my boys. We shared in simple summer pleasures like making homemade popsicles and running through the sprinkler together.

Meanwhile, I tried to figure out what Karl and I still needed to do together. I looked at his photo and meditated on our connection, but I couldn't *feel* him – it felt closed, like we had cut each other off. I felt a certain agitation and I could almost imagine a shouting match between us. At the same time, I felt grateful for our meeting and for all that I had learned from him.

Then one morning, Karl's friend Diana called to let me know that Karl's mother was in the hospital. She said, "Since you and Karl have such a deep connection, I thought it would be good if you held his mother in your prayers."

What? I could not understand why *she* had called me – why, when Karl had said we were 'done,' did she want *me* to be involved in praying for his mother? Had Karl asked her to call me?

I called Basil and told him the story, and he said, "Rita, using the second chakra energy incorrectly creates contracted states of mind which show up later in the heart as vibrations of mistrust and suspicion. Remember, the only thing – *the only thing* – you have control over is how you choose to react.

"At the heart of every connection is Love – It gets distorted because of people's patterns. Open to love and serve the beings around you. Open your heart to others and then you will automatically see the love with Karl. Don't fixate on him or on Diana – just practice serving the beings around you.

"And as for you and Karl – when I say that it's not done, I don't mean that you have to live with him, I just mean that there is more to blossom. There are matrixes of connections established through lifetimes and it just has to ripen – the karmic connection just has to ripen. Don't worry – just notice.

"What's underneath the worry in you now is possessiveness and what's under that is no sense of Self. You have to learn to fill from the inside and to stop grasping for beings on the outside. A fully purified heart has no exclusivity and basically no preferences. Everything is non-dual, with absolute equal vision."

I asked if he preferred Luna, and he said, "With Luna, it's not a preference – our relationship is arising out of our connection." Then I asked if Ramana Maharshi ever had a partner, and Basil said no – Ramana said that God had taken mercy because he was so fastidious he would've driven a partner crazy!

Next Basil gave me a writing assignment... he said to write five small poems in appreciation of the service offered by the checkers at the natural food store. I balked at that assignment, and he said, "Rita, you have to turn the discerning power of intellect – which is quite formidable in you – into service. You have a fairly good capacity for writing, and if you do this writing assignment, it will help to develop your power of discernment, which, if used correctly in you, is the masculine. Then you won't need to go seeking the masculine outside of yourself."

Before we hung up, Basil said, "You have great potential, Rita, and that's why I can't cut you much slack – and that's also why you have to be rigorous with how you hold yourself."

The next day, I wrote the following in an email to Basil:

"You said that I have a "fairly good capacity for writing." I'm not sure what you mean by fairly good. Before, you advised me to make the creative descent into my first lover and you said that my vocation had descended. And at the last retreat you said that I have important things to write which are not my stories. I took all of that to heart and I have been rearranging my life to put writing first. Now, are you implying that I should be doing something else?"

Basil replied:

"Fairly good writer?

"A really good writer would jump at an assignment to render into words the experience of the world... it's not about your writing ability... it's about your approach, or your view... don't fret... writing is important to you..."

I read Basil's words again and again, and then I cried for the rest of the day. I felt like a failure. I felt angry at him for pushing me beyond what I could handle. I wanted to quit being his student...

... And, after eleven at night, when I was crying so hard that I could hardly breathe and I was feeling suicidal and desperate, I called Karl's friend Diana. She was the only person I could think to call at that hour. At one of Basil's retreats she had told me that she never goes to sleep before midnight.

Calling Diana turned out to be a good move. We talked for almost two hours and she offered me really good support. I felt most grateful for her presence, and through our sweet connection I let go of the suspicion that I had previously felt towards her.

The next day I continued crying. Fortunately, Karl called that night from a business trip. He sensed that I needed support, and he was so right. I read Basil's email message to him, and he listened, and then he said, "Rita, you *know* that you are a good writer. You *know* that writing is your calling. You *know* that you just finished writing an amazing novel. Hold to yourself, to what you *know* is true."

Then Karl sat quietly for a while and tuned in to my energetic state.

After that he said quietly, "I saw a masked woman and an owl. My sense is that you need to give the following message to your personality self: *'I honor the opening you've gifted me with in the second chakra in past lifetimes. Know that you will not be lost – you will be fully integrated in the Heart, in the Bliss.'* Rita, in your heart, I saw wings, like the Sufi winged heart – you are so ready to fly!"

The next day I felt very tender, but I did not cry. I felt like Karl was holding me – like his support was keeping me afloat. I wrote in my journal:

"In all those hours of crying, I realized that I had traded in my attachment to a man for an attachment to a teacher.

"Fall back into the Self. My Self, my intuition, is more important than anything – it is more important than being a "good student" and doing Basil's assignments correctly. What is most important is finding my true Self, and only I can do that – I don't need Basil. I release my attachment to him."

Chapter 34 – Exploring sexual energy, remembering What Is Important, and shifting into Juiciness!

In early August, Karl called again to see if I was doing better. Oh, was I ever doing better! I was feeling stronger each day, and I was even beginning to laugh at Basil's message. I told Karl, "A fairly good writer is better than a really bad writer!"

To my surprise, Karl acknowledged that he and I might not yet be 'done.' We talked about what our unfinished work together might be. He shared that he thought he might serve me by helping me publish the novel... and, he thought that I might serve him by giving him something of my knowledge of how to use sexual energy for healing. He said that he wasn't asking me to show him physically!

I said that I didn't really understand what he meant, but whatever it was, I was at his service.

The next day I wrote in an email to Karl:

"Since we talked, I have been thinking about how you think I will serve you. I keep asking myself, 'How will I teach him something about the wisdom of using sexual energy for healing, when I don't even know myself?'

"So, today I went to the bookstore, looking for a book which would explain how to use sexual energy for healing. Unfortunately I did not find one, but I did find a book called *Tantrika: Traveling the Road of Divine Love* (by Asra Q. Nomani, HarperSanFrancisco). It looks interesting – maybe I will learn something by reading it."

Karl replied, "I know when the time comes the transmission will just happen vibrationally or in words of wisdom."

I wasn't so sure, so I got on Google and typed in "sexual energy for healing," hoping to find some clues. I found lots of information on how sexual energy is healing, but it was all about how having sex is healing for people. I didn't find any information about how one might channel sexual energy into healing, without having sex.

As I read *Tantrika*, I learned a lot more about Hinduism, Islam, Buddhism, and Tantra, but I did not learn anything about using sexual energy for healing. Rather, the focus continually returned to the Self. I learned that in true Tantra, one of the key ingredients is *Atman*, true Self – one has to realize the Self before they can join in tantric union with another.

My favorite part in the book was actually when the author cut her hair short. She wrote:

Cascading long hair was a trademark of a woman's femininity.
"Please cut it short, like a boy."
My hair fell to the floor with each snip, and I watched myself rid my
identity of more than my hair. In Tantra, cutting the hair also
amounted to shearing our egos.

That was exactly how I was feeling about my buzzed hair. I felt as though I was shearing my ego, and joining in Union with Lord Shiva. I read that one of Shiva's names is *Shankara*, which means *Giver of Peace*, and I liked that name so much that I started writing in my journal, "*Rita Ann Shankara.*" I really liked the sound of that name.

While I was busy exploring sexual energy, Luna came to town for a few days, and we had a lovely visit over tea. She served as a wonderful barometer for me, because as I told her how I was doing, I could tell that I really *had* changed – that I wasn't still telling the same old story.

I told Luna that the email and phone contact with Karl now felt fine because I was finally understanding the bigger karmic picture. She was very accepting – she was not at all judgmental.

Karl called the next evening to talk about his request for me to teach him about sexual energy for healing. First, he wanted me to understand that he did not want us to re-hook in that way – feeling desire for each other – he really wanted us to continue holding a pure vibration together. He then shared that he sensed that what I would teach him was not for him – it would actually be in service of someone else.

I asked what he meant by that, and he said that he had a friend who had experienced a lot of trauma early in her life, and although she had healed a lot, there was still a lingering knot associated with the early abuse. He had a psychic sense that he was going to learn something from me that he would then use to help her heal further.

In the days that followed, I felt mostly whole in myself. Bryan took the boys camping, and I enjoyed the time alone.

Although I felt much stronger in myself, I also felt dismayed at how easily I would slip into longing for a man. So, I called Anastasie and Sina, and invited them to buzz my hair again.

Over dinner and red wine at the picnic table in my backyard, I asked them what they could see me doing in life. They excitedly talked about what they saw as my strengths, and it was all so juicy that I ran and got my notebook and pen.

The next day, Sina dropped off a book for me to borrow: *What Should I Do With My Life? The True Story of People Who Answered the Ultimate Question*, by Po Bronson. I began reading it at once and I delighted in realizing how many people struggle with that same question.

The second buzzcut felt very liberating. I actually buzzed it myself – a little shorter, on the number five blade. I later wrote this poem:

O' My Lord Shiva,
I say that I buzzed
my hair,
but really it was You.
You keep guiding
my hands
and my heart
to open
to You.
The current of Durga heat
has become
an idling pulse
in my being.
O' My Lord Shiva,
It is with rushing Gratitude
that I come before You to sing
this cricket-chirping night.
But really
I don't come
'before You' –
rather, I fall back
into all the
layers of myself
*which **are** You!*
O' My Lord Shiva,
I am Yours.
Adorn me
with Grace,
Wisdom,
and Compassion.

A few nights later I had an interesting dream:

> *Karl and I went into this very big tent – a tent made of hard canvas and olive green in color – and we lay down on the floor... a sparkling blue jewel lay nearby. We were holding hands – and I felt the pure Bliss of Enlightenment. I felt so happy, so whole, so complete, so connected, while just holding his hand. I didn't want anything else. Holding hands was more than enough.*

Life was really getting more interesting and more enjoyable. I loved it that I was starting to have enlightenment dreams. I felt more and more bliss in my days, even as I continued to experience contracted dips of fatigue and despair.

But even when I felt tired, I found myself melting over little things, such as the boys' laughter as they played in the yard. One warm summer evening I joined them in the yard for a game of "barber shop" – I buzzed their hair too, and we all delighted in the wonder of our matching buzzcuts!

One night I wrote in my journal:

O' My Lord Shiva,
with fresh figs
juicy strawberries
and the utterly strange
taste of pumpernickel,
I offer my fatigue
up and out
for healing.

My love for food was gradually returning, as I felt more and more at Home in my true Self.

Karl went on retreat with Basil and Luna for a week, and when he returned to San Diego, he called to share the latest shifts in him.

He said, "I asked Basil for an assignment and he discerned that I need to go on vacation with Martha this Fall, so it looks like my visit up your way will be postponed. Martha and I plan to go to Paraguay for our 25th wedding anniversary in October, after I return from my business trip to Australia. I feel grateful for the opportunity to see if we can re-ignite what once was. We hope to discover whether or not we truly need to dissolve our marriage."

I heard such relief in Karl's voice and I told him so. I felt happy for both him and Martha. And, I felt relieved when he told me that she knew that we were still in contact. I told him how well I was doing, and he was happy for me too.

Talking with Karl felt really grounding to me – my crown chakra remained very open for the rest of the day. I delighted in my boys' antics and enjoyed their beauty. Joshua was learning to read and to swim, and Benjamin was – well, he just WAS. Full of his mama's red fire, but also very gentle and charming, he was an amazing little guy.

While I was feeling so expanded that day, I wrote:

"I am too expanded today to go into that constriction over wanting a man. And anyway, that pattern feels so repulsive to me. When I'm in that vasana, it is as if I'm saying that the most important thing in life is being with a partner.

"And that is *not* true!

"Here is the truth: my children, my parents, my brothers, my sisters-in-law, my friends, my community, my work, my service to others, and my path to enlightenment are all very important to me! I am showing up for my Self and my life!"

That night I re-read the introduction of Nomani's *Tantrika: Traveling the Road of Divine Love.* (HarperSanFrancisco, a Division of HarperCollins Publishers.) The following passage jumped out and grabbed me in tight embrace:

To practice Tantra well is to be a Tantrika, a woman who isn't defined by anything, living compassionately, lovingly, blissfully, and fearlessly with appropriate wrathfulness when necessary. To master Tantra is to become a dakini, a woman who dances in the sky, flying free of the things in life that keep her hostage to ego, fear, and boundaries. She is a sky dancer whose flight takes her through a spiritual voyage of clarity, fearlessness, and ecstasy that liberates her from worldly existence. A Tantrika is a divine creation, a goddess with a small g, respected, honored, and worshiped, liberated from shame, fear, expectation, exploitation, and suppression. She is free to be adventurous, aggressive, and bold in her efforts to find enlightenment. **She is a yogini who has awakened her inner fire and helps others light their own.** *She isn't defined by the dualities of wordly life. Man. Woman. Old. Young. Good. Bad. Sane. Insane. East. West. She moves beyond those boundaries to a place of non-duality where she exists with simple honesty, compassion, and wisdom.*

(Bold lettering, mine.)

After I read that passage several times, I thought, 'I no longer feel like the 'other woman,' like the woman having an affair with a married man. I, as an aspiring *dakini*, cannot be labeled like that! I simply AM!'

That night I had another enlightenment dream:

I went on a retreat with Basil. He and I hugged for a very long time, and while we were hugging, my whole being relaxed and I felt the pure Bliss of Enlightenment. It was serene.

On *Janmastami*, Sri Krishna's birthday, Julianna and I took our young friend, Melena, with us to a celebration. We chanted the Mahamantra for hours: *Hare Krishna, Hare Krishna, Krishna Krishna, Hare Hare. Hare Rama, Hare Rama, Rama Rama, Hare Hare.* I felt such Bliss... and I could feel the addictive love pattern loosening... and I realized that I was no longer suffering.

I remembered Basil often saying how important it is to "authenticate the changes," and so I meditated on all of the ways my life was getting better – I felt much happier, healthier, and lighter. Even the migraines visited me less frequently, with less pain.

The next day Melena's mother, my dear friend Kaitlyn, told me that Melena had really enjoyed the Janmastami celebration. Melena had recently begun studying Indian classical dance with Julianna, and when Kaitlyn asked her if she wanted to also take a hip hop dance class, Melena declined, saying, "I am an Indian dancer. My skin is white, but my feet are from India."

136

I got really strong chills when Kaitlyn told me that, because I had taken care of Melena often when she was a baby, and now Melena was – like me – drawn to India.

The following week Melena turned thirteen, and Kaitlyn held a Blessing Way circle for her. After the circle of women gave her their blessings, more people arrived for an Indian dinner. Before the meal, people took turns going up to speak with Melena.

When her father, Tom, spoke with her, he cried – both at the beauty of his daughter and at the sadness he felt over his father's recent death. I cried so hard as I witnessed his loving heart – it was one of the most beautiful and healing moments of my life. Suddenly all of the work with Basil made sense, and I was released into an experience of utter bliss and love within myself.

Later, at home, I reflected that Melena's ceremony had healed the thirteen-year-old in me who did not have a ritual like that. I felt honored to be a part of that circle, and I realized that the experience had softened my heart tremendously.

I wrote in my journal:

"I feel such gratitude for being in that circle with Melena. In this open heart space, it suddenly feels as though a lot is living in me that wants to come out.

"What is it that needs or wants to come out? Well, an idea for a book called *Rita: Journey of a Western Yogini* is downloading. It is the story of my path to Union. There is so much God everywhere I go now."

In the following days, my heart stayed soft, and I realized that being there in that circle had helped me to remember What Is Important in life. Suddenly I felt fully present in my life and the desperation to be with a man was gone.

One warm September afternoon, at a little boy's birthday party, I shared with an older woman that I didn't know what I was going to do with my life. She asked, "What have you always wanted to do since you were little?" Without even thinking, I said, "writing and teaching," and she said definitively, "then that's what you're going to do."

Another woman at the party commented on my haircut. She said, "Besides looking very chic, it has a very spiritual feeling."

Later I wrote:

"O' My Lord Shiva, divinity dances in sun sparkles on the beaks of blue birds feasting on sunflowers, and I radiate the warmth of Durga heat as I try out these new wings. Little flights are growing bigger – Whoosh! Whoosh! Whoosh!

"Ah, behold the pink of September sweet peas! The setting sun feels good on my forehead as birds explode into patterns of union and reunion in a blue sky above the ripe blackberries. I am almost ripe – tasting the sweetness of pink in my soul. O' My Lord Shiva, behold this wondrous transformation! I offer all to You."

So many deep connections with both gods and people continued to enhance my days. I saw the Hindu Pantheon as one rich, colorful tapestry. I wrote:

"O' My Lord Shiva, I am no longer afraid of unfolding my true Self for I see that I am not losing the good parts of me. Becoming my true Self is easier and more fun than acting from ego. I feel like I am falling back into a place in which all of the happy times of my life are rolled into one Big Happiness which is *now* and is Eternal. It's like all the Bliss I have ever felt and will ever feel is imploding and exploding all at once in my being."

Julianna invited Melena and me to go with her to a *Radhastami* celebration for Sri Radha's birthday. Thankfully, Julianna and I were connecting as soul sisters once again. She delighted in what she sensed in the new me: "a baseline spark coming up."

I giggled as I told Julianna and Melena that I felt like a "closet Hare Krishna." Then we all laughed when we read in a book that George Harrison also considered himself to be a closet Krishna – he described himself as a "plainclothes devotee" and a "closet yogi." (*Chant and Be Happy: The Power of Mantra Meditation – Featuring Exclusive Conversations with John Lennon and George Harrison*, Bhaktivedanta Book Trust.)

Later, after we took Melena home, Julianna and I made dinner together, and I told her that ever since Melena's Blessing Way, it seemed like the addictive love pattern was released.

I then thanked Julianna for her honesty with me. I told her that even though her "judgment" had pained me, in time I had come to appreciate it. I honored her judgment about my contact with Karl. I said, "Even though I am so concerned about integrity, I acknowledge that I still continue the contact anyway. I am finding my way through though, and I am truly happy that he and Martha are going to take a trip next month."

Just as I was really feeling myself shifting into Juiciness, I got slammed with a big overwhelm kriya – a big contraction that came to help me purify further. I sensed that hormones induced the meltdown. Thankfully, I could feel the underlying current of Connection even as I cried.

I cried a lot. I felt overwhelmed by the boys, by finding a career, by my car breaking down... by not having enough time to write... and by Bryan's comments to me.

Bryan and I were being polite partners in raising our boys, but underneath the nice surface, I sensed a hot pot of animosity brewing. I feared that if the pot boiled over, we might all get burned. I asked myself, 'How can I transform the hot pot of animosity into a comfort stew of loving kindness?'

The answer was always the same – to keep praying for Bryan and to keep holding the vision that one day we would truly be friends, free of the negative energies that bound us in conflict.

Just as I was really losing my ground, one morning Benjamin's kindergarten teacher called to say that he had gashed his head on the wall. I had to take him to the doctor to have his head glued back together, and so I missed a morning of writing, which just contributed to the whole overwhelm kriya.

I felt like such a complete wreck. My womb felt weak, achy, and vulnerable. I longed for the strong support of a man, and I asked, "O' My Lord Shiva, are You asleep to me?"

While sitting in the doctor's waiting room with Benjamin, I looked at a magazine through my tears. It was a Buddhist magazine, called *Tricycle*, in which I started reading an article about happiness. The author explained how we can be happy even when we are facing challenges. When I read that, I suddenly popped out of the kriya and my whole being expanded again.

Late September brought cool winds and many attractions! Julianna said it was as if I was in Spring – I found myself suddenly attracted to so many different men. I started baking bread again, which helped ground some of that sexual energy.

Julianna came over for hot tea and homemade bread. She told me about the man she was dating, and she shared that another friend had given her this dating advice: "Live your life and pray."

I said that I felt as though I would burst because I was so full of sexual energy. She wondered if maybe I could pay a tantric healer guy to have sex with me – to see how I would feel if I got that need fulfilled.

Later I told Dana what Julianna had said, and she asked "Isn't that illegal?" I laughed, as I questioned if sex was really a *need*... or was it just a *conditioned* need?

On the last night of September, Basil called from Canada. He again sensed rising bliss in me. As we hung up, he said, "Rita, bake your bread, write your poems, and continue to enjoy deepening in Being."

It was perfect that he called. Earlier that evening I was feeling so alone and I even thought that I would rather be in bed with a lover than anything else in life. I prayed that the Universe would give me a sign that I was still on the right track, so when Basil called, I took that as a sign from Krishna.

Chapter 35 – Meeting Baron

On the first of October, Krishna presented me with another track to follow. That morning, I awoke to rain and a migraine headache. I went to the natural food store to get some flour for baking bread, and while in the bulk section, I kept bumping into this man. I hardly looked at him, but I felt his energy go into me.

Then I drove across town to drop my rent check by my landlord's house, and as I turned a corner, there was the same man I had just bumped into at the store! I waved, and he waved, and I kept driving.

That evening Julianna came over for dinner with the boys and me, and I told her about the man I had seen twice that morning. I could hardly remember what he looked like, but I could feel that his energy was both very strong and very gentle.

Julianna rolled her eyes at yet another Rita attraction, and we got into talking about other things. But as soon as she left that night, I once again felt that man's energy. All week I felt his energy and I kept thinking, 'I am really going crazy now – now I am obsessing over a man who I don't even know his name!'

I felt a tender root feeling when I thought of him, and I wondered if we were sending each other sexual medicines. I sensed that he was thinking of me also.

I "threw the *I-Ching*," the Classic Chinese Book of Changes, asking the question, "What do I need to see about that man?" I got the hexagram for *Peace*, which was characterized by the harmonious union of man and woman. I got chills and tears flowed. I could feel that man's energy so deeply in my root.

The next night, I cried as I wondered if I would ever see him again. I felt annoyed with myself for focusing on him, so I decided to buzz my hair again. First, I wrote this poem:

> *With this hair buzzing,*
> *I bow to how little control I have.*
> *With this hair buzzing,*
> *I greet the bubbling union*
> *of yesterday's sorrows and*
> *tomorrow's joys.*
> *With this hair buzzing,*
> *I invite Light and Strength*
> *into my whole Being.*
> *I thank my Lord Shiva*
> *for His many blessings.*
> *I pray,*
> *O' My Lord Shiva,*

guide me to Brahman,
purify my heart,
make my character impeccable,
heal my patterns...
Let me rest in the current of Durga heat...
Hare Krishna Hare Krishna
Krishna Krishna Hare Hare
Hare Rama Hare Rama
Rama Rama Hare Hare
May all beings be free and at peace.

I read the poem aloud three times, then plugged in my clipper set and buzzed my hair with the number seven blade. I felt much better after that!

I sent the hair buzzing poem to Luna, and she replied, "She who finds blades and shears, opens to the definite... in symbolism of release and surrender, she opens to the Infinite. May this expression make room for nothing... my hands on soft head with you now..."

As the week went on, I felt more and more crazy in my desire to see that man again. I started calling him "the gentle and peaceful one," and I looked for him everywhere I went. I could feel his yummy energy throughout me, and I whispered into space, "O' gentle and peaceful one, I like how you feel inside me."

Oh, that pattern was so strong in me! That pattern that I *thought* I had released... that pattern of fixating on a potential lover... it was made of a thick, magnetic substance, and when my hormones got going, it could be downright gripping. Basil had said that I would need discipline. That was for sure. I also knew that I would only be truly released of the pattern by the Grace of God.

Everything always came back to God. No matter what the problem was, the solution was always to sit quietly and Connect. So why did I still need to fill up all of those journals? Why track all the clues, when the mystery was already solved?

Overall, I actually felt more patient with myself. I realized that the attraction to the gentle and peaceful one was not *bad* – there was no God waiting to punish me. I was just unraveling and purifying so that I could live more fully in the Light of God. And, the One who wound me up was the same One who was unraveling me – I *knew* that there was a *Plan*.

Still, I wanted to know if I was just making it up about the gentle and peaceful one – were we really connecting, or was this yet another of my psycho-sexual fantasies? I wanted to find out, so I convinced Dana to go out with me to a chanting concert on Friday night, in hopes that I might see him again.

Before the concert, we went to get a bite to eat, and I saw a man who looked like the gentle and peaceful one. He walked by our table, and I said, "Dana, I think that is the man!" And she said, "Well, if that's him, I know him – that's *Baron* – I used to teach with him at a university years ago."

141

I couldn't believe my good fortune! Dana actually knew him! Soon she walked over to him and invited him to join us. As he shook my hand, he said, "I know *you*! We've met before – at the food store and again on the street! When you waved at me, I wanted you to stop and pull over." He remembered me too. Thank God. The connection was *real* – I didn't make it up.

As the three of us sat talking, I could hardly focus on what we were saying – I was so entirely aware of my desire to be in his arms. When it was time for the concert, we left Baron there, and all through the concert I felt his energy in me – strongly.

After the concert I realized that we had not exchanged phone numbers. How and when would I see him again? Dana couldn't remember his last name, but she thought that her husband Marc might remember it.

That night when I wrote the date, October 7th, in my journal, I suddenly remembered that I had met Bryan, my ex-husband, on October 7th, twelve years before. That was too much! I then wrote:

"Baron, O' gentle and peaceful one, I am sorry that I didn't tell you that I was thinking of you this week and hoping to run into you again. I am terrible at playing the game. I invite you to contact me. My heart and arms are open to you. ~ Rita"

The next day, I felt as though I would go crazy waiting to see Baron again. I went on a walk, and I kept repeating to myself over and over, "*All significant partnerships are completely predestined.*" If that was true, and I believed that it was, then there was no point in *hoping* to see Baron again – we were either destined to be together, or not.

By the late afternoon, I hit a big kriya – reactions upon reactions at my desires and my inability to trust God. I really wanted to be okay with *not knowing* what was going to happen.

I felt a lot of pain and I cried deeply as I consciously focused on pulling back any projections of need or expectations that I may have already put onto Baron. I kept telling myself that it was not about Baron and it was not about how we felt about each other and it was not about whether or not we would be together.

I *owned* that it was entirely about that strong pattern in me that rips me off center... and when that pattern gets going, then I can't fill from the inside and so I look outside for someone else to fill me.

I prayed to Lord Krishna to teach me how to fill myself. I felt so awful inside, like a no-good nothing. I wondered, 'How did they let *me* on the Yoga Path?'

And then I laughed. For a brief moment I could see the humor in the fact that I was already *on the Path*, so there was no going back, even if I thought that I was undeserving dirt.

So many thoughts of Baron swirled in me – it made me feel absolutely crazy. I could hardly sleep that night, and when I awoke in the morning, I felt desperate to see him again.

It was Durga's Puja Day – Her special day of the year – so I focused an intense amount of energy on that great Hindu Goddess who rides a lion and slays the demons of illusion in our minds. All morning, I burned incense and candles to Her, I kneaded the bread dough for Her, I chanted to Her (along with Krishna Das and Jai Uttal CDs), and I prayed intensely to Her to help me let go of wanting to control the connection with Baron.

At noon I finally made it out on my walk. I walked farther than usual, hoping to run into Baron, but on the way back home, when I had still not bumped into him, despair crushed my hope. I thought, '*I am looking for you everywhere you aren't, Baron.*'

Just after that thought, I stepped into the street by the railroad tracks, and out of the corner of my eye I saw a man on a motorcycle in a black leather jacket stopping to let me cross. I looked his way, because Baron wore a black leather jacket, and as I turned, he saw me too. It *was* Baron! He pulled his motorcycle over and motioned for me to come over to him.

Baron pulled me close to him, and we stood there holding each other for a very long time. I kept thinking, 'What if I can't ever let him go?' Then he said, "Maybe we both really needed a hug like this." I said, "with each other, perhaps."

We found a place to sit together in the brilliant sunshine. While we talked, I touched his hand and he touched my neck. He smiled as he touched my buzzed hair, and he asked if I liked touch. When I said yes, he said, "Maybe I'll give you a massage   or a thousand."

I softly whispered okay, and then I admitted that I felt scared. He said, "I feel intrigued!" The connection between us felt very deep and we looked into each other's eyes for long moments. We learned that we were both raised Catholic in the Midwest, and we exchanged last names before we parted that afternoon.

That evening I felt so expanded, so high. I bowed to Ma Durga and thanked Her for bestowing that Blessing of tender love – on Baron and me – in the sunshine of Her day.

A few days later Baron called, and we talked about our beautiful meeting in the sunshine. We agreed it had been intense, and we shared that we were both still feeling very strong waves of the energy of our connection.

Sounds great, right? Now we ride off into the sunset of blissful ecstatic union, right?

Wrong. As it turned out, Baron was still in a relationship with another woman. When he told me that, I told him that in the past two years I had fallen pretty hard for three people, two of whom were not available because they were in other relationships. And then I got upset, questioning out loud to him WHY I would have to face that test of integrity again – I said that if he was with someone, that was really hard for me. He said quietly, "Don't despair yet."

I wanted to get off the phone. He asked if he could call again, and I said yes. I hung up and threw a good Rita fit! Crying and angry, I went out on my walk. I stomped out all of my anger. Then I went to buy starts for a winter vegetable garden.

When I sat down to lunch, I felt excited about planting my own garden, watering my own soul. I offered my disappointment to Lord Shiva and my anger to Ma Durga. And suddenly, my fit was over and I felt so connected to All... and then the waves of Baron's energy and the energy of our connection came rushing back through me.

In meditation that night, I could feel his energy so strongly. I sensed that the energy of our connection was sensual, sexual, primal, heart, and divine. The pleasurable currents which rippled through me felt almost orgasmic.

I wrote an email to Luna. She responded:

"Oh me, Oh my... Wow Rita, this sounds like a ride... Are you up for it? It will definitely be exciting and dramatic, feeding an important part of you/one. *But can you rest there?*

"I can totally imagine your state of realizing that the integrity dance song was playing again, wondering if the steps to this dance are gonna be harder cuz you're ready for them, or different, cuz you already did all that work. Uhhhh...

"I just want for you simplicity. Not that you and an "other" wouldn't have work, but that you would get to rest into him. So wonderful you have your connections with Shiva, Durga, the unknown... seems to really hold you for engaging in such an adventure.

"Anyway, you are following a course, which has its own life force, laid before you, not much to do but stay awake and honest, it sounds like you are. He showed up for a reason.

"Basil's ears are perked up now... let him know what was going on. Of course, he says what a "character" you are. I say "why, what do you mean"... he says "she's just so Rita." Gave him a good giggle though... you guys have your own little jokes going on in all those tracks. Anyway, he's tickled... and wants you to remember what you know about yourself."

By Friday morning, Baron called again and asked me out on a date. I said that I would only feel comfortable going out if he told the other woman. He agreed that would be fair, but he wanted to think about it. Half-hour later, he called back and said that he had made the call: he told her that he would like to go out on a date, and she said, "Well, we are off then."

When Baron arrived at my cottage door for the first time, we were each shaking with nervousness. While we hugged, he glanced up at the Krishna art on the wall behind me, and said, "You have Krishna-Radha... that's reassuring."

We drove to an Indian restaurant in a nearby town, and while we ate, we kept gazing into each other's eyes and I sensed that much recognition was happening at the soul level. Later, we sat on my couch looking into each other's eyes for long comfortable moments. Baron said, "I think I prayed for you," and I said, "Oh, you are *precious*," and he said, "you are *projecting!*"

One wonderful date led to the next, and it wasn't long before we realized that we were quite the pair of wild characters... and quite the lovers. Once he said to me, "Let's study Krishna and Radha and Rama and Sita, and see what we can learn from them – or what *they* can learn from us!" I smiled and said, "They are playing through us – the *lila*, the divine play."

Baron was another Rooster, like Karl, only instead of being one twelve-year cycle older than me, he was two cycles older than me. Although we had some concerns about our age difference, the age difference mattered little when we were together. Baron greeted life with a rambunctious spirit. He enjoyed partying and singing with friends.

The energetic feelings between us became like holy food which sustained us, so that even though we were very different people, in our union we found such bliss. We talked about our differences and we recognized that at some point they might come between us, but we were each willing to continue exploring the connection.

Meanwhile, I got the following email from Basil:

Rita,

The moods of the divine mother are manyfold. Sixteen moods, if contemplated regularly through the day, form the antidote to drama, projection, and sexual/astral polarization, and the ensuing anger, attachment, grief, and withdrawal that are the inevitable results of such polarization.

Contemplating the divine mother is a way to bring peace to the restless turmoil of the western psyche... always looking for fulfillment beyond itself, and the enduring thirst and hunger which this catalyzes...

The invocation of bhavas, or moods, is a higher tantric practice that helps stabilize the passions...

May you find solace in the sixteen moods of the divine mother.

Basil

I felt upset by that message – what was Basil trying to say? Did he tune in to my relationship with Baron and see something that I was not aware of?

The next day, when I felt calmer and more appreciative of Basil's message, I wrote him back:

"Thank you for writing. I will consider what you said and contemplate the divine mother. I am actually feeling quite balanced and not in a state of projection/attachment at the moment.

"Going out with Baron, and we are being very open in sharing what we know about ourselves and our patterns. I've learned so much from you – from your guidance with the pattern (with Anastasie, Karl, Eric), that I am much more aware now. I am feeling pretty grounded with Baron and in myself. I feel that my expectations are in check.

"Having said that, I know that there is always room for more growth and more solace within myself. I will contemplate the sixteen moods of the divine mother."

Later, I wrote in my journal, "Baron is painting new tones on my heart and soul, and I am blessed by his affections. Durga likes him. I am grateful that I am capable of such deep connections – connections that are getting ever-deeper with each person."

Basil replied to my message: "Glad that you are feeling grounded in yourself... and, your pattern is deep, which is why practice before and during its manifestation in the world is so critical... this will only open the door for sustained and true relationship, which at your heart I know you are longing for..."

Each precious moment with Baron was absolutely wonderful for me, but when we were apart and he would wait a few days to call me, I would go into unpleasant reactions. Although I felt pained, I sensed that the reactions were necessary, because they gave me the opportunity to release any attachments or expectations.

One night I wrote:

"O' My Lord Shiva, Please help me remember the Truth. This crying, this pain, is the result of engaging in this world of maya. Please guide me with Baron, to a higher connection where the pain of maya cannot touch me. Please take these tears and throw them on your Fire! O' My Lord Shiva, cradle me this night, as I am longing for Rest – please let me rest in the current of Durga heat."

The next weekend, Baron and I went out to a party together. At the party, several women commented on how beautiful I was. On the way home, Baron shared his insight about the women's reactions to my beauty: "There is a quality of Beauty that they are not ready to see in themselves, but they can see it in you. Let them project, if it helps them to discover their own Beauty."

Later that night, while sleeping beside Baron, I could feel threads going back and forth between our hearts, bodies, minds, and souls... energetic threads which felt like *Red* silk – silk that was beautifully spinning bonds between us. I felt deeply connected to him... and, I felt a little scared.

A few days later Karl called. We had not talked for a few months. He had big news: he had fallen in love with a woman in Australia, and instead of going on the anniversary trip to Paraguay with Martha, he was dissolving his marriage and returning to Australia to be with his new love, Karen. I told him about Baron, and we had a good check-in. When I told him emphatically that I needed to hear my own inner voice and not be so dependent on Basil's, Karl laughed and said, "I hear you, loud and clear, not just physically, but energetically as well. I hear you, I get it."

Karl and I agreed that we still shared a deep spiritual connection. Before we hung up, I wished him well in Australia, and he offered blessings for my relationship with Baron.

That night I wrote,

"O' My Lord Shiva, Delight abounds as I watch myself unfold. Following the Path is leading me to the Core of my Being, and There the vocation appears, Destiny has me over for tea, and the Great God Shiva purifies my Heart... and, as the conditioned self unravels, the Joy of Self rests in the current of Durga heat... and I, Rita Ann Shankara, greet the Sun of hope in my heart. I shine forth the brilliance of stars, planets, dinosaurs, rocks, minerals, and the green, green earth."

That night I had this short little dream:

*Basil looked inside me and he said that something was gone... some pattern or personality trait was **gone**!*

When I awoke, I could not remember *what* Basil had said was gone, but I felt good about the dream. It felt like a good omen.

After Baron left that morning, I wrote this poem:

Dear Baron,
Sunlight on pine needles –
You on me –
it's all good.
Oh, so good.
I delight in the Sun
of NOW
with you, my darling precious one.
What else is there?
Yesterday and tomorrow
are illusions
Today, this moment
of sunshine on pine needles,
and your breath still warm
on me –
***This** is delight. **This** is now.*

I felt immense gratitude for meeting Baron. It felt as though we had been Divinely placed together, like puppets in a Grand Love Play. We were the stars of the show... the lovers wrapped in red silks... and yet we did not get to know how the play would turn out. We were watching the Play unfold – what else could we do?

Chapter 36 – Opening on the Yoga Path in a catawampus world, anchoring my awakening, and bearing the fruits of sadhana

The day before Halloween, I attended a workshop with Basil. I arrived early, feeling a little nervous. Basil looked up from his laptop and said, "Oh, Rita, you are going to stand out like a vibrating fork today!" I smiled and asked what he was doing. He said, "I'm reading about quantum entanglement... something every good Tantrika should know about!"

As usual, my whole being relaxed as soon as everyone sat down and we began chanting. After a long meditation session, Basil talked about the intrinsic joy of the universe. He said, "The Universe has an enormous sense of humor. The flowing of ego states is so humorous – just ask Rita!"

Basil then described the following difference in View: in the Western view, reality is hell to be survived and then you get released into heaven, whereas in the Eastern view, there is, in Reality, an abiding quality of Presence available to every being in every moment.

"Interpersonal relationships are the ground for the exploration," Basil explained. "At the end of the day, review: did you see the Absolute inside of all the hearts of the beings you experienced? It takes courage to hold to deeper perceptions, because your own ego material – and the ego material of others – is quite strong. Attractions and aversions are reactions – it takes a strong stability of Being to not get pulled into attractions and aversions... and to keep the View.

"When you have a quality of willingness in your heart center, and you are willing to expand into what *Is*, then you feel in Love with All. The human heart is designed to love all of Creation, but we have been trained to try to put that love into one place." Basil looked at me and said, "If you're a fundamental Lover, then you may as well get on with it."

Someone asked Basil how we know when we have found the correct way to serve others. He answered, "When you are on-line with your calling, your crown will feel open, warm, and connected, and your heart will feel warm. When the soul has evolved to match the essence, you will get massive instructions from the Absolute, that Field that determines the moments of your awakening and that also guides your work.

"Don't worry – relax – don't take things so seriously. You can't get fundamentally off your purpose – you can get distracted, but the Totality of Being will keep pulling you back to your unfolding purpose on the Path. The Great Intelligence gives you exactly what you need for your growth, and not what you need for your relative wants. The Great Intelligence listens. If you follow the fruits of the inner prompting, you will have continuous Support.

"Watch the timing in your life and have the grace to follow it. Part of our timing is linked to the timing of the Collective. Personal enlightenment is only possible through the Collective. Great gifts are only activated in the service of the Whole. If you watch the elegant dance of history, you see that inventions only appear when humanity is ready for them. The Universe *knows* what it's doing. Our job is to polish the mirror, tune the instrument, and show up."

After lunch, Basil talked about the process of awakening. He explained, "In Yogic structures, they study the moral precepts first and then get awakened, but here, in our catawampus world, we get awakened first, and then we go back and learn how the moral precepts line up. Then we look to see if we are recognizing the Presence revealed in all encounters. If so, the energy exchange is more accurate and our relationships become cleaner. Energy that is reciprocated correctly builds in its intensity."

At the end of the day, Basil tuned in to my heart and said, "Rita, the next piece for you is this feeling in your heart, and not all that you are writing down." Then he told the group, "I have a story for Rita, and if I tell it correctly, it will help her to ground the vibration that just came down in her."

> *Once there was a lake building behind a glacier – she could feel herself building. Now, lakes on the earth can last a long time, but lakes behind glaciers eventually have to let go... so, each day she lost a bit more of herself, until finally she let go – finally she had sacrificed enough of her self to the Sun...*
>
> *... when the ice melted enough and she finally broke off, she flowed down in flooding torrents... she traveled down through known valleys, and there was no way not to go back down to the Ocean... so the Ocean returned her to her Self... along the way, she remembered all the aggravated feelings, and all that she had gone through, and she understood it all... and now, finally, she had a container big enough to hold all of her!*

Tears blurred my vision as I bowed in gratitude to Basil. I then left to meet Baron for dinner, and I told him the story that Basil had told for me. Baron said, "You are *a lot* – I'll grant you that! And, I am a vessel big enough to hold you – you can be way out there, and I can hold it." I said that I already knew that, as I felt so *met* – so strongly *met* – by him.

The next night, Baron and I went out to a costume party for Halloween. We dressed as Lord Shiva and Ma Durga, and we had so much fun! As we walked home, Baron said, "We should get some Indian clothes and adornments that we could wear out with friends... or we could wear them just when we want to celebrate each other."

Late that night, while eating cheese and crackers in my kitchen, Baron gazed into my eyes and said, "Maybe you are one of these holy people who should be on stage? Maybe you should just say that you're enlightened and people can line up to see your smile and look in your big brown eyes... and they can leave donations!" I laughed and protested, "I can't do *that* – I'm not really enlightened! And who knows if I will be this lifetime or not?"

Baron smiled and said, "Rita, thank you for inviting me into your home and your life." I responded, "Thank you for showing up," and we both laughed. It felt good to laugh so much again.

In meditation the next morning, I offered *All* with Baron – the connection, the love, and the worries about whether or not we were really *right* for each other – up to Lord Shiva's spiritual fire, and I immediately felt *Trust* descend. Tears dropped in my lap as I experienced the absolute *Beauty* of what a moment of true Trust feels like.

The following weekend, Baron and I went to another party and my ex-husband, Bryan, walked in with his new girlfriend. Baron and I went right over to them and we all talked for a few moments and it felt a little funny, but okay.

Later, I asked Baron if our sweet, nourishing connection was *real*, and he said that it felt adventurous with us because we dared to be so *present* with each other. He said that he felt so *seen* by me.

Somehow I found the time to be in a relationship, while still mothering, chanting, meditating, and writing poetry and prose. One night I wrote:

"O' My Lord Shiva, my Being is a magnificent temple of gold. I step into the temple's kitchen and prepare a hearty soup for the Beloved. We drink from the kettle of Infinity... and my Heart smiles – a smile of tremendous proportions... Warmth streaming down the descending currents of Grace upon grace upon Grace."

I read that prose aloud several times, and each time I read it, I cried when I read the part about *descending currents of Grace upon grace upon Grace.*

That night in meditation I fell into a very deep state of consciousness. I sensed that I was just about to fall off the edge of myself into the Void, and I felt scared. In that instant, I recognized my fear of the depth of connection with Baron. I told myself to just relax and let go and be okay with the depth... but then instead of relaxing into the Void, I came down a notch. My body felt very heavy and weighted down. I realized that if I had let go, I might have gone into a deeper samadhi realm.

I appreciated the conceptual understanding of deeper states that I had learned – mostly from Basil. I appreciated Basil so much, and, at the same time, I felt as though I needed to ask him to let me go, like a child asks their parent to let go. I thought of how he had held me like a precious daughter – guiding me, scolding me, encouraging me, praising me, and *seeing* me.

So, before Basil's next evening group, I sent him the following email:

"I'm writing about a little internal struggle I'm having – I'm feeling a bit of a father-daughter dynamic happening in me with you. There is a part of me (the daughter) which wants your (the father's) approval of Baron. And there is an even bigger part of me that just wants to listen to my own intuition, even if it means I make mistakes, and even if it means I trip and fall on my face!"

When I arrived for the evening group, I asked Basil if he had received my email. He nodded and said, "Rita, it's not about Baron. It's about *you*!" I sighed as I sat down for the chant.

After we chanted *Om Namah Shivaya*, we meditated and I relaxed into ecstatic Bliss. I felt much heat in my system. Then Basil talked about the importance of anchoring our awakenings. He said that he anchors his awakening through teaching.

Before we parted that night, Basil talked about the importance of cultivating the *Witness*. He described the Witness as the *reference beam* that has noted everything throughout all of our lifetimes. He said, "The more you do inner work, the more the bandwidth of the Witness expands."

The next morning when I sat down to write, it hit me that I anchor my awakening through writing. Suddenly, writing this book became the most important thing in my life. More important than Baron, even.

Suddenly, the words began to flow, through the Goddesses Saraswati and Durga, through Lord Shiva, through me as the vessel, through my fingertips on the keyboard letters... to the pages that will eventually be bound in this book.

That afternoon, Eliza called. She was the woman who I had fallen in love with the decade before. I hadn't heard from her since the Thanksgiving that rang with the bells of honesty. Oh, it was good to hear her soothing voice again. She called to share the following dream:

> *She went to this big house for an estate sale, and there were all these places where you could look at things, but you had to really dig for the gems. One area was all **blue** glass that was sparkling with blue light, like blue jewels...*
>
> *Eliza realized that it was my – Rita's – house, and she wondered if I should be selling **everything** like that, but she looked at me and I was obviously feeling happy and free!*

What a stunning dream! I shared with Eliza all that I had experienced on the Yoga Path over the past few years – all of the attachments that I had released and all of the deeper states I had experienced. We agreed that she must have tuned in to my expanding state of consciousness. I told her that I had just recently sensed that my witness was *blue*, and she said that there is a samadhi state in which one sees a blue pearl.

I told Eliza that *sadhana* – which for me involved daily chanting, meditation, writing, and finding a path of service – had become *the* most important part of my life. She shared that she had also found a spiritual path that had become the most important part of her life. *Of course!* As deeply connected soul sisters, we often lived parallel lives.

That night I received the following email from Basil:

"Rita, you are in the process of a profound transformation of your sexual/spiritual energy. Correct alignment of your energies is essential during this period of your sadhana. Guidance is critical and it comes in many forms.

"You have an important window in your sadhana. It will take lots of conscious awareness to not re-activate very powerful latent vasanas at this time.

"Your practice is bearing fruit and worthy of notice."

I sat in meditation and allowed myself to savor the sweetness of the fruits of sadhana. And I vowed to keep my eyes open in the relationship with Baron, so that I would not re-activate that latent vasana.

Baron and I shared a lovely Thanksgiving Day together. We wrestled on my living room floor and my strength surprised him! He agreed that I needed someone to push up against. I told him that I appreciated the way he held the masculine energy, and he said that he also loved how I held the feminine energy. In our relationship, the harmony between the masculine and feminine polarities allowed us each to relax.

After our wrestling match, we cooked some delicious food together and took it over to Dana and Marc's home for a wonderful meal with them and their little girls. Bryan and his girlfriend took our boys to a different party. It was the first time we separated on a holiday, and it felt a little strange, but okay. I felt so much gratitude that day.

That night I told Baron that he was like my big grizzly bear, and he said that I was like his playful little otter. We laughed at the image of the bear and the otter playing together by the side of the river! In the coming moons, we began calling each other Bear and Otter.

The next morning when I turned on the computer to work on this book, an email message popped up from Raya, the woman who led evenings of kirtan. While traveling in India, she wrote this to me:

Dear rose gopi,
I'm now in Vrindavan, the land of love and devotion. The land where the gopis offer their hearts to Krishna in the form of roses. Sometimes I remember you and I see a bright beautiful smile, so sincere and enthusiastic. I hold you in my prayers, and I offer your roses at the feet of the Goddess Sri Radha.
With love,
Raya

I felt so touched by her message that I printed it and hung it above the kitchen sink, where I could read it again and again while washing dishes. It meant so much to me that Raya had thought of me in Krishna and Radha's land.

As I continued writing this book, I realized that I was finally fulfilling Basil's advice from the year before – I was finally showing up each day for the creative descent and treating it as my first lover. I felt as though I was merging with my soul's purpose.

December arrived and I attended a one-day workshop with Basil. As we were all getting settled, Basil said, "Rita, your job today is to *not* contain it – to do that, you have to let go." I said, "It's so big," and he said, "So is the Sun. Relax into the non-physical spaces that you exist in, and there, your heart is more powerful than the Sun. Your power is your connection – your Joy will,

152

like the Sun, warm the space around you, once your personality is refined. Relax into Connection, and things will be less jangling." Then he laughed and said, "This could be the day that Rita melted down."

After the chant and meditation, Basil described how we are all living inside of each other's hearts – we are not separate and isolated. In fact, the heart is receiving the pulsation of the Universe at every moment.

Basil explained that once you embrace an expanding sense of Self, then you get to play with others. "For example," he laughed, "when I look into Rita and see the intensity there, I see 10,000 Roman Candles going off, and that's very interesting! And then, if I look inside of that, I see a crystalline blue intellect with incredible capacity to see the mysteries of existence."

Basil continued with the following lecture:

"We take these large Fields of vibrations and step them down into form, and to the degree that we do that without ego, we enlighten others around us. To the extent that a being purifies, they can help a lot of people.

"When you are purifying your vehicle, and you are contracting, it is important to re-frame your attitude: rather than asking how you can get rid of the contraction, ask *'What is the Field out of which I am contracting?'* This question pre-supposes that you are already existing in larger vibrational fields, so they are not something that you have to work to go to.

"When you relax into the Field that is already holding you, this is when *Faith* enters. And, it's either true that this is a connected, conscious universe, or it's not true. The deeper your faith, the more everything lifts up around you... and then you are less contracted and there is less for you to do."

I relaxed as I listened to Basil, because everything he said resonated with how my life path was unfolding. He looked at me and said, "Rita, you are so full, so to not be that full makes you hyper. When I reflect that fullness back to you, you calm down."

I thought about that for a moment, and then I asked, "Do I need someone to reflect the fullness back to me, or can I just feel it in myself and calm down on my own?" Basil answered, "Because you are so tantrically trained, Rita, to some extent you *do* have to find your fullness through others. You need to be with people who are also open and willing to let you be in deeper states." I thought about Baron's assurance that I was not too much for him to hold, and little shivering chills rushed through my being.

During the morning break, Luna said something about me being "insufferably cute," and I asked, "I'm not so much anymore, am I?" Basil said, "You're much less cute – now you are insufferably *beautiful*." I sighed loudly and he said, "Insufferably isn't *bad* – true Beauty is just hard to bear."

When we all sat down again, we chanted *Om Hiradyam Shanti Ma*, which means *Peace of the Heart Cave through the Great Mother*. I fell into a very deep space in which I felt a lot of heat – I wondered if it was the true current of Durga heat? When we came out of the meditation, Basil said, "Rita's like that frothing machine that you froth milk with – she makes bubbles of joy!"

Before lunch was served, Basil approached me and again tried to convince me to go on the next Bali retreat. I said that I had already decided not to go, but he pressed on with his case:

"Rita, I see all of this Light above your head which is ready to descend – you are ripe; there's a window now for you, and given the state you are in, it would be very good for you to be immersed in deep states regularly. The Bali retreat would give you eight days in the Field, and you wouldn't get Enlightenment, but you would move a big piece – you would shift your matrix and then all of the overwhelm wouldn't be there anymore."

I explained that I didn't feel ready for such a long retreat with him; that when I went on the three-day retreat in June, it had almost been too intense for me. Basil looked into me and said, "The mind will nearly always rationalize away from sadhana – it has an investment in keeping its own strategies going, so one should generally be suspicious of choices away from the opportunity rather than towards it. We only have so long here, time is truly of the essence.

"The Field is intense, yes, but as you probably have noticed by now, you are as well. And intensity needs to be met with intensity. The overwhelm you were feeling at the June retreat was in large part because you were sitting in the midst of your own intensity... and *that* is the fire that changes us."

Basil tracked some suspicion in me and he asked what the root of the suspicion was. I sensed in, and tracked that I felt suspicious that I was going to give my power over to him again and not listen to my own voice. I told him that I felt compelled to put any extra time into writing this book. He heard that, but he asked that I temporarily put aside my tendency to lock down on forms and just feel into my *being* – to feel what my being actually needed. "Then," he said, "you can pick the forms back up and make your decision."

In the afternoon lecture, Basil talked about Enlightenment in concrete terms. He said, "It's not about feeling better – it's about realizing the full awareness of all the states possible. Liberation is the awareness that you ARE everything. The veils were placed for them to be removed. Shifting to higher states contributes to All – cultivating awareness is definitely a form of service for the planet. As you un-pack the story, you bring through vast qualities of existence, and then you serve by giving them back out again."

For the last topic of the day, Basil explained the difference between an *acharya* and a *Guru*. He said that he was an acharya, that he could not claim to be a Guru. He then gave the following definitions:

"*Acharya* is the Sanskrit word for an accomplished teacher. A teacher inspires, instructs, motivates, offers skillful means, and provides a field for projections and resistances. Sometimes the *guru function* comes *through* a teacher – as it comes through everyone at times – but a teacher is not a Guru.

"A *Guru* is someone who abides continually in a Connected State and they don't do anything out of personal will. A Guru takes on full responsibility for your spiritual awakening. A Guru has burnt through the veils of illusion and they can help take you There.

"The appointment with the Guru is not something to plan or set up – when strong Consciousness is at work, things line up without any effort on your part."

Someone asked if the Guru needed to still be alive, and Basil said no, they could already be dead. Someone else commented on Neem Karoli Baba, and I laughed out loud – I said, "Oh, I love Neem Karoli Baba," and Basil said, "Of course you do, Rita. He was a consummate rascal! He used to bonk people on the head and absorb bullets into his body and throw fruit out into the crowds of devotees!" Basil suggested that I read *Miracle of Love: Stories about Neem Karoli Baba* by Ram Dass.

Next Basil talked about all of the times he went to Baba Muktananda's ashram. When he told of the time Muktananada had instructed him to come to India, he looked at me and said something about how he was advising me to go to Bali. I retorted, "but you're not a Guru!" and he said, "No, but I can see the state you are in, and I know that it would be good for you to go," to which I replied, "but I can listen to my own inner voice and know what's good for me too!"

Before I left the retreat, Basil gave me a hug and assured me that the decision was up to me. He said, "Rita, you've made great progress!"

I felt so happy when I arrived home that night, and then, like a cherry on top of a full cake, I listened to a wonderful message from Baron on my answering machine. He welcomed me home, and offered to bring dinner over.

I felt so touched that my Bear had cooked a nourishing meal for me. After we ate, I took the page down from the fridge door – the page on which I had written forty-nine times "It is exactly the same pattern." Even if I was acting presumptuously, with Bear I hoped that it was no longer the same pattern.

Chapter 37 – Loving Bear

One morning I awoke to the flashing lights of a migraine headache, and for a few days my brain felt foggy. In that state, overwhelm seeped in, but then I thought, 'This is a pattern, a tendency, a vasana. Focus on the *Field* that I am contracting out of. *Who* is contracted? Fall back into the Absolute…'

In meditation, I thought, 'I *should* go to Bali, but I *can't*. I should go because Basil so strongly recommended it, but I *can't* go because I am so wrapped up in writing this book.'

Julianna invited Baron and me to watch a performance of her young Indian dancers. The dancing touched me deeply. Tears welled in my eyes as I understood the vital importance of any transmission of ancient India into this culture. After the show, I gave Melena a long hug and told her that my favorite part was when she smiled at me while she was dancing to *Maha Lakshmi*. Her eyes twinkled as she said, "You can't *not* smile at Rita when she's smiling at you – and *that's a fact!*" I delighted in the new quality of sassiness in her teenage voice.

The next night Baron took me out to a fun Winter Solstice party. I wore my new gold lion pendant on a sparkling gold chain about my neck, and I felt elegant in a blue velvet shirt with black silk pants. Inside, my soul vibrated like the loud purr of a well-petted cat. We feasted on chocolate truffles and danced with Julianna. She kept laughing and saying over and over, "You are *out*, Rita!"

We got home several hours past midnight. Still buzzing from the chocolate party, we sat in meditation to calm down. The next morning, my Bear said that he felt so lucky to have met his svelte otter, and I said that all of his longing had been witnessed. He asked what I meant by that, and I said that he wasn't just *lucky* – he was *blessed*… even if he didn't *believe* that. He said, "How could I *not* believe in angels, when I've met *you*?"

The week before Christmas, Basil sent an email from New York, asking how the writing was going. I wrote back saying that the writing was wonderful when I had time for it, but with the boys off of school for a few weeks, and all that I was doing for the holidays, I was feeling frustrated that I didn't have more time for writing. I shared that I was anchoring a lot through writing this book and I asked if he would want to read it.

Basil replied, "Your book sounds important. I will read it. Patience creates time."

I practiced patience through the holidays. Julianna and I took the boys ice skating on Christmas Eve… then one of my brothers came to town and shared Christmas day with the boys, Baron, Julianna, and me… and after all of that fun, I was full-to-overflowing with so much love. Baron laughed and said, "Rita, you are so *bhakti!*"

On the last day of 2005, in a hot shower with nag champa incense burning, I soaped my body while looking out the open window at the hills covered with snow. As I looked back and forth between the gold lion glistening on my chest and the light shining through the white clouds onto the snow, I wondered, 'Will I be standing in this same shower on the last day of 2006? What incense will I be burning? What thoughts will I be thinking?'

After an amazingly delicious New Year's Eve dinner, Baron and I went to walk a labyrinth at a church. As I walked the paths leading to the labyrinth's center, I became aware that I was walking faster than most of the people around me. I laughed as I thought to myself, 'That's *okay* – I've got things to do in 2006!"

As I continued walking, I wondered what to focus on for the New Year ahead. The only thing that kept coming to me was "*Just keep deepening.*" In the center, I sat down to meditate in the spot where a huge pomegranate and an ear of Indian corn lay on the floor in front of me. I whispered to those harvest offerings, "I pray for fertility for the book I am writing." As I walked back out of the labyrinth, I prayed to Lord Shiva and Ma Durga.

At the stroke of midnight, the Bear and the Otter kissed and joined their voices with more than one hundred other beings in chanting *OM* several times.

The next day, after cooking a yummy black-eyed pea stew, I chose an angel card for 2006: *Responsibility*. I meditated on the many things I had to be responsible for, until I came to the core of why I picked that card. At the Core, I knew that I had a responsibility to bring forth that which was within me… and to let that Love shine, even if I felt some fear about doing that.

A few days later, Benjamin shared the following dream with me:

> *my cottage was just sticks on the ground, and there was this big screaming noise, and it ended up to be a big blue thing falling down on top of the sticks, and the blue thing caught the sticks on fire.*

The dream sounded exciting to me, but Benjamin said that it was a very scary dream, so I sent it to Basil, asking him about its meaning.

Before Basil replied, I wrote him this second email:

Dear Basil,

Greetings from holy firecracker land...

I have a sense that my witness is blue...
is everyone's witness blue?

My experience of the Witness is deepening,
so that once a contraction begins, I pull back
just slightly, and there is the Witness, and
very quickly I feel Bliss there.

Tears flowing, laughter exploding,

157

falling back into my Self
again and again...
Blue Witness loving it all.
Love,
Rita

Basil replied to both of my letters:

"Regarding the blue space... yes... the inner space is often a deep blue... And a heads up on Benjamin's dream... I had a feeling when you first reported it... your comment on the blue confirms it. His dream may indicate that he is experiencing your dives into deeper planes as a threat to his emerging structure. Be sure to spend quality time with him for a while to reassure him that Mom is not going to disappear into the vast blueness and leave him behind..."

I focused on Benjamin as best I could, although my mind was mostly focused on writing this book. And, when I wasn't writing or mothering, I was melting in my Bear's arms.

One rainy night, after Baron and I fed each other pomegranate seeds on my red mohair couch, I gave him a card with an otter on it. Inside I had written this poem:

> *I am melting into you*
> *my darling Bear*
> *I want to dive into you*
> *under your skin*
> *and swim in your blood*
> *and know how you feel*
> *inside –*
> *and that feeling*
> *of wanting to be inside you*
> *is entirely new to me.*
> *I have never known*
> *a desire for union*
> *which burned*
> *in me*
> *with such consistency*
> *and such depth.*
> *O' my darling Bear,*
> *I adore you –*
> *and even as I am afraid*
> *of our depth,*
> *I want to dive deeper*
> *into the Ocean*
> *of Love and Laughter*
> *that is you*
> *and me*
> *holding the bigness*

of our vessels
in the container
that is the pulsation
of our Love
    Now
        Now
            Now
In your tender touch
I am overwhelmed
with emotion –
I could scream
into the stars
of eternity
and burst open
into billions
of shooting flames
and sparks
of Light.
You send me There, dearest Bear.
With utter love and bliss and gratitude for you,
Rita Ann ~ your svelte otter

Baron read the poem, and he said, "You touch me so deep, Rita. Your eyes are ablaze of divine, and when you meet me in my core, you rescue and reassure me." I looked deeply into his eyes and said, "Sometimes it seems like you are feeling the same thing as I am, and I just want to jump in there and see if it feels the same!" He nodded and said, "It *does* feel the same – it is so much bliss."

In meditation that night, I clearly saw the *divinity* of Baron showing up in my life just when he did. That realization made me weep, and I expressed deep Gratitude to Lord Shiva.

The next day I wrote:

"Such Bliss this afternoon: bigger perspective – mind and crown are expanded – heart feels soft and tingly – understanding fabric of existence – and seeing the pathways of contractions – and sensing that all of the universe and its endless possibilities are vibrating in me and in everyone all the time – and in that state of endless vibration, we are All intricately Connected."

While I sipped a cup of hot white tea, three little boys made mud balls in the yard, and I delighted in the cheerful chatter amongst them – they sounded like little bird people! I felt good, but I also felt a tad bit worried about something with Baron. I wasn't sure who to talk to about my worry.

Suddenly I remembered that at one of Basil's retreats, when he was talking about how once you trust the inner Being, a Unification of Being takes place, he had said, "Does this split you open in one Rita-like moment of ecstasy? Occasionally. But not usually." I smiled as I remembered all of the times that I had sat in Basil's loving presence. I *did* trust Basil…

159

... so I turned on the computer and wrote him the following email:

Dear Basil,

I am wondering about your perspective on something in my relationship with Baron. We are connecting deeply, having fun, enjoying the nourishment, and, at the same time, I feel a bit conflicted. In a few weeks, he will begin public speaking again, and I am concerned about the religious ideas he will talk about.

Although I see his deeper connection and I witness how he lives from the heart, he is very much a thinker and a scientist. He describes himself as a naturalist, deist, and humanist. Even though I see where he has faith, he insists that he doesn't have faith – that he doesn't *know* that the supernatural exists. To him, maybe it does, maybe it doesn't.

We've talked about this before – my concern about whether or not it can work to be in a relationship with someone who is out there publicly sharing ideas that I don't necessarily agree with – and we've talked about all the ways that we are different, and we kinda look at each other in amazement that we are still together. It is perplexing why we have been brought together now – we are both continually surprised.

He is a mystery to me. He says he doesn't believe in the supernatural, and yet, years ago, Baron had a teacher from India. He traveled with his teacher to India... and the Hindu gods and goddesses are close to his heart, especially Krishna, Radha, and Shiva...

What is your perspective on this, Basil?

Love,
Rita

After I sent that message to Basil, I realized that I was not only asking for his perspective... I was also asking for his *approval*.

Basil replied,

Rita,

to be in relationship you have to let go of control...

particularly the control of another.

trusting the arising of their being is the only medicine that is true and good.

without this

all relationships degenerate into some form of control battle.

try not to figure him out.

try loving him.

160

let go.

and if you disagree then don't participate.
but don't hold it against him.

all roads lead home.

eventually.

love,
Basil

      Try loving him. Yes, that was exactly what my heart was saying to do… and, in fact, I was already doing just that: *loving Bear.*
      What a relief it was for me to read those words from Basil. We are *all* on the Path – regardless of our religious ideas, we are *all* returning *Home.*

Chapter 38 – Grounding and Stabilizing

After attending a few of Baron's weekly talks, I realized that his religious ideas weren't so different from mine after all. There were even places where our ideas merged, so I felt silly that I had worried about that. As that worry faded away, a new one emerged: our differing beliefs about monogamy. We talked about the issue a little bit, and I had a few dreams of him with other women, but for the most part that tension just brewed beneath the surface.

Over the next few months, I really enjoyed the times Baron and I shared together, but when we were apart for a few days, I still worried and got emotionally triggered. I wanted more regular, daily contact, and he needed more time to himself. The dance of *wondering* exhausted me and I longed to be able to rest into him. Each time we talked about it I felt reassured by his words, but then a few nights later I would again find myself crying when he didn't call.

I wrote out some healing visions for my relationship with Baron and for my mothering journey, and I once again endeavored to put meditation first before my duties as mother and lover. I knew that when I felt Connected to the Heart Oneness I trusted life more. I thought of all that I offer my boys when I feel Connected: juicy humor, colorful stories, hearty laughter, delicious food, an intense example of the vibration of creative expression, and, most importantly, a steady Field of mama attention.

When I shared my intentions with Baron, he said that he could see how meditation was harmonizing for me because I have such a dynamic system. Yes, I knew that I needed more regular meditation to integrate all of the energies going through me.

One night after crying because I felt as though I was more sexually attracted to Baron than he was to me, I took a long hot bath by candlelight. I held a hand mirror and looked deeply into my chocolate brown eyes for a very long time, and I experienced that the Witness and the Essence are One. Later I wrote this journal entry about that bath experience:

"Renewing rose oils and salts… Renewing body, which is sexy but that doesn't matter, as body is temporary. Renewing mind, which has been unraveling patterns and spinning out in imaginings and is as temporary as the body. Renewing heart, which has felt stuck but is softening in these warm waters. Renewing soul, ahh yes, I feel you there… But what is **that**? The witness and the essence are together, **one** in utter Bliss of Self. Why didn't Basil tell me they were one?

"Yes, the witness and the essence are one – One with eternity – which is not about sex – It is this Beauty, this Power in your eyes of Light – you *are* this Beauty – Karl was right, "remember to breathe" – it *is* breathtaking!

"You can drink a cup of coffee in celebration of this Beauty, this Rita Ann Rose renewed – and in this renewal, you can let all that raw, beautiful wildness come forth by simply *Being*. In each moment let this Beauty rest in your heart and shine through your eyes."

When I shared that writing with Baron, he looked at me with such tenderness. He said that maybe we needed to get away together for a while so he could just focus on me without the usual daily life distractions. I agreed.

A few weeks later we took a trip to Harbin Hot Springs. When we returned home, I sent the following message to Luna and Basil:

Hello dear Luna and Basil,

Baron and I just returned from relaxing at a hot springs resort. We enjoyed soaking in the healing waters, eating delicious food, and meditating together.

By our second afternoon there, I felt as though my ego had dissolved into the water. It felt so blissful, but then I experienced many fears arising, so we went to rest in our room. I asked Baron to chant *Om Namah Shivaya* in my ear. We then sat in silence for quite some time.

After the meditation, we lay down and I told Baron that I wanted to run away from myself. He asked where I would go and I said Paris. I told him that I used to fantasize about an imaginary woman in Paris, a woman who I might one day meet. While we lay there, with him holding me, I suddenly thought, 'I do need to go away from myself, I think I will go to Paris right now.' So I did. I left my body and went to Paris:

I approached a woman standing on a street corner. She wore a little black dress and a red lace see-through shawl. I entered her body and we drank a strong bitter cup of cocoa and I felt the warm liquid come down us, and then we went into a little bookstore with a few small wooden tables. We sat down and she took out a black book and wrote in it for a while... I wondered if she wrote in English since I was inside of her? Then we walked down the street and saw a black cat... and then we went up to her flat and started a bath, hot water running... and I thought that I should leave her with peace, so before I left her, I filled her with Love and Light and prayed that she would be free of suffering and stress...

... and then I was back in the bed in Baron's arms, and right then he asked, "The woman in Paris, that you fantasized about, what was she like?" Too much. The next morning at breakfast I looked up at the sign which listed the movie they would be showing that night: it was called *"The Girl from Paris."*

Now we are back in the embrace of the sacred mountain, where I am taking care of boys and running the cottage life. It's all good. The biggest challenge I face presently is how to be more regular with sadhana. It's a juggling act with all that I'm doing, but I do manage to chant and meditate still, although not with the regularity that I had before and that I crave. I trust that it will come in time. Meanwhile, I am consciously viewing my roles of mother and lover as spiritual practices.

March is a really busy month for our family here. Lots going on, including Bryan and his girlfriend Lela going to Brazil for ten days... she is seventeen years younger than him and Baron is twenty-four years older than me... funny stuff. They invited us to their Chinese New Year party and we went, and it was good for the boys to see that we all feel comfortable together and that everything is okay. Joshua and Benjamin are doing great. Amazing little beings. I am enjoying them more and more. I think they are enjoying me more too.

My parents and all three brothers will be here spring break... I'm really looking forward to that... and I am curious how my conservative Catholic parents will receive my wild boyfriend – who is *their* age!

I think of you both often and hold you in my heart.

Much love,

Rita Ann

Basil replied with the following note:

Rita,

Nice to hear from you...

Sounds like your life is grounding in a good way... and the relationship with Baron seems to be stabilizing an important part of you...

Regarding more time to meditate...

It doesn't just come. The ego has a million excuses which nibble away at deep inner contact. It takes discipline to make it happen.

Immersion in a retreat setting is helpful because it re-frames ego content in such a way that there is more "time" for meditation. Hope you can make it to Bali sometime this year.

love,

Basil

Soon thereafter, I once again committed to a daily meditation practice, and I joined a meditation group. One evening after the group meditation, Julianna told me that when she tuned in to me she saw *Ripeness*. She said, "Rita, you are really filling out your true self and it has a crystalline quality to it. Maybe I've been giving Baron too much credit – maybe it's actually *you*, and he showed up because this was already happening in you."

I felt encouraged by Julianna's words, but the next evening I had a big breakdown over Joshua and Benjamin's fighting. I cried and cried, and I asked them, "What if this never changes for me? What if I won't ever be able to stay calm and loving when you fight? What if your fighting will always trigger fears, anger, and sadness in me?" In that moment of naming a possible truth, I felt some kind of transformation happening in me, and just then Benjamin said, "Mama, stop crying so you can hear me. You know how all those gods have that yellow circle around their heads? Well, I see that around your head right now."

Later I told the boys about how I used to feel the same negative feelings when my younger brothers would fight, and I would yell at my Mom to make them stop. I just wanted the fighting to stop. Benjamin responded emphatically: "Mama, you have to go into your heart and remember what I

164

just saw around your head."

After the boys fell asleep that night, I felt such gratitude, and on top of that I received the following wonderful email from Baron:

"Monday evening, processing e-mail, thinking often of you with thankfulness and delight. How beautifully you live! How loving and patient you are as a mother! How open, willing, and honest you are with me! How pure you are in your quest!

"I love sleeping with you especially, face to face, sharing breath, close and warmed by each other's embrace.

"You, busy with duties, need to know this is how you are regarded. I may be a few miles from you, but I am, oh, so close."

As I wrote this memoir, I found the highlights of the Karl-Rita novel weaving themselves throughout, and I realized that I would not publish that novel. I suddenly saw how the story with Karl was just a small part of a much bigger picture. I let that story get absorbed into this book, and I breathed in gratitude for all of my growth.

The next weekend, Baron and I took Benjamin on a trip to see Krishna Das in concert. During a pause between chants, Krishna Das talked about his Guru, Neem Karoli Baba, whom the devotees fondly called "Maharaj-ji." He said that someone once asked Maharaj-ji, "How do you know if your spiritual practices are working?" Krishna Das said that Maharaj-ji's answer was simple: *"Through the constant repetition of the Name, the presence of Grace becomes apparent in your life."* I thought about that, and I recognized that even with all of my struggles and dramas, I *could* see Grace working increasingly in my life.

When I got home I sent the following poem to Basil:

Climbing the rungs of consciousness

Hey Ma Durga,
as I climb the rungs
of consciousness
I lose my footing
when the level below
burns in Your Fire.
Tears swell
as I recognize
that so many rungs below
have melted away
in Your Heat
and there is a Quiet
around the spaces
where worries once gripped.
At once it feels empty
and oh, so full.
This rung is much more quiet,

even during the busy days.
Gratitude rings in the multidimensional levels
of my being
as I know the One within and without.
Quietly I sing, "Hey Ma, Ma, MA!"

My parents and brothers came to visit. They all really liked Baron, and he liked them. Of my Mom, he said, "Your Mom is just as cute as can be. I can tell she's a really good-hearted person."

While we hiked in the mountains with my family, Basil sent an email saying that he liked my poem. He wrote, "Rita, you are a rare and precious gem. Not too many of them come along."

I began reading *Miracle of Love: Stories About Neem Karoli Baba* (by Ram Dass, A Dutton Paperback, E.P. Dutton), and I found much inspiration in Neem Karoli Baba's words. My favorite teaching was, "*It's better to see God in everything than to try to figure it out.*"

While I practiced seeing God in everything, I felt inspired to undertake a study of many great beings. I made a list of the books I wanted to read, and then I realized that I had already purchased the first three books.

As I breathed in gratitude, I looked around my kitchen and noticed that I had hung up photos of the three great beings who I was going to study next – Neem Karoli Baba, Anandamayi Ma, and Ammachi. It felt as though those three Gurus had lined themselves up in my cottage, without any conscious effort on my part.

I especially resonated with Anandamayi Ma, a beautiful Indian saint who had no formal schooling and no Guru. Highly intelligent and capable of entering deep states of Consciousness, she gave herself Guru mantra and became enlightened. Crowds of people gathered around her, happy to experience her Bliss while listening to her pithy teachings.

Utterly inspired, I continued to sit in meditation each evening, building inner strength and riding the waves of emotional intensities coursing through me.

Chapter 39 – Learning and Practicing

Basil and Luna decided to hold a summer retreat in Hawaii after the spring retreats in Mt. Shasta. My ears perked up at the mention of Hawaii, and I told them that I would consider joining them there.

At the April retreat, the first thing Basil said was, "Rita, you have a tremendous amount of excess energy. As you are getting more comfortable with yourself, the energy is starting to move out and that actually expands your consciousness."

He then gave us a meditation teaching which I found very helpful:

"With your meditation practice, don't try to "get better," but rather, go in, release, and let the outcome descend from a different place. Trust that the inner connection is actually intelligent. Be suspicious of your intentions when doing inner work – wanting to "get better" takes you to the threshold, but it isn't enough to penetrate the deeper realms. You must have purity of heart and be doing it for something bigger than yourself.

"The test of your practice is how available you are to the ongoing qualities of the world around you. As you expand, can you hold that expansion when you return to what you know of as your anchored sense of self? This is the challenge of practice. How do you land again? And how do you work with the material that arises when you land again?

"Just remember that the Witness Consciousness is present and watching in all of the states. That energy allows us to watch ourselves from the detached place of the Witness. That energy will take care of us if we keep connecting to it. Whatever we pay attention to, we vibrate to."

In talking about high beings, Basil commented, "They are extremely particularized. They are very much themselves – very dynamic and full of themselves. There is a lot of juice in their personalities." I found myself feeling very inspired any time Basil spoke of high beings. I wanted to be one of them. I laughed to myself as I realized that I was a wannabe-saint.

Before the morning break, someone asked why they didn't always hit the deeper states in their meditation practice. Basil answered, "You don't get to the deeper states all the time because you are being worked on. Relax about not always hitting the deeper states – you are being re-made by the Universe with millions of years of back-story. Enjoy being worked on, especially in the inner realms, but also enjoy being worked on in the outer world – by accepting and bowing to the circumstances that appear.

"Remember that Eternity is eternal. Relax into the re-working that is happening. The Universe watches attitude more than anything else – It doesn't care about the back-story – It cares about the purity of intent. The Universe is conscious and very subtly tuned to the heart chakra."

I sat next to Basil at lunch that day and he told me that I was the metronome of Krishna, that I kept time for Krishna. He said that he saw all this steam above my head and that I was more fun to watch than cartoons! I asked him how my masculine was doing, and he said, "Your inner masculine is good, but still a little too much – it just needs to be pulled back a little. It's more intense now because Baron is mirroring it. Your inner masculine wants to have things named correctly, and when they *are*, you rest, but only briefly."

That night Baron and I got into an argument about polyamory versus monogamy. Polyamory means "many loves." Baron said he believes that love comes in many forms during our lives. For nearly forty years he had held the ideal of being in a primary relationship with a life partner in which they were each allowed to explore other loves, including other sexual encounters. He said, "Fidelity transcends monogamy."

As we talked into the night, trying to find the standards that we could agree upon for our relationship, we each got reactive and we quickly fell into a downward spiral. I went in the bathroom and cried, imagining that our relationship would soon end.

The next morning, before going to Basil's retreat, I wrote the following:

Last night
I hit the bottom
of my Well of Grief.
There I met
two shining knights
named Gratitude and Humor.
they picked me up
dried my tears
and held me
through the long hours
of the sleepless night...
... and I trusted that the Universe gives me
exactly what I need for my growth.

With a strong cup of tea in hand, I took my puffy-eyed self to the retreat. My throat hurt and I felt dull, but I listened and took notes anyway.

Basil first talked about the importance of going into your core. He said, "Put your identification in your core and then witness the surface material that arises at the personality level. The surface material is a pattern that has been elegantly arranged through generations. It is incredibly well organized. The solution to the imbalance of personality does not lie at the surface level. Self-help at the personality level doesn't resolve the fundamental imbalance, because when you fix one thing, that often messes up something behind it."

He explained that the solution lies in the correct identification with your core. In the West, because our psyches are so damaged and we have a basic unease in our psychic structures, it's better for us to work in group fields rather than alone. The consequences of contact with Light are fear, fear, fear, so Basil advised us to feel into our fears and ask what those fear vibrations need. He said that those fears usually need connection and warmth. Being in community breaks the illusion that you are separate. Connectedness relaxes your limbic center.

Basil continued, "Maturity occurs when you understand the causation of events. Astrology can be a helpful tool in not taking things personally because it shows the patterns of large-scale motions. Having said this, remember that you can't get over yourself in a hurry. Your structure is what you are – if you lost all of your structure at once you wouldn't have the ground to anchor you. Prior to being purified, if the Absolute showed Itself directly, your vehicle couldn't handle it. So, your personality balances gradually. The fundamental parts of you – your fate, your karma – remain, and you work through them. Have patience as you work through them."

Basil then talked about the importance of living our purpose; of merging with the destiny that holds us. He quoted Rumi:

> *Every night we relax into the arms of a loving nowhere*
> *and every day we pour ourselves into our appointed work.*

(*The Essential Rumi,* by Jalal Al-Din Rumi (Author), Et Al Coleman Barks (Translator), HarperCollins Publishers.)

That afternoon, we sweetly sang *Alleluia* for more than thirty minutes. During the chant I thought about how Basil had said that our surface problems are designed to take us to the center, and how we should not try to resolve the surface problems in the center. I reflected that, at the surface, especially in the relationship with Baron, I could not rest. So, I fell into the center and *rested*, and I recognized that *That* was the only place where I could truly find rest. I looked out at the surface and saw the humor in the fact that I couldn't rest before when I wasn't in a relationship, and now I couldn't rest *in* a relationship either!

I thought, 'Maybe I manifested a relationship that I can't rest in, so that I will be forced into the center to rest *There*.'

After the meditation, Basil explained that conditioned karmic structures make it difficult for the Light to stream through us all the time. He said, "As children of the West we have to redeem the stream of the Western line. We have to understand what karma we are working with – and stay within it – in order to blossom. We have to solve the problems of the West – problems such as the mind-body split, the flesh-spirit split, issues springing from the patriarchy and technology, and so forth – and when we unpack these problems, we develop skill sets to correct the imbalances."

That night Baron and I continued wrestling with our problems. I pushed and pushed until he basically said that he would agree to my standards, which included noticing attractions but not acting on them. He said that those would not be his standards, but since he was with me he would honor them. I felt somewhat better, but even so, I went to bed crying again.

I was glad that I pulled myself to the retreat again the next day because Basil talked a lot about relationships between men and women. Julianna asked him about her current partner, and in response Basil gave the following lecture:

"Julianna, with Paul, don't blow him off because he's not perfect. Serve him, support him in becoming perfect. Five times each day, really see his beauty. Beyond that, rest yourself in the organized perfection of Beauty around you – surround yourself with flowers and beautiful music. And understand that every couple has a mutual annihilation pact going. Every being embodies the force of Kali and Shiva. That force of Being wants to annihilate that which isn't perfect in the beings around it.

"So, you are being used – by the Universe – to annihilate your partner's ego. Don't get so attached to all the reactions. True unions have to be supported from the inner planes. Watch your dreams.

"Also understand that the correct alignment of the masculine and feminine – within and without each being – is integral to our sattvic approach to life. When the masculine and feminine are in balance, nature smiles and the gods visit. When they are out of balance, things quickly become out-of-whack."

Someone asked Basil about sexual energy, and he answered, "Sexual energy is potent medicine. If you have too much sexual energy going with your partner, it creates conflict in the relationship. When your sexual energy gets going, rising up from your second chakra, it will hit whatever content hasn't been cleaned up – such as mother or father issues – and then you can't see the other being anymore, and so you start projecting onto them.

"So in the West, where our psyches are already messed up sexually, if we have sex first, it almost always drives us apart. It's better to lay down roots of deep connection first and then have sex. Once you have connection in the higher centers, bring the sexual energy into it very slowly and watch to make sure the higher connection remains. If the higher connection breaks, then you no longer *feel* the other being and then you have to work the issues.

"In an unprocessed psyche, the force of the issues pushes the partners apart, and the heartbreak is tremendous. Unfortunately, culture can't blossom until the male and the female are in balance. This balance is fundamental in existence.

"So in looking for the correct balance of masculine and feminine, we experience many inevitable attractions on the way to finding a soulmate. What we attract reflects something in us – something in the other person completes something in us. We can move through attractions skillfully and with integrity, and we can learn a lot and heal a lot in various relationships.

"You are already destined to be with the one you're going to be with, so you can relax. Do your practices, and let the one you are destined to be with arise. Let the relationship come up from under you. You'll know when it's a soulmate union when support comes from other planes and the relationship opens you to the community. Correct union is in service of all beings. When a higher purpose brings the two souls together, you feel a Higher Self connection above your head.

"Some couples come together with a contract – a purpose to complete in a certain amount of time. Soulmates are different – they are constant companions who find that being together physically is very harmonious, and they have very significant work to do together. The agenda arises from inside them.

"At the deepest level, the purpose of coming together is to liberate the souls. The purification of the ego makes the person's essence more apparent.

"Not everyone meets their soulmate. If it's not meant to be, it won't happen. However, even if you never meet your soulmate, they are still supporting you on another level from somewhere."

During the lunch break I hiked through the trees around the retreat home, and I contemplated the relationship with Baron. I reflected on Basil's description of soulmates, and I wondered if we each have only one soulmate? It seemed as though Michael, Karl, and Baron were all my soulmates.

At the end of the day, Basil talked about *The Day of Brahma*. He said that all of the *Yugas* (ages) were within The Day of Brahma. I didn't really understand what he was talking about, but when he said, "We are at the end of the Kali Yuga now and when it ends, the whole thing will shut down," I blurted out, "Is that why I'm so drawn to Durga?" Basil laughed and said, "Rita, you are a sucker for intensity, so all of the gods and goddesses love you!"

I asked when this yuga would end, and Basil said sternly, "Rita, I'm not going to get involved with you and Baron because when you two figure this out, it will mean the end of the yuga." I said, "So do I have some kind of destiny with Baron?" He sighed, saying, "I'm not going to answer that. You will have to learn to discern certainty from your heart. Ponder certainty."

Before I left the retreat, Basil said that he liked my lion necklace. I told him that it could be either Durga's lion or the Christian lion. A friend had recently told me that the lion was a symbol for a disciple – someone who had the courage to carry the message. Basil added that in Buddhism, the Lion's Roar is a symbol of waking up, of awakening. I said that I was definitely waking up. He nodded.

The following Saturday I spent eight hours in solitude, in a state of receptivity. I felt as though my intuitive channel was really on. In that state, I received instructions to make art collages to the Divine Mother, and to learn more about the Mother through studying the life of Ammachi. Suddenly drawn to meet Ammachi, I signed up to attend her June retreat near San Ramon, California.

After finishing the book about Neem Karoli Baba, I read Shankara's *Crest-Jewel of Discrimination*. Then I read books about Ammachi, Anandamayi Ma, and Ramakrishna. Each of those high beings intensely loved the Divine Mother. Neem Karoli Baba said, "*See all women as mothers, serve them as your mother. When you see the entire world as the Mother, the ego falls away."* (*Miracle of Love*, by Ram Dass, A Dutton Paperback, E.P. Dutton.)

I felt so much love emanating from Neem Karoli Baba. Reading his teachings helped me to relax about the mothering path. I thought, 'It doesn't matter if my mind wants to be somewhere else, because the mind isn't real anyway! Let the mind do what it does, but keep my heart open to loving these boys.'

In the coming months when I struggled with mothering, I found myself approaching it more from the voice of the Witness. For example, I would think, *'Oh, there I am resisting mothering again...'* As the Witness voice gained strength, I slowly perceived a shift in the way I experienced mothering. I felt Grace descending.

I attended an evening of kirtan and dissolved into total ecstasy. I felt merged in Absolute Delight. I felt as though I didn't need a house or anything – as though I only needed devotional chanting.

Yet, even as I felt the effects of God's Grace in my life and I witnessed my sword of knowledge getting stronger, I still found the maya difficult to transcend, especially in the relationship with Baron.

As Baron and I continued our dance, I also continued to sit in meditation each evening, with an ever-evolving practice. I visualized a sacrificial fire in my heart. I imagined Mother Durga, in all Her splendor, standing in that fire, and I offered Her my ego, asking Her to burn it in the Fire.

Chapter 40 – Stop Spinning!

A few weeks before the pilgrimage to meet Amma, I journeyed through a big set of kriyas with Baron Bear. Our usual dance played out: I felt so in love when we were together, but then I felt disconnected when we were apart.

I observed my energy state when I was with him – I tracked that my heart softened, currents ran through my physical and subtle bodies, and my crown opened with much tingling. According to Basil's teachings, these were good signs. I thanked Ma Durga again and again for the gift of Bear in my life.

But then, when Baron and I would be apart for a few days, my energy state would shift into worry, paranoia, and despair. One night we talked on the phone and I expressed how I felt disconnected from him. I shared that it seemed as though I was more into him than he was into me. He agreed that our relationship felt a bit lopsided.

Baron said, "You have more pizzazz with me. I'm more flat with you. You're more giving and heartfelt with me." That hurt my ego and I burst into tears. When he heard me sobbing, he said sweetly, "Rita, you're this young bhakta with this old hard-hearted rationalist who hasn't had enough time with you yet to soften his heart to the level that you have. But he can work on it."

That night after our phone call, I cried for two hours. I wrote the following in my journal:

"Hey Ma Durga, I keep trying to grab onto You! Why do you let me drown in this ego still? How many more spins must I endure? I am so tired. And so exhausted by the magnetic pull of the content. Intellectually I understand Advaita Vedanta and all That, but the samskaras are so strong! I know that an earthly man will never satisfy my deep longing for union, but I ignorantly continue to pursue that mission with gusto! Hey Ma Durga, what if I'm not destined to be a great saint like Amma or Anandamayi Ma? What if I'm just another ordinary soul who is destined to spin around her whole life? Oh, Durga, I cannot bear the thought. Kill me now – please kill my ego! Please let me rest in You."

After sitting in meditation, I wrote:

"Hey Ma Durga, thank you for that peaceful, almost blissful feeling – it gave me hope to continue on the path. Ayyh! What sheer hilarity is your Lila! The way You bounce me between pain and pleasure with Baron is so obvious! You really want me to **get it**: I am **not** this body, **not** this love with Baron, **not** the content and stories that flow through me. I AM BRAHMAN, the Totality of Being. I surrender to You, Durga. The Mother designates the moment. I pray IT will come soon!"

The next afternoon, Baron called, but he seemed distant. After that call, I fell into unbelievably excruciating pain. I tried so hard to hold onto thoughts of God, but I felt really crazy inside and I cried for several hours.

During dinner with the boys, I told them that I felt frustrated with the Universe. Benjamin asked why and I said that I didn't like how God makes people suffer so that they will long to go back to Him and then see the Light. It didn't seem to me like God had much compassion for us, so I felt frustrated with the Universe. Benjamin replied with a hilarious Indian accent, "Mama, you are not supposed to do *that* – you're supposed to be okay with what happens. You're supposed to be okay with what's happening, even if you're walking the plank!"

Later I wrote:

"No one else can be in this for me. This part was assigned to me and I have to play it out. Take courage and be determined. Hold onto God. Oh, Durga, take me to Your Radiance... grant me the Grace to live through this intense purification."

The next night proved to be the worst of that string of kriyas. Baron went out with friends and didn't call. Somehow I remained calm in meditation and I wrote this prayer after:

Hey Ma Durga,
tonight You ARE
the essence of Beauty
dancing in the sacrificial Fire –
drunk on the ecstasy
of Being the entire Universe –
You take my offerings
and burn them in the Fire.

When I got in bed the calm left me and the tears flowed. I turned on the light and wrote:

"Durga, Please help me hold onto that expansion. As midnight draws near and there is still no call from Baron, I feel another contraction building... my heart is beating faster and I feel a little panic. So maybe he will break up with me. Trying to see that only God exists and only God acts. So if he breaks up with me, it's really God separating from God through ending the union of our two forms. And I will be okay. I *am* okay. If I am Durga who IS One with Brahman, then how can I allow myself to grieve in this limited story-line with this one guy in this one lifetime? Hold onto God!

"With ferocity, hold onto Self. And, at the same time, be gentle if grief waves do come – if we separate, it will take time to disentangle. Can't hope one way or the other – if we are meant to be together we will be, and if we are not meant to be together we won't be. My job is to keep purifying, meditating, studying, and practicing forbearance."

As I read the biography of Ammachi, I wept at the incredible level of forbearance she displayed throughout the challenging circumstances in her childhood home. Due to her dark skin, her own family treated her worse than a servant and beat her regularly. Amma faced their tortures with a loving, cheerful attitude. She prayed fervently to Krishna and eventually became enlightened. Although some people – including her own relatives – tried several times to kill her, Amma persevered and went on to become a world saint who has hugged millions of people while launching dozens of humanitarian organizations that serve the suffering.

The *Bhagavad Gita* describes the lover of God as *one who remains spontaneously content with whatever comes.* I contemplated that, but continued to cry over Baron. I wrote:

> *O' Durga,*
> *in bed alone, again,*
> *my heart is breaking.*
> *How can I bear this pain?*
> *Is he really leaving me?*
> *Nighttime is the hardest part*
> *when grieving the loss of a lover.*
> *Nighttime, alone in the bed,*
> *can break the resolve*
> *of the strongest yogini.*

The next day was Friday. Baron called to see if he could come over that evening. As I braced myself for what I assumed would be our end, I cried a lot, and I left several very long, anxious messages on Julianna's answering machine.

By the time Baron arrived that evening, I was exhausted. I turned off my phone and we sat down to talk. When I told him that I had been going through such devastating turmoil, he explained that he had just been busy and focusing his attention on other things. He was surprised to hear what I had been going through, and I was surprised to hear that he had absolutely no intention of breaking up with me.

While we talked, Julianna left a very stern message on my machine. She said, "Stop. It's not about Baron. Stop spinning! Drop down into yourself."

Basil once said that I would burn through my tendencies through passion. He said that I needed to feel all of my emotions fully without trying to dampen them down. I thought that I was doing that by allowing myself to grieve, but Julianna's message helped me to see that I was spinning in a way that was wearing out myself and others. Still, I wondered how to stop looping without feeling like I was dampening down an emotion?

I thought of how I was able to hold onto moments of connection with God, but then emotional intensities would grip me again. I felt as though I needed mirroring from another seeker or from a Guru. I reflected that even though I had surrounded myself with holy images and I sat regularly in meditation... and I was reading about the inner lives of saints... I still felt the need for direct initiation and transmission. I wondered if maybe I was purifying for meeting Amma?

The next day I sent this email to Baron:

Be free O' wild one,
and I'll see if I can be more okay with it.

I'll be here, steady in my love for you,
and you see if you can dive in more.

And when we find those places where we can meet,
may it be fulfilling and good for both of us.

He replied, "*I do dive in when you open so beautifully and trustingly.*"

That afternoon I wrote the following:

"Piercing desire to merge in absolute splendor with Your Radiance, O' Ma Durga. Piercing desire to **be** Compassion Itself – to serve others without regard to this form and its constructs."

As I sat contemplating how I could serve others better, I realized (again) that the best way to serve Baron was to take the pressure off of him by striving for total absorption in God. Suddenly I realized what should have already been obvious: I was doing *exactly the same pattern* with him – the pattern that I thought I had burned through, the pattern that Basil had warned me was a deep tendency in me.

Indeed, I was projecting my need for union with God onto Baron and expecting him to fulfill what an earthly man cannot possibly fulfill. I hoped that through regular meditation I could attain higher levels of consciousness and deeper absorption in Divine Reality, which would enable me to meet Baron in a place of more relaxed stillness.

I thought that it was important for me to realize that when Baron didn't meet me the way I wanted to be met, it was not about *him*. He was being used to show me that what I was really longing for was to be completely MET, in full Radiance, by God.

Julianna called to check on me. She said it seemed as though I was experiencing a profound existential anxiety about not feeling loved. I admitted that I wanted to experience total Union. She asked if I felt better after talking with Baron, and I said that rather than feeling 'excited,' I felt 'calm.' She laughed and said, "Rita, you wore yourself out so that you can finally relax."

That night in meditation I felt an intense sexual fire energy rushing through my system. I focused on directing that wild energy toward my longing to merge with Mother Kali. Rather than directing the energy onto Baron's form, I focused it all onto Kali. I thought about how I kept alternating between Kali and Durga, both manifestations of the goddess Parvati, and I felt grateful that my journey to finding the Mother was unfolding so nicely.

Over and over I chanted:
Kali Durge Namo Namah
Kali Durge Namo Namah

A few nights later, at meditation group, a couple visited to give us *diksha*, a transmission of the state of Oneness. They explained that enlightenment is a neurobiological event, and so our brains need to be re-patterned. When someone has been trained to give *diksha*, they can transmit the state of Oneness through their eyes or by laying their hands on people.

During and after the experience of the couple laying their hands on my head, I felt an intense longing to merge with the Radiance of the Mother. Here are the thoughts that danced through my mind during that time:

'Kali Durge Namo Namah, please help re-pattern my brain so that I know that I am the Radiance of the Mother. Kali Durge Namo Namah, fill me with Durga's fierceness, strength, tenderness, and compassion. I am Freedom, Wildness, Colorful, Zesty, Juicy. Echoes upon echoes of the Mother... the Mother within and without... Jai Kali Ma!

'My projection of what I think it will look like to merge with the One Radiance is holding me back. I am afraid that if I really let go, I will be too wild and I won't wear clothes! Fear of being too wild and naked. Fear of not being a polite, good girl. Fear of being socially inappropriate. Fear of singing in public.'

After the diksha transmissions, we discussed our experiences, and I laughed out loud when I shared my fear of being naked. It was good for me to name that fear and to laugh at it. That helped me to relax about it all, and I felt a bigger vibration of Patience enveloping my being.

The next night Baron Bear and I went to a party where we saw a statue of *Ganesha*, the elephant-headed god who is the Remover of Obstacles. Bear prayed aloud to Ganesha to remove any obstacles in our relationship. Then when we were dancing, I felt us melting into each other.

Later in the weekend we went to a dinner party with some of my relatives, and they told Baron that they were so glad to see me happy again. My aunt said, "She's found her groove again – she's laughing like when she was a teenager." That really surprised me, because I thought that during my unhappy marriage I had put on a happy face for others. Apparently not. People had actually noticed how unhappy I was.

Hearing my aunt say that I had found my groove again really affirmed my heart opening. I felt like crying for all of the years that I had closed down, but I also felt like celebrating for the renewal of joy in my heart.

The week before going to Ammachi's retreat, many wild animals, including panthers and tigers, appeared in my dreams. Life with the boys felt difficult, but my meditations were strong.

One night in meditation I felt strong chills throughout my body. It felt like an electric charge – like all of my cells were sexually awake – and it intensified each time I directed my mind to Durga. I continued to sing *Kali Durge Namo Namah, Kali Durge Namo Namah*. It felt as though that chant was landing more as mantra medicine for me.

The relationship with Baron was good, and yet I continued to worry. I offered my worries to Kali Durge. I talked with him about my concerns, and he said that he was happy with me and he wished that I would just relax. He said, "Cut yourself as much slack as you cut me."

I picked an angel card for the Amma week: *Responsibility.* I hadn't picked that card since New Year's Day. I remembered that I had felt a responsibility to bring forth *That* which is within me, and I took that seriously. I prayed, "Oh, Amma, please grant me whatever I need to bring forth *That* which is within me." I bowed to her with patience and humility.

Two nights before the trip, Baron and I sat in meditation. Afterwards, I asked how it was for him, and he said, "It's always good when I meditate with you. I felt Bliss." I asked what that bliss felt like in his body, and he said, "a vast, vibrating emptiness."

The night before the trip, I hit another kriya in which I didn't feel the connection with Bear. I prayed, "Oh, Kali Durge, how can I unravel this pattern? You made this pattern – please unravel it for me!"

That night I dreamt:

I was in a small group with a wise man from India and the music was playing "Celebrate good times, come on!" and the sage said, "What is this music? It's just based on scientific law!" Then he proclaimed that the people who have progressed to know Shiva are **There***. I started crying because I knew Shiva, so I thought that maybe I was almost* **There***!*

At breakfast I told the boys about my dream and they asked what it meant to be "*There,*" and I explained about merging in God; about knowing that you are One with everything in the whole Universe.

I said that I believed Amma was a being who had merged with the whole Universe like that, and the boys asked if I would really want to be like Amma. They said, "then we would have thousands of people coming to the cottage!" I joked back, "You guys would have to learn how to make chai," and Joshua wisely blurted out, "We could just get those cartons of chai and add milk!" Spoken like a true modern-day child.

I took the boys to school, and Julianna picked me up to begin our journey to Ammachi. I felt both excited and nervous. After reading several books about the lives of saints, what would it be like to actually be in the presence of one?

Chapter 41 – Meeting Amma

Julianna and I arrived at the Mata Amritanandamayi Center just in time to see Amma enter the ashram for the evening program. Dressed in a pure white sari, Amma radiated the warmth of absolute Love. I thirstily drank it all in – the pujas, the prayers, the rose petals, and the colorful shimmering decorations. We sat among a few thousand people and I loved smiling at all of the beings around us. As I smelled the incense and felt the music deep in my bones, tears swelled in my eyes. I gazed at Amma's Beauty and at the bright orange robes of the *Swamis* (teachers) surrounding her.

During the Swami's lecture, I felt the intensity of the connection with Baron, and then I felt the vasana rising. At that moment, the Swami translated Amma, saying that the *vasanas* (tendencies) "come up to be exhausted." I watched as my mind brought up some doubts. I felt disillusioned with the spiritual path as I looked around at all of those people who were trying so earnestly, and yet, I wondered, 'How often does a person really break free?' I felt like giving up.

I went to bed feeling mentally agitated, but I awoke early the next morning with my inner voice chanting *Kali Durge Namo Namah*. Once we arrived in the hall that morning, I relaxed into the meditation and prayers. While waiting to go up to Amma for my first *darshan* with her, I felt a deep yearning to offer myself to others in selfless service like Amma does.

I didn't know how to offer more service. I felt the panic of losing myself, but I also kept remembering the deep sense of mission that I had felt as a child. Now I just needed to figure out what that mission was…

When it was my turn to go up to Amma, I felt nervous. I told myself that whatever happened would be fine. Later I wrote in my journal:

"I didn't think that I would cry, but the instant Amma took me into her arms, I started crying so hard. I'm not sure what happened except that she kept saying "MaMaMaMaMa…" and then she gave me two chocolate kisses, and I wanted to make eye contact with her, but I don't think that I did… and afterwards I cried so hard that I thought I would burst. And now, hours later, I still feel tender and raw… Amma was talking and laughing while hugging me, but I don't know what she said. Afterwards my mind felt calm and I was thinking of ways to serve others."

As I sat listening to the continuous *bhajans* (devotional songs), I wept as I tuned in to the world's suffering. I felt some currents of heat pulsing throughout my being, and I kept 'hearing' that I would teach meditation. I realized that I feared really dropping myself and stepping into my calling. I felt fear of teaching and fear of responsibility. Yet deep within, I knew that meditation was really helping me, and I longed to teach that beneficial life skill to others.

179

That evening during the teachings and bhajans, I thought, 'Sitting in this sea of people, I am filled with patience, understanding, and hope... the disillusion has faded. Doubts are dissolving...'

During the evening talk, the Swami said that Amma doesn't blame or judge us. Rather, she observes us. She says that our minds are like dry twigs, and if she bends the dry twigs they will break in two, so she has to slowly bend our minds! He then talked about the importance of meditation. The goal of meditation is to free people from all bondage. Meditation isn't to make us special – it is to make us humble. Meditation enhances our capacity to act; it gives us more clarity and makes our actions more effective in the world.

The next day Baron met us at the ashram for the weekend retreat. That evening he and I went up to Amma for darshan together. We held this question in our hearts: 'Are we good for each other's spiritual growth?' First she hugged him, then me, and then the two of us together. Then she kissed each of our hands and she gave Baron a really funny mischievous look! We took her 'answer' to mean that yes, we were good for each other's spiritual growth.

That night the Swami explained that Amma's goals are one with the Universe's Goal, which is to put the Universe back on the right track. He said that because her goals are one with the Universe's Goals, there are no obstacles for her. Seeming obstacles just melt in front of her.

During the guided meditation, my mind relaxed. The Swami said, *"Feel every cell awakening and buzzing with an ecstatic golden light. Every pore is open to divine energy. Peace flows out of our hearts, engulfs us, and we become One with that Peace."*

The next afternoon Amma held a Question and Answer session out in the sunshine by the pond. As I gazed at the stately swans gliding through the water, Amma commented that it is good to be in the sun after 3pm because after 3pm the sun's rays contain particles of gold.

I felt nervous about asking her a question, but I did it anyway. I asked, "Amma, I understand that the Divine Mother stages this universe as Her Divine Play and that the vasanas are designed to take us back to Her, but if She wants us to come back to Her, why does she make it so hard? Does she really want us to merge with Her? I mean, You were born enlightened, but what about the billions of other people on the planet? How many people can really break free of their vasanas and get back to union with the Mother?"

A Swami translated my question, and Amma laughed. She said, "In India we are used to British English. When we hear American English, it sounds like Wah Wah Wah!" Then she gave the following answer:

"Amma's desire is that her children should always be happy. Amma and her children are not two – we are One. There is no separation. Amma's only desire is for her children to laugh and love, and laugh and love... and to share other people's sorrow. Our hearts should melt when we see the pain of other people. That is real spirituality.

"As we live in the world, our main goal is to attain Self-Realization. We live in the world, perform our duties, and keep our focus on God. Lack of knowledge is the biggest impediment. We have to develop alertness and awareness. Only from spirituality will we get complete Freedom – everything else is like a bundle that is wrapped with pleasure, but inside it is filled with pain. We have to understand the nature of the world and its objects.

"Once the Light comes, darkness and ignorance will spontaneously be removed. God is writing a drama, but God is not identified with His role or with the characters... unlike us. We are identified with our roles and with the characters."

That evening Baron and I went up for darshan separately. Amma hugged him for a really long time. Twice he tried to pull away, but she held him closer. He said that his vision went to deep, pure black. After that, he looked so radiant. He said that she looked in his eyes for a while before the hug, and I said maybe she saw the ancient yogi from India that I saw in him.

When I went up to Amma, I held this question in my heart: 'How can I be a better mother to Joshua and Benjamin?' I took a photo of them with me. She kissed the photo before hugging me. I started shaking as I sat down afterwards. I looked at the photo of my boys and thought of how the three of us get stuck in boredom and irritation, and then I cried remembering how my own mother felt bored and irritated with my brothers and me.

I thought of the cellular imprint I received from my Mom, but then I looked at Amma and thought about how she had received many, many beatings from her mother, and she was not beating people! She was not imprinted forever by what *her* mother did – there she was, hugging and loving everyone! I realized that I needed to stop focusing on the imprint, because I was locking it down by fixating on it. It seemed as though Amma's 'answer' was for me to simply love and hug my boys.

After three darshans with Amma, I noticed a cumulative effect building with each hug. I felt as though she was going deeper and deeper into my heart. I felt so in love with her. She was so adorable. I began to cry for God and for the Beauty of the world, and it felt good to cry for something beyond my own sorrows, tendencies and fixations.

I thought of the intensity with which I had been wrestling with God. I realized that in my noble efforts to burn through the vasanas, I had actually been locking them down. I began laughing at the absurdity of it all. I felt as though Amma had given me a transmission of love and laughter when she said to laugh and love, and laugh and love.

The last night was *Devi Bhava* night, the night Amma dresses as the Divine Mother. After special *pujas* (ritual worship), she hugs people all night long. Often she hugs people for fifteen hours or longer – without even taking one single pee break! When I went up to hug her at 3:30am, I took a photo of my family with me. She really looked at it before she kissed it. She seemed pleased by the photo. While she hugged me, I said, "I love you, Amma," into her chest, and then I asked for mantra. She said yes, so I went to get in the mantra line.

A devotee named Prema prepared a group of us to receive mantra. She explained that the disciple-Guru relationship is not one-sided. Amma agrees to guide the disciple forevermore to Liberation, and the disciple agrees to chant their mantra at least 108 times each day, to develop an outer and/or inner relationship with Amma each day, and to see the Divinity in each and every being they encounter.

Prema gave us each a slip of paper on which to write our chosen aspect of the Divine. One woman wrote Jesus, one man wrote Peace. I couldn't decide between Kali and Durga, so I asked Prema for advice. She said that praying mantra to Kali can make life more intense. As she said that, she noticed my lion necklace, and then she said, "Choose Durga – although Durga is fierce, She is also a very tender, loving Mother." I agreed that I needed the tenderness of Durga – I certainly did not need Kali stirring up any more intensity in my life! I was intense enough already.

I received *mantra diksha* from Amma, a Sat Guru, at 4:30am. In accordance with ancient Yogic tradition, she held rose petals on my head while she said the mantra two times into my left ear. It was a truly amazing experience. I could hardly believe my good fortune to have received mantra from her.

An hour later, when my heart was stirring in the same way that it quivers during the poignant moments of weddings and funerals, I knew that receiving Guru Mantra from Amma had been a peak moment of my life. I knew then that she was my Guru. I thought, *'Durga is Kali is Amma is Durga!'*

The next day, I read through the notes that I had taken at one of the Swami's lectures. The following really grabbed me:

"We have personal dreams, goals, and desires, but we should watch Amma's example. Her desires are for the poor to have food, for violence to end, and for all beings to know God. We should get closer to Her Goals. When our goals get closer to the Universe's Goals, everything flows.

"When we are open to all situations, life becomes a flow, an unfolding. Amma refers to her life as a river flowing. She flows around obstacles. She is constantly flowing. She doesn't plan where Love is going to go, and this is how Love is: with Love there is no planning; it is so spontaneous. As long as we insist that things go according to our plans, there is suffering and struggle. But when we allow things to unfold, life naturally flowers.

"Humility must come first – it purifies us and allows us to see nothing as inauspicious, and then we behold Amma's Grace and Presence in everything. In fact, there is nothing inauspicious in this world. Everything is auspicious. Everything is for the best. Humility melts Amma's heart. Bow down and all will come."

When I returned home from meeting Amma, I shared a beautiful, loving day with my boys. I told them that Amma had hugged people for fourteen hours without taking a single break, and Joshua said, "She is energy-packed!"

I gazed at the photos of the three Gurus on my kitchen walls: Amma, Neem Karoli Baba, and Anandamayi Ma. I realized that receiving mantra from

Amma linked me more directly to Anandamayi Ma, since Anandamayi Ma had clairvoyantly perceived Amma (from across India), and she had sent people to Amma before she left her body. I cried with gratitude and felt closer to God.

I felt Amma's Grace in little ways throughout my days. I felt her Grace even in the difficulties with Baron Bear. Even though he was fulfilling my request of calling every day, and even though he was saying he loved me, I still didn't feel as though he really *wanted* to see me. I felt hurt and disappointed and I noticed how much that drama dissipated my energy. I wondered if our relationship really was serving my spiritual growth? I wondered if we should break up?

Instead of breaking up, I decided to try just accepting exactly what our relationship was – and what it wasn't. Rather than insisting that it go according to my plans, I would watch it unfold and stop trying to mentally figure it out.

As I sipped hot tea in the sunshine, I listened to the boys playing a war game. Benjamin asked Joshua what surrender meant, and Joshua replied, "Surrender means I'm tired enough, I'll join your side." I laughed out loud and thought, 'Hey Ma Durga, O' dear Amma, I'm tired enough of this vasana – I'll join *Your* side! Please let me join Your side!'

Chapter 42 – Orchestrated Drama in Divine Lila

The day after I 'decided' to just let things unfold with Baron, I attended the first day of Basil's June retreat. I was thinking a lot about my purpose in life, so I was happy to hear Basil talk about purpose:

"In meditation you can burn through some vasanas, but there are two classes of vasanas that you can't burn in meditation. One class you can only live through (Ramana Maharshi called this *prarabdha karma*), and the other class you can only burn through by finding your purpose. And once you merge with your purpose, you find that your purpose here actually turns out to be quite universal.

"Rather than finding "your purpose," it is actually a *Quality of Being* that is refined enough to come through you once It knows you are capable of it. There is another agency that flows through these interrelated streams of vasanas, and that agency is Grace. With Grace, you will still have intense tests and you will still have pain, but you will *perceive* less suffering.

"If you get your practice and your service both well-anchored, you can burn through the middle stream (the prarabdha karma) easier and faster."

On the second day of the retreat my stomach hurt and I felt really nauseated, but I persevered and learned a lot. I asked Basil about the voice that gave me a play-by-play rundown of what was happening, even when I was in deep meditation states. I asked him if I needed to try to get rid of that voice.

Basil answered, "In meditation we are generating a body of experience that will be the foundation for the next level of experience. The voice you are hearing, Rita, is like a translator that is building a body of understanding. That voice is the Witness voice and it is important, especially for you with your writer/philosopher constitution.

"The voice will lay down at some point, and then you will go deeper into samadhi realms. So there's nothing for you to do – there's actually nothing you could do. The voice will lay down when the body of understanding is built. As you go deeper, you will realize that the purpose of meditation is that the Universe is teaching you to become Itself. Remember that the goal of spiritual life is to know the Infinite – not to figure out your own problems!"

We chanted *Om Namah Shivaya* and then sat in meditation. I fell into a wonderfully deep state, but then at lunch I once again approached Basil with my own problems. I asked him about the pattern which was flaring up again with Baron, and he reminded me that the feminine has a voracious appetite to be met which no man can ever fill – it has to be met by the Divine Mother. Then he asked what I experienced during the chant and meditation.

I said that I saw the vastness of the Self – I felt It directly. I saw that the stories of my life were outside of me, like a film playing on a screen. I tuned in to the vastness of the Self in all the beings in the room, and I felt the absolute connection of all of us. Basil smiled, and said, "Rita, this is one big impersonal stew, but each person thinks it's personal. Just remember that it's not personal. Also remember that as the mind gets stronger, it gets more disciplined and then it doesn't entertain sensations very long. Weak minds work things. Rather than reacting to Baron when you feel him pulling away, deeply contemplate his being, and see if you can understand how it's all arising."

That night I still felt nauseated. Baron called from a loud party and asked me to join him there, but I didn't feel well, so I went to bed early. I felt sad that he seemed distant – he seemed more interested in partying than in connecting with me. I felt fearful about our relationship.

At the retreat the next morning, Basil talked about our illusion of attaining enlightenment. He said, "Except for very advanced beings, it's an illusion to think that you're going to complete the journey in one lifetime, but all of the high states you achieve are never lost. All of the energy states keep vibrating."

I questioned him on that one and I expressed despair at the thought of not reaching enlightenment this lifetime. Basil laughed and said, "Rita, nothing is set in stone, not even your enlightenment moment!" Later in the morning he joked about that again, saying, "A good moneymaker for the sangha would be to have everyone place bets as to whether Rita's going to get enlightened this lifetime." One man in the room said, "I wouldn't want to bet against her!"

Basil nodded and said, "Rita, when you hit a deeper state, that Light uplifts everyone and then they see that possibility in themselves. Every time you go beyond your questioning mind, you leak that expanded state out and when it expands rapidly, time stops. If you loosen up, play more, and relax, you will be astounded by the rapidity of remarkable changes. It is very helpful to relax into what's happening. Remember that there is continuous help flowing into you at all times. The energy holding you in an expanded meditation is the same energy holding you during a family crisis."

After lunch, Basil described the social climate in India 5,000 years ago: "The purpose of politics then was to support people's openings and their spiritual evolution. In Vedic times, there existed the correct alignment of spiritual energy into the form world. Amma is now intentionally creating the conditions for the Vedic structures to re-activate.

"You are all very courageous and the planet needs you. The fact that we can have such openings in this time of density is truly amazing. In your spiritual practices, connect first with your courage.

"According to the Yogis, this Kali Yuga is the densest age. For the culmination of the Day of Brahma, everything has to grow and complete itself before Brahma can lie down and go to sleep. At the end – at the Night of Brahma – he's had his milk and cookies, but then Rita's there with one question left, so all the celestial beings and angels gather around her and bat the question away, and her mind stops cold, and Brahma goes to sleep, and the whole thing shuts down and everything goes back to Pure Consciousness vibrating.

"But before the Night of Brahma, we all have to wake up and experience a Golden Age. So the point of this whole thing is the Awakening of all beings. And since Rita still has vasanas left, Brahma still has to get up for another day!"

My ears perked up at that, and I asked, "only for another *day*?" Basil laughed and said, "Rita, rita, rita, you've got a long life ahead of you – you're going to live to be an exotic old bird. Remember that increased longing and outer service speed up the process."

I expressed frustration that I wasn't merging with my purpose and I wasn't finding a career of service which would also support me financially. Basil said that I wanted bells and whistles to go off, but maybe it wasn't going to happen that way for me – maybe my calling and service and job weren't all going to line up to be one thing.

He continued, "Our life movement is predicated on our gifts. The more potent the gift, the deeper the tests. Deficiencies are contracted gifts waiting to unfold at the right time. The Intelligence *knows* what It is doing – the gifts are not for us. The gifts are for the service of the Whole.

"Sometimes you just have to surrender to deep states and know that you are energetically contributing to others... and once you are re-patterned, you will give more physically. The outer service will appear when it's ready. Remember that the outer service is *given* by Consciousness through you."

As I left the retreat that day, I told Basil and Luna that I would join them the following month in Hawaii. I hugged several people goodbye, and one woman said to me, "I think you're going to get it this lifetime!" I wasn't so sure about that.

The following week, as I contemplated the teachings which came through Basil so beautifully, I endured a painfully dramatic test with Baron. A few weeks later, when I was able to write about it, I sent the following email to Basil:

Hello dear Basil,

I hope this finds you not too travel-weary. Hopefully your time in New York is restful and inspiring.

I am still high from Amma and from your retreat – thank you so much for that retreat. I loved so much of what you said, especially that nothing is set in stone, not even my enlightenment moment!

Since the retreat, life and Amma orchestrated a painful test which transformed into a delightful theater. Even as it happened, I shifted from holding tightly to my role to watching the lila unfold. I am in awe of Amma's Grace. Here's the story:

For many years, Baron has wanted to find a polyamorous relationship, and although he has never found a woman to agree to it, he's pretty attached to the ideal, and it has caused much pain in his relationships. This was the subject of the kriyas I had with him during your April retreat. At that time, he basically agreed to my "line," although he didn't think it was wise to relinquish his ideal.

186

Well, on the second night of your June retreat, he went to a party at his friend Sallamae's house. He called me from there, but I didn't go because I felt too sick and tired. Well, it just so happened that Sallamae's dear friend Kalima was visiting, and she happened to look attractive to Baron. He ended up staying the night on a mattress on the living room floor with her, and although they did not have sex, they did kiss a little, and they did hold each other. Somehow I was only dimly in his awareness and when she asked if he was in his integrity, he was evasive in his answer. The next day he told her about me, and a few days later he told me about her. As you might well imagine, I felt a bit hurt and angry.

I felt so ashamed and embarrassed that I had stayed in a relationship in which I knew that was likely to happen – I felt strong self-loathing. Sallamae was the only person I could talk to. She felt really bad because it was her friend. I called her and she held a container for me to let the anger out. I yelled and I got really clear about what I could and could not accept in the relationship with Baron. I found a clean sense of power and clarity, and I was ready to break up with him if he didn't show up and commit in a way that felt okay with me. I reached a place in which I knew that the anger was appropriate, and I began to feel it vibrationally as a state which was not only okay, but also necessary for burning that particular veil. In my meditations, strong burning sensations filled my system.

After I talked with Sallamae, Baron called to say that they were all going to the circus that night. He asked if I would go with him. Yes, yes, the circus! The perfect place for such a drama to unfold. It was in that moment that I switched from holding tightly to my role to letting Amma's Grace unfold the play.

Baron and I walked over to the circus together and met our circle of friends there. When I met Kalima, my internal response was, "She's cute, but **so am I!**" I just felt so powerful and so full of myself, and so clear that she had nothing to do with any of it. I felt this red-hot vibration of anger at the situation but I didn't feel any anger toward her. We all went in and took our seats and of course Baron and I were sitting directly behind her. I was burning, burning, burning, throughout my whole being, with what felt to me like a very high vibration of anger. It didn't feel at all malicious or revengeful; it just felt pure. Baron correctly named it when he said, "It's enlightened anger." And then he said, "It is with trepidation and gratitude that I sit next to you right now."

I continued burning as the anger merged with Divine Power and Strength. After the circus, we talked late into the night. We finally came to an agreement and a commitment. While I held to my line, I also opened more to love and I even expressed an interest in talking with him and Sallamae and Kalima.

The next day, while booking the Hawaii flights, Baron, Sallamae, and Kalima arrived at my door. We all sat down in the grass in my backyard, and we each put intentions in the center for what we hoped to get out of the meeting. Amazingly, when I first came out and sat down, Kalima saw *Durga* in me.

She said that she hadn't seen or thought about Durga in years. I told her that I had just received Durga mantra from Amma, and we were all astonished by that syncronicity. We had a good long talk and we each said all that we wanted to say, and Kalima cried a little. She felt really awkward. By the end, Kalima and I had our arms around each other and we were cuddling with Sallamae...

For his part, Baron told Kalima that although he felt an attraction and a desire to explore it, he was not going to, but rather he valued the relationship with me and he was committed to going deeper with me. He then said that although he has held the polyamory ideal close to his heart, he was now curious to see how it would be for him to approach attractions differently. He saw his pattern of going from one woman to the next... and he decided to *not* do that again right now, but to instead fully commit to me. Sallamae strongly urged him to tell me *before* something happens, and he agreed.

In the end, I joked that I should get to spend the night with Kalima to fair things up. She and I hugged for a really long time and I told her that I really was sorry that I couldn't sleep with her. Instead of hugging him, she bowed with palms joined at her heart and said "Namaste" to him, and he did the same in return.

It was a very healing meeting for all of us, maybe particularly for Baron, who, in all these years and in all his relationships, has never had that opportunity to sit and talk and allow love to be there in the midst of a painful pattern. I told him that his true nature is that he has so much love and he wants to give all that love out, and the way that he has expressed it through sexual love encounters is not his true nature but rather it's a pattern of behavior. He somewhat got that, but my eyes are open to the possibility that the pattern is strong enough that it may continue in some form at some point.

But right now, he has made a choice to be here, and he has really shown up. I still see the value in being with him. I have grown and continue to grow so much through being in relationship with him. We are both reading *Conscious Loving, The Journey to Co-Commitment: A Way to Be Fully Together Without Giving Up Yourself* by Gay and Kathleen Hendricks, and that book is helping us a lot at this juncture.

So! That was quite a lila! The day after that healing meeting was Luna's birthday and we were blessed to share a meal and kirtan with her. It was such a treat to be with her on her birthday – she looked utterly radiant. I'm sure you are glad to have her back with you in New York now.

I'm looking forward to the Hawaii retreat – I'm finally going to make one of your longer retreats!
love,
Rita rita rita

P.S. Have you heard from Karl lately? A strange thing happened with him. During your June retreat I sent him an email in which I shared that I was thinking of him with love during the chants. Well, Karl replied from France the day after Baron and I met with Sallamae and Kalima. He said that he was cutting off all contact with his previous life and going off into the Void! He also said that he *knew* that Karen (the woman he fell in love with in Australia) was his beloved for the rest of this life and for all future lifetimes! I wrote back saying that I respected that, although I still wonder if he and I might have some more karma to complete someday? For now though, our contact is over.

As Baron and I continued to strengthen our bond after the Kalima episode, I shared with him one of Basil's teachings on relationships:

"The goal of relationships is to liberate the beings, and to the degree that a relationship functions like that, there is shakti... and that is not always comfortable. There are lots of secondary goals, like massages and getting needs met, and they're nice, but they are not the main goal."

We agreed that there was a lot of shakti in our relationship, and we both felt closer to each other after the Kalima lila. I said that I could see the good that came out of the whole drama, but that did *not* mean that I wanted it to happen again!

As we lay in bed holding each other with my head on his chest, I heard this echo from our hearts that kept saying, "*Here we go skipping and dancing together through the ages...*"

I fell asleep filled with gratitude for finding Power through anger and Love through relationship.

In the morning, Baron whispered in my ear, "What an incredible week, Rita. I am so in love with you and I want to explore that more deeply and assuredly. I feel so blessed."

I felt so blessed too.

Chapter 43 – Hawaii Retreat

July brought much activity and several migraine headaches. With Joshua's ninth birthday, the Fourth of July festivities, my parents' visit, and getting ready to go on the Hawaii trip, I got a little wound up. I wrote the following in my journal:

"One breath at a time. Remember that I am not the doer. The Play coming through me this summer is not my doing. Pull off of the story, remember Amma, chant mantra japa, laugh, love, and enjoy the Show! The Mother's Divine Lila. O' Ma Durga, guide me deeply into Your Radiance."

One night while Baron and I were holding each other close in bed, I awoke with the sense that Amma was in our embrace. Just then, Baron awoke and said that he had just dreamt that he was necking with Amma! He said they were kissing and touching each other.

I shared Baron's dream with Julianna. We laughed and agreed that Amma must have visited him to help clean up his sexual karma.

Five nights later I wasn't laughing anymore when I myself had a sexual dream with Amma! In waking life, we were at the Oregon coast, camping in tents with my family. That day I had spent a long time communing with Ma Ocean and with a little brown lizard on a rock. That night, sleeping in the tent beside Baron and my boys, I had the following dream:

> In a classroom, Amma was on stage. She asked the class what things were needed for enlightenment and a woman listed a few things, but then Amma said that she forgot one thing. I raised my hand and she called on me. I opened my mouth to speak but nothing came out... so I opened my mouth again and I said very slowly and clearly, "I will open at the right time." Amma said slowly and clearly, "Yes, you will." Then she wondered if I had answered her question, and I nodded, saying that one of the things necessary for enlightenment was **timing**.
>
> Then I went in the room behind her stage and she came in and started kissing me on the lips! She kept changing between Amma and this Queen, and the kissing was sexual, and I had two thoughts: 'Maybe she's speeding up the timing of my opening,' and 'Maybe she's come to clean up my sexual karma too!'

Later I shared the dreams with Basil and he agreed that Amma was helping to clean up our sexual karma. I asked him if he had read the dramatic story I sent him on email, and he said no because he had gotten really sick in New York. Just before we hung up the phone, Basil said, "Rita, you are the most extremely pure adamantine jewel of clarity." I asked if he had just said adamantine jewel of clarity, and he said, "That's what I said. You live up to it, girl."

Baron decided he would visit his sick aunt in Minnesota while I attended the retreat in Hawaii, and then he would join me on the island for a week of vacationing together. I would be away from the boys for twenty nights total – the most time we had ever been apart.

I got some little straw bracelets with blue glass beads on them, and the boys and I tied them around our ankles. I also got us little pouch necklaces with a stone inside each one. We put them on and we touched each other's stones, filling them with love from our hearts. I told them that while we were apart we could think of each other and feel each other's love in the bracelets and stones. They liked that, and they didn't seem at all worried about me leaving. They were excited to go on some camping trips with their papa.

The night before the trip, I picked an angel card for the Hawaii journey: *Freedom*. How perfect.

On the first flight, such a depth of happiness and gratitude arose in me that I felt as though I would burst from the utter sorrow of such pure elated joy. I cried as I wrote in my journal:

"I feel such a sense of mission and purposeful work ahead of me, but I also feel the humility of what a speck I am in the Cosmos… Last night it suddenly occurred to me that I don't care about "enlightenment." I care about being my true, happy self and spreading that happiness to others. I care about doing whatever work the Mother wants me to do.

"It feels so good to break out of my little cottage and mothering world. This metal bird is already carrying me to Freedom! I pray that this trip will help me break through the barriers of my little self, symbolic of me breaking out and working in the world again. I feel like I am bursting through golden streamers, liberated from the restricted cell of the mothering bubble."

On the flight over the ocean, I delighted in the surreal view of clouds stretching all the way to the blue horizon. The intense sunlight made the clouds look like bright snow-covered fields. As we got closer to the islands, I watched a most spectacular sunset over the ocean. Then I smiled at the sliver of crescent moon as I read the following quote by Amma:

> *When you behold the entire universe as a play of consciousness, what is there to do but smile? Spirituality is a deep, genuine smile at all situations in life.*

> (*Embracing the World: Images and Sayings of Sri Mata Amritanandamayi Devi*, Mata Amritanandamayi Mission Trust, M.A. Center.)

Luna greeted me at the airport with a big hug. The warm Hawaiian air kissed my skin as she placed a fresh flower lei around my neck. Oh, it felt so good to be there.

The next morning I awoke to an intense migraine headache. I lay on the floor of the sanctuary room while Basil worked on my body and Luna fed me bites of banana with macadamia nut butter. Basil said that I needed to get clear about the expression of my sexual energy. He saw that I had too much backed-up sexual energy in my second chakra and then when that energy moved up to the brain centers it created the heat of the migraines. He told me once again to focus on bringing the sexual energy up to my heart.

I thought that I *was* bringing the sexual energy up to my heart. Perplexed, I said, "I'm in a relationship with one person and I think my sexual energy is clean and clear, so I don't know what you mean." And he said, "yes you do, you just don't want to do it."

Do what? I didn't know what he meant, and Luna didn't know what he meant either. I didn't think that was a helpful thing for a teacher to say to a student. And, as the week progressed, he made more comments about sex that confused me. My perception was that Basil held a real rigidity about sex.

Even though I felt irritated with Basil at times, I appreciated the many good, insightful teachings that came through him during the retreat. I found myself dropping into really expanded states of consciousness.

The first evening I gave Basil a quote by Swami Vivekananda, and he read it to the group as a way to begin the retreat:

> *Each one has a special nature peculiar to himself which he must follow and through which he will find his way to freedom.*

(*Wisdom: 365 Thoughts from Indian Masters*, by Danielle and Olivier Föllmi, Harry N. Abrams, Inc.)

Later Basil said to me, "Rita, it's a delight to have you here. This week, practice letting the Ground of Being carry you. Stop apologizing for yourself. You have many more meltdowns ahead of you, so just relax. Let the meltdowns go through you and purify you."

The next morning Basil said, "Rita, you are doing uncommonly well – you are about to get uncommonly happy." I said, "Well, I'm pretty happy now," and he said, "It's about to get worse!" After the morning session we packed a lunch and headed to the beach. I walked down to some rocks and offered Love to Pele (the Volcano Goddess), to Ma Ocean, and to Amma. I set an intention to expand into more Love while on the island. That afternoon I felt like a gleeful child when Luna and I ran into the water, splashing in the salty waves and laughing as we rolled together in the sand.

At dinner Basil said, "Rita's about to have a divine transmission." I didn't feel any different than usual, but sure enough, he was right: during the chanting that evening, I went into a past life experience of death by drowning. I expanded into the soft, blissful space that a being can go to after death. Rather than feeling scary or traumatic, it felt amazingly peaceful.

The next afternoon Luna took me snorkeling at a rocky beach with strong waves. I quickly got overwhelmed by trying to breathe only through my nose while also trying to avoid touching the sharp coral. Suddenly I felt an urgency to get back to the shore. I felt exhausted as I swam with all my might, and I felt afraid that I wasn't going to make it.

Just as I reached the rocks, a little Hawaiian girl slipped over the rock in front of me. Without thinking, I intuitively grabbed her and handed her back up to her mother. Shaking, I went to sit in the sun. In an effort to calm myself, I ate some chocolate and gazed out at the ocean. I wondered if I had overreacted in grabbing the little girl, but just then the mother came up to me and said, "Thank you so much – she doesn't know how to swim."

When I told Basil the story later, he laughed and said, "This will all be written in a book some day." I asked what he meant, and he said, "This past twenty-four hours: last night you experienced that deep state of death by drowning, today you panicked in the ocean and feared you were about to drown, and then you just happened to get back to shore at the exact moment that a little girl needed rescuing. That's a good one, Rita."

That evening Basil once again addressed my ancient lines of confusion between sex and power. He said that I had used sex for power subtly in past lives, and I was still using sex in this life too. I didn't understand, so he said, "Notice how you use sexual allure to maintain Baron's attention to you, and notice what you do when his attention sways from you."

He instructed me to go inside and track the sexual energy in my body. I closed my eyes and went inside, and I hit upon an ancient place, like sand dunes, and I went into a similar state of peace and bliss as in the death by drowning experience. I didn't see any content, but I felt amazingly peaceful.

I shared the experience with Basil, and he said, "You are seeing landscapes where you have done sadhana before. That becomes your guideline: only run sexual energy when you can have that feeling. Running sexual energy with too much objectified desire structure overwhelms the open expanded space and then you confuse the male with that space. Those inner states you experience – you should preserve them with scrupulous attention and not give them away for lower sexual pleasures. Sexual energy is very potent and should be used correctly and not often.

"In past lives you used sexual energy to get to high, expanded states. That still lives in you, so you can still use it to quickly get to expanded states… but, if you put our culture's way of sex over that, it creates irritation in your system which then shows up in your emotions and then you push the man away."

I protested that I wasn't pushing Baron away, but Basil insisted that it had shown up with Baron when I got so irritated that he took his attention away from me.

I thought about that as I rushed to the computer to see if there was an email message from my Bear. There was. While visiting his aunt in the Midwest, he was feeling close to me even though we were half the world away from each other. I delighted in the very loving emails he sent me daily. In one message he shared that at a big party he didn't even feel like flirting with the women there. Rather, he was enjoying thinking of me and sending me loving energy.

I could feel Baron's energy around me, and Basil saw it, too. He joked with me about my boyfriend coming and asked if he was going to get to see my boyfriend. I said, "I don't know – I'm still feeling a bit of a father-daughter dynamic with you, and the daughter is afraid that the father doesn't approve of the boyfriend."

Basil replied, "I have no judgment of your relationship with Baron. I'm not saying that he's not a good lover – I'm just saying that you need to understand that a deep archetype of the Lover lives in you. I'm just naming the energy structure I see."

In the next session, Basil reiterated that the physical body always develops symptoms. He referred to me as an example of someone who is learning to *not* identify with the symptoms. He said:

"Rita, since I've met you, you are doing so much better – you are emotionally doing better, your health is better, your intensity is more sattvic, your creativity is up massively. You are dialed for intensity, highly creative, and tremendously connected. You have all this expansiveness and you run so much current, but then you identify with your symptoms.

"When you try to fit your symptoms into a small container, you suffer. The worst kind of suffering is the suffering of identifying with too-small of a container. As you know, when you do this, the symptoms boil. You have to expand the symptoms out and let them float so that they will stop burning so hot.

"Turn the magnifying glass of your attention toward the Absolute and then you will become large enough to not burn so hot. When you turn the magnifying glass of your attention toward body sensations, men, boys, a frustrated sense of self, or incorrect creative expression, then those things heat up.

"The Absolute made you so intense so that you would turn that intensity toward the Absolute. We can climb your ladder of situational pissy-ness up to this exquisite blue light inspiration stream. Rita, you are meant to surrender into the current of curious language – you are meant to do that for others. It's not for you.

"I see the inspiration of a scribe or a divine poet continually flowing into you. You are saturated with a written stream of inspiration coming into you. You are deepening in the shakti of creativity and heartfulness. Saraswati, the Goddess of Knowledge, is really with you.

"Right now there is a poem vibrating all around you. The poem is waiting for you, like Baron was. Run to meet it like you ran all around Mt. Shasta looking for Baron! Fall into the poem's arms. For this evening's session, write the poem."

That afternoon, when I passed by Basil, he said, "Look, there goes a poem followed by a girl." At dinner he teased, "That's a poem cloaked as a woman."

The following poem came through me that day, and I shared it with the group that evening:

Vibrant green-blue shimmering peacock of Eternity
lifts Sun kettle

194

and pours pure gold stream
into the seed of Anandamayi Ma.
The child is born, walks the Indian earth, and matures.
At maturity she receives the Full Vedic Wisdom Structures
and gives Herself Guru mantra.
*Gives **Herself** Guru mantra.*
"Hey Ma Durga!" the beings around Her sing.
The gold of Eternity radiates from Ma.
Laughing, laughing, laughing
She offers the gold to all.
Playful Red Grandmother
feeds Her many children.
Big Monkey Brother comes running –
"Ma! Ma! Ma! Feed me! Feed me, Ma!"
Giggling merrily, the two embrace
and feed the seas of hungry seekers.

Across the Indian landscape
Anandamayi Ma sees in her mind's eye
a small fishing village
where a dark woman is merged in ecstasy
with Krishna and with Devi.
Anandamayi Ma
lifts Sun kettle
and pours pure gold map lines
for Her seekers to reach Amma.

Across the oceans
in an old Mediterranean village,
the fishermen cast their nets
and remember
that a long, long, long time ago
their ancestors received a starseed transmission
from the Sun kettle of Existence.
They reflect that one day their descendent –
a daughter –
will find those stars shining warm in her belly.

So here I am today –
Mama Rita –
held by my Red Grandmother
and Her Monkey Brother
and their Sun Child, Ammachi.
Amma, Radiant Mother,
You hold and bathe me in Expansion.
Amma, Radiant Mother,

I hear you whispering,
"My child, it is time for you to serve.
Offer others the laughter
of the gold star children
who shimmer warm in your belly."
With streaming tears of Gratitude,
I offer my work to You, my Amma.
Om Amriteshwaryai Namaha.

Basil nodded and said, "See, I told you that there was a poem shrouded as a woman."

The next day we began honoring our ancestors. Basil had asked each retreat participant to bring photos of their ancestors. This turned out to be my favorite part of the retreat. After each person showed photos and told family stories, we sat in meditation and energetically held their family line. Each time it felt so powerful.

I intuitively understood the Truth of what Basil taught: "The ancestors really appreciate attention. It brings them so much love and takes the heat off of the karma. It is very important to honor the ancestors. Every culture except for ours makes shrines to the ancestors. It is essential to claim the lines and take responsibility for them. All of the ancestors, with a little bit of attention, go to Love."

When we honored my ancestors, Basil said, "Let's give thanks for the gift of Rita's intensity." I looked around the room and smiled with gratitude at the heartful beings around me. I thought about all the history behind each person there, and I agreed with what Basil had said: "The value in looking at each other's ancestral lines lies in building compassion for each other. When you start to see everything that each person holds in their structures, you feel more compassion for them."

One woman at the retreat, Trish, was also the mother of a nine-year-old boy. She too struggled with mothering. She shared with the group that she felt so giving in her career as a therapist, but she did not feel giving with her son. Basil said, "If you can't give to the beings closest to you, then that means core material is being touched." After giving Trish some good insights, he shared the following with me about my boys:

"Joshua and Benjamin are so exquisitely tuned to your system that they are among the highest teachers in your life. The purpose of them pushing your buttons is to teach you about yourself. A lot of their behavior is designed to trip you up and get you to slow down. They need deep regard of their being. Try to see them forming. If you can see their deeper beings forming, you won't be so reactive with them.

"When the boys are acting up, stop and open up the space within, and when you open that feminine place of receiving, they will be able to give back to you with good behavior. When you demand, they push back. You will get what you need when you open up the space to receive it. You have such deep capacity in there, but then you also have this demanding masculine overlay. When you open, they will be sweet.

"Really contemplate, 'Why are these beings with me?' The irritation you feel with your boys is a reflection of your power structure. As your power purifies, they will have less need to irritate you. And, if you practice serving Bryan, that will help your boys, and you will find more support showing up in your life."

Basil advised me to practice serving Bryan by doing several nice things for him each week. He said, "You weren't able to surrender to Bryan's way of inquiry, and because you need to do inquiry and it wasn't flowing between you two, everything got backed-up. When you serve him, his instinct of wisdom is going to blossom better and that's going to help your boys so much."

In the next session, Basil talked about his current Guru, Amma. He said that Amma was reconfiguring social and political structures so that a few generations from now the Vedic structures would reactivate and blossom in society. He perceived that most people would not realize what she was doing until centuries after her life now.

Several of the retreat participants had just gone to see Amma the month before, and Basil joked with us about that, saying, "It is very dangerous to see a saint. You can expect very deep vasanas to pop in short order!"

Even as he said that, I was trying to keep my mind on Amma. Basil saw that and gave the following instructions:

"If you are opening through Amma, you can't just think Her Name. You have to actually focus on her long enough to feel the Unconditioned Reality through her. If you just think about her flippantly, that only puts a bandaid on your sensations.

"Rita, for your enlightenment program, all you need are these two things: 1. The mind becomes that which it dwells upon, and 2. By placing the mind on the highest state, you become the highest state.

"Putting your mind on energetic structures helps you to open. You have to gain strength in keeping your gaze on the highest state. Remember that we reinforce conditions by dwelling on them – we are all doing this. We are all there, oscillating and learning to put our concentration on things that expand us.

"We each come in with veils of doubt that we can only each burn through on our own, through meditation. After you burn through them, you understand why they were there. However, you have to get out of your own misery to be sensitive enough to feel those higher dimensions."

The next morning at breakfast Basil said, "There's Rita stumbling into the ecstasy of herself." I told him that I was thinking about the father of Laura, one of the retreat participants. Laura's father had committed suicide when she was a little girl. I asked Basil if her father had reincarnated, was part of him still with Laura? Basil sighed and said, "Rita, you think that you're here? You are pouring tea in a writer's nook in Calcutta... and you're putting too much sugar in the chai!"

That afternoon, as we prepared to go to the beach, Basil said, "Bring your boyfriend," and I said, "My boyfriend's not here yet." Basil sighed again, saying, "What do you think, that you end at your body? Your boyfriend is already here. He's all around you, so you can bring your boyfriend to the beach!"

The retreat was supposed to end that day, and I was planning to have a couple of days free to integrate the retreat before my Bear arrived. However, since it was a small group and no one was leaving yet, the retreat did not end on schedule. I already felt 'done' and a bit scrambled up inside from not having enough time in solitude that week, so by that evening's session, I was feeling quite irritable.

At one point Basil gave me yet another assignment, and I lost it. I told him that I had too many things to do already, and something would have to go. He laughed and said, "Yeah, your *self* has to go. What's exhausting you is tension control and strategic fear. It's not your life that's exhausting you – it's how you are *holding* your life. The resistance to landing your capacity is making you tired. Once you land your capacity, it will open up lots of energy.

"You will have to hold to your writing discipline so precisely that it will become Everything. Through your craft you will pierce through... whining all the way Home! What limits you is the resistance. However, you are in a relentless process of opening yourself, and the act of opening continues to reformat everything even if you are holding on tightly."

I said something about not caring whether or not I got enlightened, and Basil quickly stated, "Even though you have let the demand for enlightenment go, you still need aspirations. You need Amma's To-Do List! And you need to make peace with yourself – Rita, you will be intense your entire lifetime; that is not going to get better.

"You have a responsibility to become *aware* of what is happening. When you practice *noticing*, then you are less at the whim of what's happening. Witness, see it, and truly understand... then your vibration goes up, and then you are more sattvic."

The next morning Basil told the following story for me:

> Once a long, long, long time ago, there was a maiden who was looking for an answer. She came upon a golden staircase, and she tried to go up, but the steps were too pure and she felt impure. There was a golden prince at the top of the stairs... he was the right hand of God. The maiden sat down to wait for an answer, and along came a cobra.
>
> This glistening, iridescent, jewel-like snake came up from the meadow and the maiden did not feel any fear. The hood of the cobra lifted up and they looked into each other's eyes and in that moment the maiden felt two points of white hot heat at the base of her spine, and the heat traveled up her body, and she felt the white heat throughout her being, and suddenly she saw all of the men throughout all of her incarnations. She saw all of the dynamics between the masculine and the feminine – all of the disappointments, the anger, the love... all of it...

All of it flashed in the maiden's vision, and then when those images settled down, she looked and there was the golden prince right in front of her, and she realized that she was looking at herself. The Divine Mother turned and embraced Herself. And with that, the Divine Mother exhaled and a big Om vibrated throughout the Cosmos.

Tears streamed down my cheeks and I bowed to Basil with gratitude. We chanted to Tara and then sat in meditation. I felt calm as we broke for lunch. At lunch I jokingly asked if the retreat was ever going to end.

By dinner I felt irritated with Basil again. I really wanted the retreat to end! That evening we held a closing circle. We each shared appreciations, and I was feeling relieved that the retreat was finally ending, but then something shifted and a couple of the women started working on some heavy material with Basil.

At midnight, when I realized how late it was, I should have just gotten up and gone to bed, but I wanted to feel complete, like we were done. I wanted to feel that nice closure feeling, like the retreat was finished.

At about 1:30am, I finally lost it. I should have just gone to bed, but instead I started complaining; saying that I wanted the retreat to be over in a nice neat closing session, and I felt frustrated that that wasn't happening, and now I wasn't going to get a good night's sleep, and Baron was arriving the next evening.

In response to my tirade, Basil gave me a very strong lecture (which he later told Julianna was Ramana Maharshi coming through him), in which he said, "Rita, you can't control life – life is arising, and everything is the Guru. So when Baron arrives tomorrow, whatever state he's in, that's the Guru. And whatever state arises in you when you see him, that's the Guru. And if you have a wonderful week together, that's the Guru, and if you have a difficult week of personality struggles, that's the Guru..."

At the time, something in me really snapped. I knew the Truth of what he was saying, and I felt insulted that he was saying it to me when I already knew it. I went to bed and cried a little and my chest really hurt. I wondered if Basil would still be my teacher after that night.

The next morning I awoke crying, with my chest still hurting. I packed my bags and went to get some breakfast. Basil followed me into the kitchen and asked what was wrong. I told him that the way the retreat went on and on and didn't end may have been what was arising, but it didn't work for me. I also mumbled something about how his lecture insulted me because I already knew the Truth of it.

He told me that when he gave me that lecture, he saw that I took it in really deep, way beyond the personality, and he was actually impressed by that. He said that I was now having a reaction that I had a real opportunity to work through. That made me mad, so I took my breakfast into my bedroom and closed the door.

I stewed for a while and then realized that I couldn't leave the retreat house in the state I was in. So I put on my walkman with Krishna Das playing and went out in a chair in the sunshine. I sat chanting loudly for a good hour. At one point Basil came out and put a straw hat on my head. I continued singing until I could finally forgive myself and everyone there, especially Basil. I then went inside and said my goodbyes with genuine warmth.

A couple of nights later, Baron and I ended up back at the retreat house having dinner, which was the last time I saw Basil and Luna in Hawaii. Earlier that day while hiking with Baron, I had cut my toe pretty badly. When I showed the wound to Basil, he said, "The only thing wounded here, really, is your pride."

Baron and I enjoyed a great fun week of adventures: touring the whole island, camping, swimming with dolphins, sweating in natural steam vents, eating avocados right off the trees... and, we also watched all of our issues come up magnified, one by one, to be looked at. We worked through them gracefully while sharing a wonderful week, with much romance and lovemaking.

We returned to the mainland on an overnight flight, and unfortunately, we got into an argument in the Kona airport, and then I cried almost the whole night of traveling. When we arrived home the next morning, I had only dozed for a few hours, and at noon I had to pick up the boys for a seven-day stretch with them at my cottage. Needless to say, I went into a pretty darn debilitating depression with all of my issues really, really up: Were Baron and I going to make it? How was I going to survive single mothering for twelve more years? Was Basil still my teacher?

That first week home by the mountain was really, really challenging for me. I missed the warm ocean and I cried often while listening to Hawaiian music. I felt scared for the future, but somehow I plugged along in my life.

Baron and I worked through our difficulties, and although we still had our issues (especially the polyamory/monogamy differences), we were feeling more in love than ever before. Although being with him definitely challenged me, I saw how much I'd grown with him and how much our relationship benefited us both.

I delighted in an otter card that Baron sent me in the mail, while we were still upset with each other. He wrote: "I was swimming with my otter in paradise when I grumbled. It scared her and she dove deep into the murky depths, deeper than a bear can go. He tried to play with her again, but she was woozy. I sure hope she's back in play mode when she gets this. I like the otter and I miss playing with her and letting her sleep on my big, furry (not furious) chest. Burly Bear Loves Otter Girl!"

With mothering, somehow I knew that I would survive. I had to. In spite of the depression, I endeavored to be present with my boys. I practiced opening to receive them.

The upset over the rift with Basil lingered in my being. Was he still my teacher? And, *who was I anyway?*

Chapter 44 – Coming Undone, Exploring Sexuality, and Landing in Humility

After the trip to Hawaii, I felt as though I had come undone, like I was completely unraveling. I felt very anxious and depressed. One afternoon I went over to Julianna's to talk with her about everything. I mentioned that Baron and I were reading *Conscious Loving* and learning about upper limits. She said, "I wonder if what Baron just went through – with the naked woman at Heart Lake – happened due to his upper limits being pushed after Hawaii?"

I just stared at her, stunned. My mind was racing so fast – Baron had gone to the lake with some friends the week before, but he hadn't mentioned meeting a woman there. My voice cracked as I answered her, "I don't know about any woman at Heart Lake." Julianna felt terrible. She said she thought that I knew. Knew what? She didn't know any details – one of Baron's friends had just casually mentioned the incident to her.

I went home and called Baron. He came over that evening and we had a long talk. It turned out that he and some friends were naked up at the lake, and there was a beautiful woman sitting on some rocks. She happened to be naked also. He went over and talked with her for a while. She reminded him of me and he told her about me. They had a really nice connection, but they didn't exchange phone numbers or anything. It sounded very innocent... except that they were both naked!

If he had told me right away, I probably would have reacted, but not as intensely as I reacted because I heard it through friends. It threw me into another tailspin over whether or not I could handle being in a relationship with someone who didn't have the same boundaries as me.

After a few weeks of praying to the Mother, I told Baron that even though we had our differences, I felt so much love between us. I said, "We just are together. We just *are*. It's not really any more mentally complicated than that." He agreed.

In the following weeks, I fell deeper into depression, and Baron supported me beautifully. I kept saying, "I have come undone. Who am I? What am I doing here?" The more I thought about Basil, the more confused I felt. After a while I realized that I wasn't really upset about what had happened the last night of the retreat. Basil was right – it was just my pride that was wounded that night. When I dug deeper, I found that what I was actually upset about were his teachings on sexuality.

One day I called Basil and Luna's friend Linda to get her perspective. I told her that Basil had once sent me an email about making love without orgasms, but I had read research on the health benefits of orgasms. I wondered what she thought about sexuality and spirituality. Did she think the two could merge, or not?

Linda told me that she personally loves sex, and she not only has orgasms, she has multiple orgasms! When I heard that, I relaxed inside, and I realized that the shame I was feeling around sex in response to Basil's teachings was actually worse than the shame I had received in my Catholic upbringing!

I then shared with Linda that on the last night of the Hawaii retreat Basil was working with two young women on clearing some past boyfriends out of their *koshas*, their subtle light bodies, and I felt disturbed by how he handled it. He told them that when you have sex with someone, you take in both their good and bad karma and then you have to eat it. He said that sexual attraction super-charges the material and you have to know how to meditate it out.

Linda responded compassionately, saying, "Rita, keep in mind that Basil IS only human and he does have opinions as well as intuitive moments." Then she explained that there are different spiritual approaches to sexuality. She also alerted me to the fact that while some research shows the benefits of orgasms, other research reveals that orgasms release chemicals that create conflict and draw sexual partners apart. Linda encouraged me to experiment for myself. As we hung up, she said that she would email me an article about celibacy, just to give me some insight into that perspective.

The next day I read that article – *The Divine Life: An Interview with Swami Chidananda* (by Bill Eilers and Susan Eilers, *What is Enlightenment* magazine). Swami Chidananda states, "… one of the things that helps you to free yourself from being caught in this physical level is celibacy. Cosmic consciousness, Absolute consciousness, is a far cry if you don't recognize the necessity of liberating yourself from your total identification with the body."

I wondered about that. What if you didn't *totally* identify with the body, but you enjoyed your body as a part of your *wholeness*? If ALL is the Cosmic Mother, then wouldn't the physical realm, including desire and sex, also be a part of the Cosmic Mother?

Why would God, who is Intelligent, create a sex act so pleasurable if He/She didn't want humans to enjoy it?

Swami Chidananda explains that if you are a spiritual aspirant, then you cannot run after two things. *You cannot run after two things.* How can there be two things if all are One? If God is All, why do we have to choose? Why can't we merge human and divine?

Swami Chidananda does say that there are certain stages when one can be highly spiritual and yet at the same time be leading a normal sex life. He says that is especially true in the bhakti path. That path does not make any distinction between a celibate brahmachari and a married householder. Throughout India there are large communities of ecstatic devotees of God, many or most of whom are married people, living a normal sex life, but are nevertheless absorbed in divine love of God.

That made more sense to me.

Later in the interview, Swami Chidananda comments on *Tantra*, the practice of "sacred spirituality," saying, "Tantra is an approach to God through all types of sense enjoyment. Everything is offered to God and so everything becomes sanctified; nothing is profane. One enjoys sense satisfaction and sees it also as part of God's bliss."

The Swami continues, "Mind you, this was an authentic path that did once upon a time exist in India, especially in the Eastern part. Even now it exists. But it became grossly perverted. People became enmeshed in it. They said they were practicing tantra, but it was only wining, dining and sex pleasure. It took them nowhere, but I suppose it took them where they wanted to go."

The true, non-perverted Tantric approach resonated most deeply with me. I perked up when I read "One enjoys sense satisfaction and sees it also as part of God's bliss." Maybe Basil was right about me living through all of those tantric past lives?

In any case, I felt relieved after talking with Linda, and I was able to lay down the shame I had been feeling. I knew that I wanted to enjoy sex as a loving part of a healthy relationship.

Suddenly I found myself really enjoying sex. One evening, after making love with my Bear, I felt the closest that I have ever felt to union. It was exquisite. I felt as though we were melting into each other and becoming one. I sensed the vibration of dolphin energy in it. It was wonderful.

Despite the beautiful sex, the depression continued to weigh down my system. I prayed to Amma, "Amma, please help me. I am so sorry that I am failing You so miserably. I want to be happy, and laugh and love and laugh and love, but I'm stuck. Please help me."

I really wanted to burst out of my self and serve others. I did not want my potential to be wasted. One afternoon I actually had the following thought: 'Maybe the Universe will call to say that there was a mistake – that I wasn't really signed up to mother two children in a small town; that I was actually assigned the task of organizing food kitchens and helping lots of people in a big city.'

I knew that was a ridiculous thought. Deep down, I knew that everything was happening just exactly as it was supposed to be happening. I prayed and prayed to surrender my life to the Mother. Each night I sat in meditation and prayed for Grace. In meditation I kept hearing these words:

Night upon night
I sit in the fire
of my self burning.

I wrote the following in an email to Luna and Julianna:
"In Hawaii, I did not feel self-absorbed like I do in Mt. Shasta. On the island, I felt Held in the larger Field of the Mother. My challenge is how to cope with the life I'm in now, here – how to feel Held here, now. I'm realizing that I am not the same person I was in Hawaii and I miss her. I felt stronger there and the Witness part of my consciousness was more expanded there. I felt ready to serve the world there. I want to deal with my problems here in a detached, sun strong way. I have come undone. Split apart. And now I'm

waiting to see how I will emerge from it all...

"... And I am feeling confused about sexuality and spirituality. I am enjoying sex and I wonder what that means for my spiritual unfoldment? Am I still on the Path? You can't ever really get off of the Path can you?

"For a while I was questioning if Basil was still my teacher, but now I've let go of the demand to know. His teachings on sex don't all resonate with me, but I do appreciate the brilliance of so many of his other teachings... so I will probably see you both here at the next retreat."

Reading *Conscious Loving* (by Gay and Kathleen Hendricks, Bantam Books) helped me a lot. I really liked the following passage:

> *When we come into a close relationship, our energy is deeply stirred by the catalyzing effect of the beloved. What we do with this increased energy determines the path of the relationship.*

I sent that quote to Baron by email, and he replied, "As we get past having to work on us we'll have more energy for your wonderful sons and this wonderful world."

This wonderful world. The boys began school again, and I pushed through the depression enough to get a job caregiving for an elderly woman two mornings each week. It was a start. I aspired to also begin facilitating meditation groups and organizing food kitchen work, but writing continued to consume a lot of my time.

Working with the elderly woman improved my mental health greatly. It felt so correct to get out of my house and out of my self! The depression lessened, although some days I still fell into it. One day when the depression became acutely painful, I sensed into it and found that it was not only caused by my own vasanas unraveling, but it was also caused by the Collective Anxiety coming into my system.

Baron told me that as much as a third of the people in the United States suffer from depression. I prayed that I would soon become healthy enough to help others become healthy. I felt grateful that I had emotional support, good food, cod liver oil, and the time for exercise, so that I didn't need to take antidepressant medication like so many other people.

One evening, just before I sat down to meditate, Dana called. She was crying so hard that I could hardly understand her, but eventually she calmed down enough to talk. Her husband Marc had just told her that he had had sex with another woman the night before. I listened and we talked for a while, until I heard Baron knocking on my door.

I told Baron what had happened with Dana and Marc, and he told me that he had just found out – that very evening – that another couple was struggling with the same issue. I was surprised to hear that it was a couple who were well-known spiritual teachers in the line of Ramana Maharshi and Papaji. Apparently the man had engaged in an extramarital affair for three years. His wife had known for a year, but they had only just told the public. I couldn't believe it.

A couple of nights later we went to Dana and Marc's house for dinner. After they kissed their little girls goodnight, we four adults had drinks, laughed, and played pool. Then we sat in the living room and they talked with us about what had happened. After a very good open discussion, they felt better. They each really needed someone to witness what they were feeling.

Baron and I continued to talk a lot about commitment and monogamy over the next week, since the issue was really in the air! He said that he was beginning to see the hurt that an affair causes, and he didn't want to hurt me. He concluded, "Monogamy is better than celibacy!"

A few days later we celebrated the one-year anniversary of our first date. That day I called a yoga studio and arranged for Baron and I to begin facilitating a Friday evening meditation. This was something that we had been talking about doing for a while. Decades earlier, Baron had attended and led such groups with his teacher, Dr. Vasavada. It felt really appropriate that on our one-year anniversary we felt ready to offer others something positive out of our sweet connection.

The next week I surprised Baron by saying that I wanted to go for a motorcycle ride! I had never ridden on a motorcycle before in my entire life, because I had always held a righteous attitude against motorcycles. I judged people who rode on them because I thought that they were behaving too dangerously.

I decided to go for a motorcycle ride as part of a conscious effort to break the righteousness and rigidity in me, but I had no idea how much I would love it! I thoroughly enjoyed riding on the bike behind my Bear with my arms wrapped snuggly around his middle.

For Halloween, Bear and I dressed as bikers, complete with black leather pants and jackets and silver-studded jewelry. With his hair and beard dyed dark brown, with a long red wig covering my brown hair, and with sunglasses on, even our best friends did not recognize us!

At one party we went up to the microphone, and I boldly said, "So, I was all serious and rigid on the spiritual path to enlightenment, and then I said, "Forget that, I'm going to become a biker!" So I got myself a biker dude, and we went for a ride, and now I am so FREE, so Open, so Liberated!"

It felt good to make fun of myself. I immensely enjoyed taking on a wild persona for a night. Several friends commented that it was the real me. It felt powerfully good to unleash the force of wildness that lives in me.

Later that night I told Baron that I was almost finished writing this book, and he said, "We've got to stop having episodes, so you can say And They Lived Happily Ever After!" I laughed and said, "Yeah, and they rode off on a motorcycle into the sunset!"

Well, we did not ride off into the sunset. Instead, we continued our usual relationship dance in which I felt frustrated with myself for still falling into the addictive love pattern.

However, as I allowed the frustrations to go through me, I finally began to 'get it' that there are no short cuts to unraveling our patterns. The same Cosmic Intelligence that wound us up in our patterns is also unwinding us, according to the supernatural law of Divine Timing. With that sword of knowledge in my belt, I found myself relaxing into the Divine Mother's Plan. Surrendering to the Mother allowed me to surrender to my deepest Self. Indeed, I began to experience Amma and my own deepest Self as *One*.

I found myself landing in Humility, in the recognition that my surface self was not the doer. I bowed down again and again to Amma, the Divine Doer.

Chapter 45 – Merging with Purpose, Getting Balanced, and Melting in Love

Dressing up as a biker on Halloween empowered me beyond what I could have imagined. It brought forth a new level of strength that I had not recognized in myself before. Everywhere I went, both friends and strangers commented on how powerful the biker costume was.

I did feel more powerfully my true self. Actually, I felt really full of myself, but not in a conceited way. I still felt the humility of recognizing that my surface self was not the doer. I recognized that the Mother was acting through me.

I was in that state of calm humility when I headed down to see Amma for the second time. It was the week before Thanksgiving. On the drive down, I shared with Julianna that ever since I had met Amma in June, I had been hoping that sometime Amma would look right into my eyes.

To my utter delight, during my first darshan with Amma, she looked right into my eyes! Her eyes sparkled with infinite Joy and Love. While she hugged me, I said into her chest, "Hey Ma Ma Ma, Mama, Mama…" and she said into my ear, "daughter, daughter, daughter, daughter…" The sound of her voice in English tickled me – it was so adorable!

The second morning at Amma's ashram, I was fortunate enough to be selected for the question line, which meant that I could go up and ask Amma a question. At the appointed time, I sat in a special line off to the side and I watched her hug people while I waited to ask my question.

When it was almost my turn, I was sitting very close to Amma, and while she was hugging someone she looked down at me. She looked right into my eyes and smiled at me. The people around me gasped, and one person even commented that she had just given me some special juice! I couldn't believe it. She had already looked in my eyes the day before, so it surprised me that she did it again. People say that she fulfills her devotee's wishes, and I was grateful that she had fulfilled my wish for eye contact.

Soon it was my turn to ask a question. I stood up with this book in my hands – well, this book as far as I had written it up to that point. My knees grew weak and I was shaking as I asked Swami Amritaswarupananda Puri if he would please translate this question: *Amma, how should I proceed with this book I am writing?*

The Swami talked with Amma about this book. She asked if there were any excerpts from her books. I showed the Swami the chapter in which I had met Amma, and he read all of the pages in which I had quoted Amma. He then talked with Amma again, and she said to tell me, "*You try, and Amma will do a special prayer.*"

I bowed before Amma, and went to sit down. I was crying so hard. When a world saint says that they will do a special prayer for your little creative work, you never know what the impact will be. The enormity of it hit me in waves as I sat crying and crying. Julianna rushed over and held me. She wanted to know all of the details. A woman sitting in front of us was listening, and she asked, "What is your book about?"

I handed her the book, and she sat reading it for a while. When she looked up, she said, "I can relate to this. I would like to read this book." It turned out that she was a creative storytelling professor at a university in California. I thought, 'Boy, Amma works fast!' We exchanged contact information, and I told the woman, who was named Shannon, that I would send her a manuscript soon.

The next day Baron joined me for a hug with Amma and then we headed to Harbin Hot Springs to enjoy a little time together. After soaking in the heavenly waters, we delighted in the décor of the room they had given us – it looked like a sexy French bedroom. The walls were red; the curtains made of rich burgundy velvet. We fed each other dark chocolate and speculated that our union began lifetimes ago in India – when he was a yogi and I was a tantric temple priestess!

On the drive home, I wrote the following in my journal:

"Lying naked in the arms of my beloved is better than the sunset. Yoni garden happily remembers lingam visit. Learning to be comfortable with uncertainty, I laugh in his softness, kiss his neck, and breathe in his chest curls. Why do I need to plan the years ahead? Allowing the bond to arise in its natural fullness, why count hours and seconds and minutes? The Mother plays Her Lila; we ride the waves: up sorrow, down joy, into the Ocean's center – and in *that* stillpoint, All is Bliss and All is Light… renunciate, lover, renunciate, lover."

Back home in Mt. Shasta I had some interesting dreams. First I dreamt:

I was at one of Amma's programs and the new President of the United States was on stage, and I was on stage with him. He and I were holding each other in loving embrace while he told everyone that this new administration would not only be about politics and money – it would also be about Spirit and music. He said that politics and Spirit would be merged.

Then I dreamt:

I was in India with this famous enlightened man who was gruff and looked like Neem Karoli Baba. I was laying my head on his chest and he was talking about not liking people, and I was surprised at that. I said, "I thought that once you were enlightened, then you would like everyone," and he said that no, there were actually very few people who he liked.

I sent the dreams to Basil by email, and he replied, "I can imagine that

Neem Karoli Baba would take a liking to you... and your first dream indicates good progress in the transmutation of your being... the correct alignment of tantric intensity is meant to blossom as leadership – that the highest functions are able to inspire the lower functions... your hugging the president has strong resonance with this process. Seems like good work is occurring in your being."

The holiday season passed like a blur. In December, Baron spent almost every night at my cottage. I watched how he enjoyed being with Joshua and Benjamin. With his own three sons already in their twenties, he knew about boys. He didn't get upset by their rambunctiousness, but rather he seemed to revel in it. He remained calm as he played with them and read them bedtime stories.

Little by little, I noticed that I was starting to relax more with the boys too. By watching Baron's example, I was learning to enjoy them more fully. I thanked Amma again and again for sending my Baron Bear into my life.

Day by day, my relationship with Amma was deepening. I found myself thinking of her often and praying to her throughout each day and night. I began to see her Grace more and more in my life. Surrendering to Amma continually allowed me to surrender to my own deepest Self.

On New Year's Day, 2007, I picked an angel card for the year: *Purpose*. For the whole month of January, I prayed to Amma for a job on the way to my purpose. I asked to begin the job on February 1st.

I was still working two mornings each week as a caregiver with the elderly woman, but I wanted to start working more hours. One day in the last week of January, I ran into my boss with the caregiving work. She said that she needed someone to work three full days per week with a woman who had broken her leg. Amazingly, she asked if I could start on February 2nd!

I wasn't sure how this new caregiving job would be on the way to my purpose, but I trusted that Amma had sent me the job for a reason. I called Randi Jan, the woman who had broken her leg, and said that I looked forward to meeting her the next week.

Halfway through the first day with Randi Jan, I knew why Amma had sent me the job. Randi Jan had some problems that she desperately needed to talk through with someone. That first day, she talked – and I listened – for over six hours. Two things became immediately clear to me: 1. I definitely wanted to be a counselor, and 2. I was very grateful for all that I had learned from Basil.

As the weeks went on, it became clear that counseling was the main purpose of the work with Randi Jan. I told her that I had wanted to become a counselor for over thirteen years, and she said, "Well, you are getting great practice with me!"

We actually had a lot to offer each other. After a while, I started talking with Randi Jan about my life issues too, and she offered really wise advice. At sixty-seven years old, she was intuitive, courageous, and delightfully funny. I often cooked soups for her, and she liked them so much that she came up with an idea for me to write a soup cookbook. From then on, making and testing soups became part of our daily ritual. It was a fun creative process that inspired us both.

Randi Jan was also a writer and she suggested that I memorize poetry to help with my writing. I took her advice and began memorizing the poems of Lalla, a fourteenth century North Indian mystic who shed both her husband and her clothing to wander around medieval Kashmir, singing ecstatic love songs to Shiva.

Working with Randi Jan really took me out of my own stories and I learned the value of serving someone else. As I served her, my own depression lifted, and I felt a passion for Life returning to my blood. Inspired by Amma's humanitarian work in the world and my own desire to pursue the counseling path, I set my sights on applying for graduate school soon.

During February and March, Baron and I met with many challenges that ultimately brought us closer together. It was a very stressful time. First, one of Baron's sons had some mental problems. Then Baron got very sick from the stress of dealing with his son and the stress of resurfacing tensions with his ex-wife. Listening to Baron cough and wheeze each night, I worried that he was going to die. Meanwhile, his beloved aunt died and a friend of ours also died. At the same time, Randi Jan told me that she was thinking about committing suicide.

I remained surprisingly calm throughout that stressful winter. It helped that Baron and I meditated together regularly and we continued facilitating our Friday evening meditation group. The Friday group gave us a place to nourish ourselves while helping others nourish themselves. One night a woman stayed after the group and told us that she needed help. She cried in our arms and then asked if we did counseling. We said yes, because we had in fact just placed an ad in a local paper, advertising our new counseling practice.

In April Baron and I began counseling others together. One morning we sat talking with his son for a few hours, and then Baron asked him if he felt better. His son replied, "Yes. I feel comfortable talking with you guys. I would go to you for counseling." Then he looked at us and said, "I'm glad you two found each other." Baron said, "Well, we work at it. Sometimes things come up that are difficult, but we keep at it." His son said, "So you are healing each other?" We answered, "yes."

It felt like the healing love between Baron and me was spilling over and naturally finding a place to flow out and serve others. I felt grateful that my service in the world was beginning to flower in so many directions, and I could see how Amma was helping me align with the purpose of my soul.

In the midst of all that, Basil came to town and offered a spring retreat. It was the first time that I had seen him since the Hawaii retreat. Before going, I wrote the following in my journal:

"Basil is a teacher that I highly respect and admire. I enjoy going into very deep states when chanting and meditating in a group that he's facilitating, and I find the information that he shares to be highly inspirational and informative. And, I no longer feel that he is "my teacher," as in, I no longer feel the need to ask him questions about my life. I no longer feel dependent on his advice in making decisions. However, I do still value his opinion and consider what he says."

Well, what Basil said to me at that April retreat was very positive and encouraging. He said, "You've brought balance into your life – good work." During one of the sessions he said, "I have to make an advertisement for Rita, my current poster child. She's brought balance into her life and that balance allows her to go deeper in her meditations." Later he said to me, "Look who's drunk with her Self – you are a delight to witness."

During one of the breaks, Basil overheard me telling someone about applying for graduate school, and he nodded approvingly. I asked if he would write me a recommendation, and he said that he would write, "This being will take any question or assignment and bite it to the bone, and your social work program will never be the same!"

In addition to Basil's feedback, several other people at the retreat made comments to me about how much I was shining. A few people said, "It's amazing how you've gotten balanced in spite of all the difficulties you've been having." (They were referring to Baron's son, Baron's health, and me working with the woman who is sometimes suicidal.) And that's when I realized that I didn't get balanced *in spite of* the difficulties, but rather I got balanced in large part *because of* the difficulties.

Once I started serving others more, I began to find more harmony – and less depression – within myself. I wondered if I might have felt better if I had gotten out of my dramas and served others sooner, but I knew that it all happened as it was supposed to happen. Even if it would've helped me to get out and serve others sooner, it wasn't time for it yet. I still had to burn through some of my own stuff before I could effectively serve others.

While working with Randi Jan, I began to see the purpose of all the pain I had endured. She was in so much pain, and I could really empathize with her. Remembering my own experiences with pain allowed me to feel true compassion for her. She often told me that I had a positive effect on her.

I told Randi Jan about Amma. She began praying to Amma, and she decided to attend Amma's June retreat. I breathed a sigh of relief when she gradually stopped talking about suicide.

One week I encouraged Randi Jan to make an altar to her ancestors. She draped a beautiful silk cloth over a table and placed family photos on top. She also put a vase of fresh roses and a few candles. I burned sage around her while she played a drum and talked to her ancestors. We both cried many tears, and later she commented that the ancestor ritual had been a powerfully cleansing experience.

After that ritual, I wrote:

"Now, in the role of counselor with someone, I can be fully present because I no longer have so much mental chatter about my own stuff. I don't feel the need to keep telling my stories. I have a lot of open internal space now, so I can hold space for others and support their healing journeys. For this I am most grateful."

Even with all of that open internal space, the month of May brought every emotional flavor under the sun. I experienced blissfully deep meditations and painfully annoying kriyas. While Baron and I continued deepening our bond, I still lapsed into crying when he didn't call or come over as often as I wanted him to. I worked hard to let go of my demands on him and to remain whole in myself. I felt grateful for his enduring love, but I felt frustrated with myself that I continued to cry deeply over small disappointments.

One night while crying, I had an important breakthrough. I wrote in my journal:

"In Hawaii, Basil told me that I would have many more meltdowns. And I am. The meltdowns, also known as contractions or kriyas, are inevitable, and that doesn't mean that I am not overall happy and healthy. I am actually feeling happy and getting balanced. After each good meltdown, I expand, and each heart expansion opens me a little wider."

After Shannon – the creative storytelling professor – read what I had written on this book thus far, she said that she longed for me to be in a place where the wonderings and struggles subsided. Well, hmmm... I wrote in an email to her, "In a way the wonderings and struggles *have* subsided, and in another way they haven't. I am an intense being and I attract intensity to meet my own intensity! And yet, there are subtle clues that I *am* becoming more sattvic... and in that way, I am victorious – even as I navigate through many more meltdowns!"

Sometimes I called Sallamae for support when I was melting down. She helped me see that when Baron didn't call, it triggered a fear of abandonment in me, and that fear did not have anything to do with Baron. He was with me, really with me. One night he even said, "I see us as being together right on through." So the work to be done was in healing myself and learning to fulfill myself.

One night, after crying deeply because I felt like Baron wasn't cherishing me as his beloved life partner like I wanted him to, I had the following dream:

> *I overheard Amma saying that she needed a regular broom. Someone had brought her a different kind of broom. I went and got the regular broom and brought it to her. Since she doesn't speak much English, she jokingly spoke to me with gestures and facial expressions. I understood that she was saying, "Don't give **me** the broom – **you** do the work!" We laughed together as I started sweeping the dirty floors, and I was so happy to be working with her and getting to casually hang out with her. Then, there was a big pot of soup and I was going to ask Amma's advice about what to put in the soup... I was thrilled to be preparing food for Amma.*

The next morning, I realized that I needed to stop crying over Baron and be grateful for that dream. It was as if Amma was telling me to put my focus on my work. Also, maybe it was a sign that Amma liked the soup cookbook idea?

In addition to the ups and downs with Baron and within myself, I struggled with Bryan over our schedule. For the past year, the boys had been coming to my house during the week and going to Bryan's house on the weekends. That was working really well for me, but he kept pressing me to change the schedule.

One night I felt so desperate for Bryan to understand my point of view that I wrote him an email letter in which I declared that merging with my purpose was more important to me than the boys. I wrote, "I see the path of publishing the book, going to graduate school, and doing counseling as the most important thing to me. And I guess it's sad, but it doesn't feel sad to me, that the boys come after that."

I continued writing, "I love Joshua and Benjamin very deeply; I care about their well-being; I feel nurturing energy toward them; I am glad that they were born; and I feel blessed to be their mama. I see that they are amazing beings. And, being a mama isn't hugely fulfilling and it doesn't feel like my purpose in life. I do really well with the school-week routine as I am routine-oriented and do well with structure. That's the gift that I can offer."

Bryan did not reply right away. The boys did not know anything about the email letter I had sent to their papa, but maybe they picked up on it psychically, because the very next evening, Joshua suddenly asked, "Could we go with you to see Amma in June?" Benjamin chimed in, saying that he wanted to go, too. I nearly fell over – I was so surprised!

For some time, both boys had been tired of listening to all of my chanting music CDs, and I couldn't imagine what had inspired them to want to go with me to see Amma. I told them again what it was like to be at her ashram: loud, crowded, and very stimulating. They assured me that, yes, they really did want to go, so I said that I would take them with me.

That night after the boys fell asleep, I sat in meditation and it occurred to me that when they asked to go see Amma with me, it was as if they were responding to what I had written to Bryan the night before. It was as if they were saying, "Don't leave us behind – we will join you on your purpose!" I chuckled to myself as I sensed that Amma had probably orchestrated the whole situation.

The next day I called Bryan to let him know about the boys' request to go with me to Amma's ashram. He responded positively. I relaxed when I heard his friendly tone. We decided to work out a new schedule after I returned from the Amma trip. I felt better after that phone conversation.

Baron lovingly agreed to join us on the Amma pilgrimage. The week before we went, I cried and cried every time I imagined being in that hall with Amma. I longed to be near her again.

Finally the day came and we packed up the car and headed south. The first night with Amma was mixed. I felt so happy to be there, but it was difficult for Benjamin to sit through the evening program, so he got a little out of sorts. We had dinner at 10:00pm, and when the boys asked for caffeinated chai tea, I let them have it because I knew we were going to be up late that night.

Benjamin's mood actually improved after the chai, and by the time we went up for darshan just after midnight, he was in okay spirits. We all four went together for darshan. First Amma hugged each of us individually, and then all of us together.

During Baron's hug, his eyes were closed, and first he saw bright white light, then his vision went totally black, and then he saw colored lights. During my hug, she kept saying, "daughter, daughter, daughter..." into my ear, and I kept saying, "I love you," over and over into her chest. I was laughing.

Then, when she hugged Baron and me together, she very animatedly kissed our hands together as she laughed and looked in our eyes. It felt, to both of us, like she very strongly blessed us. Later I asked Baron, "Was she blessing our meditation classes or our counseling work together or our union?" Baron said he didn't know.

The second day at Amma's ashram, the boys challenged me with all of their little demands on me, but somehow I managed to enjoy a fully satisfying Amma experience anyway. I still felt irritated by the boys, but with Amma's Grace I didn't feel as deeply irritated as I usually would. It was as if the agitation existed out on the surface somewhere, but in my core I felt calm and still.

I enjoyed the music, the bhajans, the chai, the spicy food, and all of the special little moments – shopping in the Amma store, gazing at the swans in the pond, watching Joshua and Benjamin climb a tree, and listening to the Swami's teachings.

When the Swami stressed the importance of meditation, I reflected on the positive results I could see in my life after meditating nearly every evening for over two years. I thought, 'The Witness part of my mind has grown a lot stronger, so now when I am upset about something, I can watch it happening, and I don't stay as upset for as long as I used to. And when I get a migraine headache, I watch it and I think of Thomas Jefferson. He got migraines, and look at all that he accomplished!'

While just sitting and watching Amma hug people, I experienced some profound intuitive moments. I cried deeply at the Beauty of Amma and the music and all the people. When I imagined going home the next day and leaving Amma, my heart physically *hurt*.

I tried to console myself by thinking that Amma is in all people in all places, but I still felt sad at the thought of leaving her physical presence. I then thought that I should have more gratitude, so I took a moment to reflect on all that was good in my life. I wrote in my journal:

"I feel balanced... clear about purpose... physically healthier... more detached from life stories... more love and less fear... and I feel very in love with Joshua and Benjamin. I hold the intention to be the best mama I can possibly be to these darling boys, even as I give my all to pursuing paths of counseling, writing, and teaching. I feel in love with Amma and I feel in love with Baron and with all beings and all things… and, most importantly, I feel passionately in love *with myself.*"

That day, when the boys and I went up for darshan together, Baron stood leaning on the railing upstairs. While we waited in the darshan line, Baron looked down at me – and at the boys – with *so much love.*

When our turn came, Amma hugged Benjamin first and she whispered in his ear, "my darling, my darling, my darling…" Next she hugged Joshua, and then me.

While my head lay on her bosom, time expanded and it felt like there was time for me to rest into her – like there was plenty of time to deeply breathe in her rose fragrance, as if I breathed the Rose of the Mother into my being. I laughed into her heart and I touched her back lovingly, sending love into her, too. It felt like there was plenty of time to give and receive love. In reality, it probably all happened in less than thirty seconds!

When Amma hugged the boys and me together, I felt like we were melting in LOVE. I felt utter Joy. It felt oh, so exquisitely blissful. In that brief moment, time stopped, and we all rested in the arms of the Mother.

Sixteen Months Later...

Five months after the boys and I rested together in the joyful arms of the Mother, I published my first book, *Rita: The Catawampus Journey of a Western Yogini*. Baron, Randi Jan, and Julianna helped me throw a book party in mid-November.

The day before the party, Luna and I spoke long-distance by phone, and some tensions that had been building between us finally erupted. I couldn't agree to disagree because I felt too much shame about the issues that came up with us, so I bid her and our friendship farewell.

The timing of Luna and I parting ways was absolutely awful. At the party, I outwardly put on a happy face and signed books, but inwardly my whole being was racked with pain. Although I sensed that Luna and I would one day reunite, I still felt chest-crushing grief over separating from her. Losing Luna was a painful lesson on the bitter reality of *impermanence*.

By Thanksgiving I was getting physically sick from the grief. At Dana and Marc's lovely holiday dinner, I smiled through the pain as I sipped a large glass of red wine. I felt really funny the rest of the evening, and later in meditation I realized that alcohol was *not* good for my system. I decided to stop drinking altogether. That decision changed the dynamics in the relationship with Baron, since he really likes to go out drinking and partying. Even though I was still pushing down the fear of us separating, that fear began to slowly rise up closer to the surface, demanding to be looked at.

On New Year's Day, I picked an angel card for 2008: *Clarity*. That winter, I wrote and published two more short books, *Praying for Orange: Spiritual Practices for Daily Living*, and *Love Soups: A Vegetarian Soup Cookbook Inspired by the Soup Devas*.

In the spring, I began preparing for the June pilgrimage to see Ammachi. Since I hadn't been able to go see her in November that year, I was feeling utterly lovesick and longing to be near her. As the daffodils opened their lovely smiles again, I focused on purifying to see Amma again. I could hardly wait for June to arrive.

During the two months prior to the Amma trip, I seriously began questioning whether or not Baron and I were correctly aligned to be in a life partnership. I noticed that my fear of breaking up was diminishing. One morning while walking through some trees, I 'heard' an intuitive voice say, "Amma won't allow you and Baron to separate until you are ready to handle it." I trusted that voice, even as I shed some tears at the thought of us breaking up.

I decided I needed some time alone to think, so I planned to go see Amma alone for five days, and then Baron would join me there for another few days.

When I arrived at the Mata Amritanandamayi Center, I immediately felt at home – singing the prayers of adoration to Ammachi, sitting by the

217

pond with the swans, eating the spicy Indian cuisine, and hearing Indian music playing. As the harmoniums and tablas radiated healing sound vibrations, I kept thinking, '*This is where my heart lives.*'

That first afternoon, when I went up to Amma for darshan, I gave her a bundle of the three books I had published since I'd seen her last. She gleefully untied the ribbon and kissed the books… and then she held me close, pushing my face hard into her strongly perfumed bosom. I laughed into her chest and I sighed loudly. I felt so relieved to be in my Mother's loving arms again at last.

During my days alone at the ashram, I continually offered myself to Amma (and to Neem Karoli Baba) more fully. Rather than saying, "I offer myself to you, *except* I want to keep the dramas and sex with Baron going," I began saying, "I offer myself to you completely – I surrender my will to Your Divine Will in all areas of my life."

On my last morning alone there, as I was driving into the ashram and singing along with a Ram-Sita-Hanuman chant on a Krishna Das CD, I felt myself go so deep into my heart, and suddenly I said out loud, "*I want to live inside the chant.*" I knew that I wanted a life of sadhana – a life in which chanting and meditating were the top priorities. As the reality of that statement hit me, tears began flowing down my cheeks, because I knew that Baron and I wanted to live different kinds of lives.

That morning, as I settled onto my cushion for the meditation, I was surprised to see *Basil* there at the ashram! We had not seen each other for more than one year. I felt nervous that he would scold me about the falling-out between Luna and me, but later that afternoon when I ran into him near the pond, we embraced joyfully and I told him that I loved him. He didn't mention Luna at all, but rather, he mischievously declared, "Time to go to India, Rita."

I told Basil that I had just that morning felt the impulse to go to India, but I knew that I had ten more years of mothering, so it wasn't time for me to go yet. As usual, he disagreed with my planning mind, saying that the Universe works from the inside out, and not from the outside in. I felt resistance to him saying that, but I smiled and wished him a wonderful day at the ashram.

The next day Baron arrived. We felt so much love for each other and I cried as we began talking about the possibility of separating. All of the issues and differences between us suddenly seemed irreconcilable to me.

On our last day at the ashram we ran into Basil. He looked deeply into Baron and said what a sweet being Baron is. I thought to myself, 'Of course, now that Baron and I are breaking up, Basil finally gives his approval!' Ahh, the sheer hilarity of the Divine Lila, the Mother's Play!

As we parted from Basil, he said to me, "Rita, see you in India, whether it's in your heart, or in the country." I smiled with gratitude that he had acknowledged my own capacity to discern correct timing in my life.

When we returned to Mt. Shasta, I decided that at that stage of my journey, it was not correct for me to engage in sexual energies. Baron and I continued our separation process, gradually spending less time together, but still loving each other as dear friends. While I did feel grief over our separation, I also felt surprisingly blissful in being alone. Rather than seeing the reality of impermanence as bitter like I had when parting from Luna, during the separation from Baron I began to perceive impermanence as a *blissful* path to God.

After Sri Krishna's birthday, I received guidance that I needed to publish *The Rita Lila: A Western Yogini's Journey to Bliss*, this revision of my first book, *Rita: The Catawampus Journey of a Western Yogini*. While reading and re-reading Basil's teachings, I became inspired to write the following story for him:

Once, a long, long, long time ago, a little girl was born in a village in the Himalayas. Her older brother, who had been a rishi in vedic times, took one look in her dark brown eyes and knew the journey that her soul was about to embark on. Though he tried his utmost to prevent her from taking that path, he was forced to lay down his efforts – for there is no way for even an ancient rishi to interfere with prarabdha karma. The girl's destiny was already in motion before she was even born.

And so she burned through life after tantric life, dangerously using the form world to attain enlightenment. Each lifetime her older brother from the Himalayas found her: sometimes as her mother, sometimes as her lover, sometimes as her doctor. Each time he tried to save her, but to no avail.

Finally the lifetime arrived in which she met him as her teacher. This particular lifetime, the girl had forgotten much of her tantric ways due to choosing birth in a Catholic family. Although she was definitely wired to fall in love, she was timid and fearful about sex. Still, she longed to attain enlightenment through uniting with the male form.

After many years of suffering over her addictive love pattern, the woman divorced her husband and met the teacher who had been her brother so long ago. She studied with him for four years, during which time she learned a lot of knowledge about the Yoga Path. He was a most amazing teacher, and she knew it, but then she began to react strongly against his teachings on sexuality.

*The teacher patiently worked with her, telling her about her tantric lives and alerting her to the dangers facing her now. He loved her like a precious daughter and he really wanted her to **get it** this time.*

The swirling motions of time and space soon pulled the teacher away from the woman. Although they were 2,000 miles apart, and although she felt 'done' being his student, this woman continued her daily yogic practices with vigor and determination.

While she thought that she was doing everything she could possibly do to progress spiritually, she didn't realize that the sexual relationship she was in was pulling her down deeper and deeper into the vasanas she was trying so hard to burn through. She felt increasingly fearful, but she did not know how to free herself from the dramas she was enmeshed in. She had sworn off the teacher, so she was on her own to figure out how to free herself.

Meanwhile, she was determined to publish a book that told the story of her journey with the teacher. She had already spent two years working on the book before she cast him off, and she was not willing to let all that effort go to waste, so she pushed against the Dao. Before the book was ready to be published, and before she was ready to stand in herself as its author, she published it. The consequences of pushing against the flow were tremendously painful.

After many months of grieving, she took a pilgrimage to see beloved Amma. The seven days she spent in Amma's Field transformed her world completely. When she returned home, she broke free of the sexual relationship, and she began to seriously engage in her yogic practices and her ever-deepening surrender to her Gurus, Amma and Neem Karoli Baba.

In preparation for beginning graduate school that Fall, she immersed herself fully in a summer of strengthening practices: meditating twice daily, eating a sattvic vegetarian diet, drinking mate tea in the sunshine, riding her bicycle, walking on mountain trails, chanting the Names of God, and bowing often before her Gurus – offering Them her whole self, not just part of herself. As she healed herself through sadhana, this yogini began to feel more and more Bliss.

*She had prayed to Amma to be protected from the grief (when she separated from the man whom she had adored for almost three years), and to her delight, Amma showered her with that Protection. Although she had been terribly afraid that she would lie in bed each night weeping hysterically, that wasn't at all the way it happened. Instead, she **wanted** to sleep alone.*

On Sri Krishna Janmastami, Lord Krishna's birthday, she prayed that Amma would help her to truly know that Lord Krishna was the Player and she was His little flute. She attended an evening Krishna Fire Puja adorned in a blue dress, a peacock feather in a topknot on her head, a gold anklet with bells, an orange Shiva prayer shawl, and a sparkling bindi on her third eye. As she poured ghee into the fire, she prayed to be released of all that stood in the way of her realizing that the Lord's energy is behind everything.

In the days following the Krishna Puja, as she chanted the Hare Krishna mantra over and over while burning nag champa incense, she felt more and more Bliss in her being.

The following week, due to many circumstances that all arose together, she suddenly decided that the timing wasn't right for her to go to graduate school. At first the shock of the decision upset her, but as she bowed crying before her altar to Amma and Neem Karoli Baba, she realized that her teacher had been right when he had said that she would keep burning through forms until she let go.

Since she was still purifying and learning to let go and let God, she was still burning through forms. She had let go of her lover, and now she had let go of the graduate school plan. As her boys began another school year, she continued to enjoy much blissful time alone during the days they spent at their papa's house.

220

At the same time, she received guidance that she needed to publish a revision of the first book. Each day when she sat down to do major content cuts from that book, she felt more and more ecstatic Bliss rising within her being. As she read and re-read her teacher's teachings, she understood how much she had finally integrated them into her life. She knew that he would be proud to see how her life was filling itself now.

After four months without having sex and without having any orgasms, she was beginning to hear her own voice of wisdom say the exact things that her teacher had said – those exact teachings on sexuality that she had reacted so strongly against! She was shocked to hear her own intuitive voice tell her that sexual energy is very potent medicine that should only be engaged in with full reverence for its sacredness.

She was surprised that although she still felt a lot of sexual energy in her being, she felt absolutely no desire to release it. Rather than feeling clogged with backed-up sexual energy, she felt clean and clear in her being, and she was actually able to successfully and consistently do the practice that her teacher had suggested: she was able to breathe the sexual energy up to her heart. This western yogini, who had lived so long ago in the Himalayas, was amazed to realize for herself that her teacher's teachings were True.

I sent that story to Basil by email, and he replied with the following:
Rita,
Thank you so much for the story… and even more importantly for the inner work. All streams become what they are meant to be eventually.
I am most glad to be gathered into your world in such an artistic and truthful way. May you continue to deepen and open.
Much love,
Basil

As the autumn breezes whisper of the wheel turning again, the Rita Lila continues. Now, with much *obvious* Guru Protection and Grace, I find myself falling into a beautiful *friendship* with a sweet older man who I was attracted to while in the relationship with Baron. This dear friend will not allow me to act on the attraction and the addictive love pattern. Although he has not met Basil, it is as though he is channeling Basil when he looks me in the eyes and says firmly, "It's not about me – it's about *you*!" After each long intimate talk that we share over tulsi tea, he reminds me that he is my mirror, and that I need to fall back into myself. Again and again, I fall back into the *Bliss* of my Self.

I thank my Gurus, Amma and Neem Karoli Baba, for sending me this special friendship in which I get to see the vasana of desire so clearly that I might just be able to purify it through this time…

Mata Rani Ki Jai! Victory to the Great Mother Goddess who is making all my dreams come true.

Glossary

Acharya – the Sanskrit word for a recognized teacher. An accomplished spiritual teacher inspires, instructs and motivates their students. The teacher also holds an energetic field for the students' projections and resistances.

Advaita Vedanta – the profound non-dualistic philosophy taught by Adi Shankara (686-718 A.D.), which states that the Absolute Existence is One with each person's inner Self.

Amma – also known as Ammachi and Sri Mata Amritanandamayi Devi – popularly known as "the hugging saint." Born in a poor fishing village in Southern India in 1953, Amma is an enlightened being who has hugged more than 26 million people worldwide. She personally runs many charitable and humanitarian organizations in India and abroad, including a hospital which offers free medical care to the poor, a university, an orphanage, care homes for the elderly, and many more. She gave one million dollars to help after Hurricane Katrina hit, and she recently gave forty-six million dollars to help distressed farmers in India. Her international ashram in Kerala, India, is home to more than 3,000 people. Twice each year, she tours the United States, where her main ashram is located just outside of San Ramon, California.

Anandamayi Ma – a woman saint who lived in India, 1896-1982. Crowds of people surrounded this happy woman who was fondly known as the "Blissful Mother." Without formal schooling and without a Guru, she was highly intelligent and entered high states of samadhi. She gave herself Guru mantra and became enlightened. She traveled around teaching and spreading bliss everywhere with her hearty laugh and pithy teachings. She was friends with Neem Karoli Baba – they enjoyed feeding people together. She also clairvoyantly knew of Amma – in her mind's eye she saw Amma from across India – and toward the end of her life, she began sending people to Amma.

Arjuna – warrior and friend of Lord Krishna in the epic story, the *Mahabharata*. Krishna gave advice to Arjuna on the battlefield. That advice is the *Bhagavad Gita*, the Song of the Lord.

Ashram – the residence of a Guru, their disciples, and religious community.

Atman – the Self; the Witness; Pure Consciousness; the unchanging Reality that is One with Brahman.

Baba – the word can mean father or teacher. In India, Baba is used as a term of endearment, especially for religious figures. Also in India, there are lineages

223

of babas who have passed spiritual teachings down from Guru to disciple through thousands of years.

Balarama – See Glossary of Hindu gods and goddesses.

Bhagavad Gita – "The Song of the Lord" – one of the most influential Hindu scriptures. The Gita is a conversation that takes place between Lord Krishna and his warrior friend, Arjuna, on the battlefield in the middle of the great Sanskrit epic, the *Mahabharata*.

Bhajans – devotional songs of worship.

Bhakta – a devotee.

Bhakti Yoga – The path of devotion.

Bhavas – moods or emotional states.

Bindi – an important symbolic mark worn between the eyebrows, marking the location of the third eye, the eye of inner vision and spiritual wisdom. While the bindi is sometimes religious and sometimes decorative, in ancient tradition it is a sacred symbol of auspiciousness that represents the cosmic sound of Om.

Brahma – See Glossary of Hindu gods and goddesses.

Brahmachari/Brahmacharini – a spiritual student who practices self-control, purity, and celibacy. Brahmachari refers to a male disciple, while brahmacharini refers to a female disciple.

Brahman – the One Absolute Existence or Reality that is unchanging and One with everything. (Note difference between Brahma and Brahman.)

Chai – tea with milk, sweetener, and spices.

Chakras – the seven energy points that exist in the subtle body. They are like spinning wheels of energy. The **first chakra, the Muladhara,** is the root chakra. It is located at the base of the spine and is associated with the color red and with the earth and home. The **second chakra, the Svadhisthana,** is the sex chakra. It is located between the pubic bone and the navel and is associated with the color orange and with sensuality and creativity. The **third chakra, the Manipura,** is the solar plexus chakra. It is located at the stomach, above the navel, and is associated with the color yellow and with the will. The **fourth chakra, the Anahata,** is the heart chakra. It is located at the heart and is associated with the color green and with love, love, love. The **fifth chakra, the Vishuddha,** is the throat chakra. It is located at the throat and is associated with the color blue and with truth and expression of one's truth. The **sixth chakra, the Ajna,** is the third eye chakra. It is located in the center of the forehead, slightly above the eyebrows and is associated with the color purple and with intuition. Ultimately the third eye chakra is the place where Shiva and Shakti unite within each being. The **seventh chakra, the Sahasrara,** is the crown chakra. It is located just above the top of the head and is associated with the color white and with connection with the Divine.

Chanting – repetitive singing. The sound vibrations purify the mind, the heart, and the surrounding environment.

Chi – or ji – is added to the end of a respectable person's name. For example, Amma is often referred to as Ammachi, and Neem Karoli Baba was fondly called Maharaj-ji.

Darshan – receiving the blessing of the Guru.

Day of Brahma – the basic unit of Vedic cyclical time, which lasts 4.32 billion years. One Day of Brahma is considered to be a thousand cycles of four yugas (ages): Satya, Treta, Dvapara, and Kali. We are now living in the last yuga of the current Day of Brahma.

Devi Bhava – literally, "the mood of the Divine Mother." Amma regularly holds "Devi Bhava" nights, in which she performs special pujas to Devi, the Divine Mother, and she herself dresses as Devi. That night Amma gives darshan as the Divine Mother, and holy water – blessed by Amma – is distributed to everyone present.

Diksha – transmission of the state of Oneness.

Doula – a woman who assists another woman in childbirth.

Durga – often called Ma Durga – See Glossary of Hindu gods and goddesses.

Durga's Puja Day – a special day when rituals are performed to worship the goddess, Durga.

Ego – that part of a person's personality that covers up their true essence.

Frida Kahlo – a colorful Mexican woman artist, 1907-1954. She was the wife of the Mexican painter, Diego Rivera.

Ganesha – See Glossary of Hindu gods and goddesses.

Ganges – a holy river in India. See also the Glossary of Hindu gods and goddesses.

Ghee – clarified butter. Often used in Indian cooking.

Gopis – the cowherd girls of Vrindavan, India, who fell madly in love with Lord Krishna.

Guru – literally, "that which takes one from darkness to light." Someone who abides continually in a Connected State – He or She has burnt through the veils of illusion and doesn't do anything out of personal will. A Guru takes full responsibility for the spiritual awakening of his or her disciples.

Hanuman – See Glossary of Hindu gods and goddesses.

I-Ching – the Classic Chinese Book of Changes.

Jai Kali Ma! – Victory to the Great Divine Mother Goddess, Kali!

Janmastami – the celebration of Sri Krishna's birthday.

Jelauddin Rumi – a great mystic and poet who lived in Persia in the twelfth century.

Jñana Yoga – the path of Knowledge.

John Fire Lame Deer – a Native American shaman of the Lakota and Sioux tribes, 1903-1976.

Kabir – an oral poet, teacher, and saint of North India, 1398-1448.

Kali – See Glossary of Hindu gods and goddesses.

Kali Durge – a chant to two forms of the Divine Mother Goddess: Kali and Durga.

Kali Yuga – the current age we are living in.

Karma – the result of one's past actions. The law of cause and effect states that all of a being's past actions will bear fruit at some point.

Karma Yoga – the path of selfless action.

Kirtan – call and response chanting, often with live musicians and fervent worship and devotion to God.

Koshas – the subtle light bodies that exist in the energetic field surrounding each being.

Kriya – Sanskrit word for "movement that purifies." A kriya can take many forms, including intense emotional meltdowns.

Kundalini Yoga – the path of understanding the channels of energy in the body and working with awakening the primal force.

Labyrinth – A maze of interconnecting passages through which it can be difficult to find one's way. In some ancient cultures, labyrinths were made of stones for people to walk into the center and then walk back out. Today, many churches and hospitals are reviving this tradition and making labyrinths for people to walk as a healing practice.

Lakshmi – See Glossary of Hindu gods and goddesses.

Lalla – a mystic poet and saint of North India, 1320-1392. It is believed that she left her husband's home and wandered about *naked* singing songs to God.

"Left his/her body" – an Indian expression that means a person has died. Their soul has traveled beyond the physical realm, leaving their physical body behind.

Lila – the Divine Play or Theatre of God. In the Lila, the Lord disguises himself as the many beings of the world, so each of our human interactions can be seen as God playing with God.

Lingam – the penis.

Lord Krishna – See Glossary of Hindu gods and goddesses.

Lord Ram/Rama – See Glossary of Hindu gods and goddesses.

Lord Shiva – See Glossary of Hindu gods and goddesses.

Lord Vishnu – See Glossary of Hindu gods and goddesses.

Mahamantra – the Hare Krishna mantra – the great mantra. The mahamantra was revealed to Shri Chaitanya Mahaprabhu in India about 500 years ago. The words are *Hare Krishna, Hare Krishna, Krishna Krishna, Hare Hare. Hare Rama, Hare Rama, Rama Rama, Hare Hare.*

Mantra – sacred syllables, words, or phrases. When repeated with concentration, a mantra can help a person to calm their mind and open their heart.

Mantra Diksha – the transmission of a seed mantra from a Guru to a disciple.

Mantra Japa – the repetition of a mantra.

Mantra Yoga – the practice of repeating or chanting a mantra until the mind and emotions are calm.

Maya – illusion.

Meditation – the practice of sitting in your being rather than your thinking. Sitting with awareness of breath, mind, and body, but not engaging with them. Witnessing thoughts (and body sensations and emotions), and allowing them to pass through without attachment. Witnessing deeper states of consciousness and relaxing into them as often as possible.

Mirabai – an Indian poet and saint, 1498-1550. Born a princess, she renounced her clan and wandered the streets barefoot, begging for food, and singing love songs to her god Krishna, the Dark One.

Mirroring – Reflecting a person's energy state back to them.

Naan – a delicious Indian flatbread.

Nadis – the subtle vibratory channels that hold the tendencies of lifetimes of experiences. There are 7,272,311 nadis in each person's subtle body.

Namaste – a greeting that means, "I honor the Divine within you that is also within me."

Neem Karoli Baba – fondly called Maharaj-ji – the Guru of Ram Dass and Krishna Das. A saint in India who was loved by many Indian devotees. Several hundred Western devotees found him as well. Many believed Sri Neem Karoli Baba to be an incarnation of Hanuman. No one knows when he was born. He "left his body" in 1973.

Night of Brahma – follows the day of Brahma. Each night of Brahma lasts as long as each day of Brahma: 4.32 billion years. During the night of Brahma, everything shuts down and becomes absorbed in Brahman – the One Reality – waiting to be re-created.

Nirvana – the final Liberation of the soul.

Non-duality, non-dualism – the philosophy of Oneness. Everything and everyone are One – we are one continuous web of energy and vibration. There is no duality between God and human – ALL is One.

Om – the original sound of the Universe. The sound of the sacred syllable *Om* still vibrates through everything in the Universe.

Om Amriteshwaryai Namaha – a special mantra that honors Sri Mata Amritanandamayi Devi, also known as Ammachi or Amma. Literally it means, "I bow to that Supreme Energy, which is Immortal Bliss."

Om Jothi – a greeting or mantra of Light.

Om Namah Shivaya – the most popular mantra – it brings both spiritual protection and material prosperity. Literally, it means, "I bow to Shiva who is Pure Consciousness and Bliss. I bow to my innermost Self, which is Pure Consciousness and Bliss." When spoken as a greeting, it means essentially "Namaste" or "I honor the Divine within you that is also within me."

Om Shanti – a greeting or mantra of Peace.

Parvati – See Glossary of Hindu gods and goddesses.

Pele – the Hawaiian goddess of the volcano.

Polyamory – "many loves." People who practice polyamory are polyamorous and not monogamous.

Prana – the vital life energy or force that moves through each being. It also moves through the landscapes of the earth. Prana is the breath.

Prarabdha karma – the kind of karma that can only be lived through. It can neither be burned in meditation nor burned through selfless service.

Projection – blaming something within yourself on another person. Attributing your own secret desires or behavior traits or personality patterns to someone else. Seeing your own qualities in another when you can't see them in yourself.

Puja – rituals for worshipping a deity.

Radha – See Glossary of Hindu gods and goddesses.

Radhastami – the celebration of Sri Radha's birthday.

Raja Yoga – the path of systemic discipline that combines aspects of karma, bhakti, kundalini, and jñana yogas. (Rita Ann Shankara is a raja yogini.)

Ramakrishna – Bengali saint, 1836-1886. Blissfully devoted to the Divine Mother, he was merged in intoxicated divine ecstasy with Her.

Ramana Maharshi – an enlightened sage and saint, 1879-1950. One of the greatest spiritual teachers of modern-day India.

Rasa – literally means "living liquids" like juice or sap. Rasa refers to the essence or flavor of an artistic creation. For example, if you are watching a dancer, the rasa of the dance would be that substance that moves your mind or greatly affects your emotions – that quality of the dance which is beyond the senses.

Ravana – See Glossary of Hindu gods and goddesses.

Rishi – a seer; a sage.

Sadhana – spiritual practices that lead one to the innermost Self.

Samadhi – an advanced state of meditation in which one is merged in the Pure Consciousness that is the Self.

Samskaras – subconscious impressions that are left on the mind by each act. These impressions then lead to renewed psycho-mental activities.

Sangha – a spiritual community.

Sanskrit – the classical language of India. Most of the Hindu scriptures are written in Sanskrit.

Saraswati – See Glossary of Hindu gods and goddesses.

Sari – a dress worn primarily by Hindu women. A sari consists of several yards of light material that is draped around the body.

Sat Guru – a True Guru. A Guru merged with Absolute Truth, Absolute Consciousness, Absolute Bliss.

Sattvic – the adjective for one of the three gunas (qualities) that make up the phenomenal world. The gunas are tamas, inertia; rajas, passion; and sattva, purity. Sattvic denotes the qualities of harmony, purity, goodness, tranquility, and meditative calm.

Self – the Pure Consciousness within each person. The Self is One with the Witness and the Unchanging Reality – the One Existence.

Self-Realization – realizing that you are the Self; that you are Pure Consciousness. Merging in that state of Oneness within and without.

Shakti – See Glossary of Hindu gods and goddesses.

Shankara – literally means "Giver of Peace." Shankara is a name of Lord Shiva.

Shanti – Peace.

Siddhis – supernatural powers attained by advanced spiritual practitioners. The siddhis can distract aspirants and make them forget the true spiritual goal of Self-Realization. The siddhis are not the goal of sadhana.

Sita – See Glossary of Hindu gods and goddesses.

Sri – title of respect for a deity or holy person.

Sri Vidya Yoga – an extremely rare path that is only followed by the highly accomplished sages.

Sufi winged heart – Sufi symbol chosen by the founder of the Sufi Order, Hazrat Inayat Khan.

Swami – a Hindu honorific title for learned priests.

Swami Muktananda – Also known as Baba Muktananda. Guru from India who traveled in the West giving spiritual initiation to many. 1908-1982. His successor is Gurumayi Chidvilasananda.

Swami Vivekananda – successor of Sri Ramakrishna. Swami Vivekananda carried Ramakrishna's message to the West. 1863-1902.

Tantra, Tantric – a system of Enlightenment. Tantra yoga is the practice of seeing everything – every form – as part of the Oneness. This practice allows one to become One with the innermost Self. A highly advanced tantric practitioner who has found Oneness within can experience further Oneness in sexual union with a highly advanced practitioner of the opposite sex. The Tantra taught in the West sometimes focuses merely on sexual pleasure, which is not the true Tantra.

Tapas – literally "heat." Tapas is the heat generated by spiritual practices that control the senses. Tapas can also mean austerities.

Tara – Tibetan Buddhist Goddess of Compassion.

The Absolute – One of the many Names for the One Reality.

The Dao – or Tao – in Chinese Mandarin, literally the *Way*. In Daoism, the Dao is the basic organizing principle of the universe.

Third eye – located in the center of the forehead, just above the eyebrows. The third eye is considered to be a place of great intuition.

Tulsidas – famous Hindi poet, 1532-1623. Tulsidas is regarded as an incarnation of Valmiki, the author of the great epic, the *Ramayana*.

Vasana – a magnetic tendency. Vasanas have been encoded in our beings over many lifetimes. They show up as strong personality patterns that do not want to let go. When you try to burn through a vasana, sometimes it will hang on with a vengeance. A vasana's magnetic quality can be quite gripping. It helps to consult a knowledgeable spiritual teacher when you are working with your vasanas. A teacher can help you cultivate skillful means in working with the vasanas. The vasanas do need to be dealt with. If you try to ignore them or pretend that they don't exist, they will come out anyway at some point. There is no shortcut to enlightenment: each being has vasanas that have to unravel – in their own time and at their own pace – before the being will be ripe for enlightenment. In facing the vasanas, it is helpful to learn three things: Patience, Acceptance of What Is, and Respect for Time.

Vedic – of the Vedas, the ancient Hindu scriptural texts.

Witness, The Witness, Witness Consciousness – that part of ourselves that simply *witnesses* our thoughts, emotions, body sensations, and actions. The Witness is One with the innermost Self. The Witness is always witnessing, and when we become aware of the Witness, we can strengthen it and cultivate it. When we strengthen the Witness, we become detached from our identification with the body-mind, and that detachment allows us to place our attention on the Self, which is Pure Consciousness and Bliss. When we put our attention on the Self, we become happy, joyful, and content. We then radiate bliss and we can help others to find their bliss. Cultivating the Witness is, therefore, one of the most important spiritual practices.

Yoga, Yogic – literally means "union." The yoga path comprises the practices that lead one to that state of union – that state of Oneness with one's highest Self and with God. Some of the yogic practices include meditation, chanting, repetition of mantras, and asanas (body postures).

Yogi/Yogini – one who practices yoga. Yogi refers to a male practitioner, while yogini refers to a female practitioner.

Yoni – the vagina.

Yugas – ages. We are now living in the Kali Yuga, meaning the age of Kali.

Glossary of Hindu gods and goddesses

There are thousands of gods and goddesses in the Hindu Pantheon. In Hinduism there is One Absolute Truth, which in the West would be considered One God, and that God has many aspects. So the One God takes many faces or forms and is known by thousands of Names, and is still One Absolute Truth.

That One Absolute Truth includes *ALL* of Existence, so It exists within and without each being. The many Hindu gods and goddesses are historical, mythological beings, and they are also energy states that exist within and without all beings.

So for example, Hanuman, the monkey god, represents devotion, courage, strength, and wisdom. You can read the wonderful history and mythology of Hanuman in the great epic story, the *Ramayana*, and you can also chant or pray to Hanuman. When you chant or pray to a Hindu god or goddess, you invoke that energy state within and without yourself. What that means is, when you chant Hanuman's name, you find that place inside where your own devotion, courage, strength, and wisdom lives, and that place inside of you wakes up a little more. And at the same time, the environment around you is cleansed by the repetition of one of the many Names of God.

Here are some brief explanations of the Hindu gods and goddesses found in this book:

Balarama – divine brother of Lord Krishna. While Krishna is considered to be a full incarnation of Lord Vishnu, Balarama is considered to be a partial incarnation of the Lord. Balarama joins Krishna on his many adventures – herding the cows, fighting off demons, and so on.

Brahma – the creative aspect of Divinity. The Hindu masculine Godhead is represented by a Trinity: Brahma is the creator; Vishnu is the sustainer; and Shiva is the destroyer. Brahma's consort is Saraswati.

Durga – one of the forms of the Divine Mother. Lord Shiva's consort is Parvati, and Parvati takes many forms, including Kali and Durga. Ma Durga rides a lion and holds weapons in her many hands. She slays the demons of the mind and protects her children with tenderness.

Ganesha – the elephant-headed god. Son of Shiva and Parvati, he is a great protector and the remover of obstacles.

Ganges – a holy river in India. The Ganges is considered to be the Great Mother Goddess.

Hanuman – the monkey god. Son of the wind god, Hanuman is the utmost devotee of Rama and Sita in the epic story, the *Ramayana*. He represents supreme devotion, wisdom, and superhero strength and courage.

Kali – one of the forms of the Divine Mother. Lord Shiva's consort is Parvati, and Parvati takes many forms, including Kali and Durga. Kali is a fierce Mother who holds many weapons in her hands. She wears a necklace of skulls and a belt of the human heads that she has severed. This is symbolic of her ability to cut through the illusions of maya and free her children from the bondage of their egos. She offers protection to those who invoke her. She also is the power of Time.

Krishna – an incarnation of Lord Vishnu. He lived in India about 5,000 years ago. He had a following of young cowherd girls called "gopis." Krishna especially fell in love with a cowherdess named Radha. Krishna represents all things attractive – he is the All-Attractive One – and Radha represents His potency. Krishna was a hero and a teacher. In the great epic, the *Mahabharata*, Krishna gave advice to his warrior friend, Arjuna, on the battlefield. That advice is the *Bhagavad Gita*, the Song of the Lord.

Lakshmi – one of the forms of the Divine Mother. She is the consort of Lord Vishnu. She is the goddess of wealth, fortune, power, and beauty.

Parvati – one of the forms of the Divine Mother. She is the consort of Lord Shiva and the Mother of Ganesha. She is the goddess of love, sexuality, intelligence, and creativity. She takes many forms, including Kali and Durga. In order to become one with her beloved Shiva, she first sat in meditation and did many austere spiritual practices. Once she attained high levels of consciousness and was an accomplished yogini in her own right, then she was able to sit before Shiva and merge in Love with Him. Civilization and culture flowed out of their creative, sexual union.

Radha – one of the forms of the Divine Mother. She was one of the thousands of girls who fell in love with Lord Krishna in Vrindavan, India, about 5,000 years ago. In Radha, Krishna found his potency. Radha represents Krishna's heart.

Rama – an incarnation of Lord Vishnu. He lived in India thousands of years before Lord Krishna. Lord Rama's noble story is recounted in the epic story, the *Ramayana*, in which the demon Ravana kidnaps Rama's beloved wife, Sita, and then Hanuman, the monkey god, helps Rama save Sita from doom. Rama is often referred to as Ram. Ram and Sita symbolize the perfect union of the male and female aspects of the Divine.

Ravana – the demon who kidnaps Sita in the epic tale, the *Ramayana*.

Saraswati – one of the forms of the Divine Mother. She is the consort of Lord Brahma. She is the goddess of knowledge, learning, writing, and music. She looks over the arts, sciences, crafts, and skills.

Shakti – the Power and the Energy of the Divine Mother Goddess. If the Supreme God is like fire, then Shakti is its burning power.

Shiva – the destructive aspect of Divinity. The Hindu masculine Godhead is represented by a Trinity: Brahma is the creator; Vishnu is the sustainer; and Shiva is the destroyer. Shiva's consort is Parvati and their son is Ganesha. Lord Shiva is worshipped by many lineages of yogis and babas in India. He represents Pure Consciousness and is the Lord of Yoga and Yogis. He wears skulls, ashes, snakes, and tiger skins, and he is most often found meditating in the Himalayas or roaming about with hosts of ghosts and goblins. The holy river Ganges, or Ganga, flows from his crown of long matted hair.

Sita – one of the forms of the Divine Mother. An incarnation of Lakshmi, she was the wife of Lord Rama. Captured by the demon, Ravana, in the epic tale, the *Ramayana*, she was freed by her heroic husband and Hanuman's monkey army. She represents the eternal female aspect of the Divine. She exhibited supreme devotion and loyalty to her husband.

Vishnu – the sustaining aspect of Divinity. The Hindu masculine Godhead is represented by a Trinity: Brahma is the creator; Vishnu is the sustainer; and Shiva is the destroyer. Vishnu's consort is Lakshmi. When humans are in trouble and need Divine help, Lord Vishnu incarnates in a human body. His two most popular incarnations in India were those of Rama and Krishna.

Referenced Works

A Grateful Heart: Daily Blessings for the Evening Meal from Buddha to The Beatles, edited by M.J. Ryan, Conari Press, York Beach, ME, 1994.

African Odyssey, CD by Putumayo World Music ("*Raki*" by Oliver Mtukudzi).

Ammachi: A Biography of Mata Amritanandamayi, by Swami Amritaswarupananda, Mata Amritanandamayi Mission Trust, M.A. Center, San Ramon, CA, 1994.

Angel cards, by Kathy Tyler and Joy Drake, Narada Productions, Inc., Milwaukee, WI, 1981.

Baba: Autobiography of a Blue-Eyed Yogi, Rampuri, Bell Tower Publishing, New York, NY, 2005.

Bhagavad Gita, translated by Eknath Easwaran, Shambhala Publications, Inc., Boston, MA, 1985.

Breath of the Heart, One Track Heart, Live on Earth, All One, Greatest Hits of the Kali Yuga, and *Flow of Grace*, CDs by recording artist, Krishna Das.

Chant and Be Happy: The Power of Mantra Meditation – Featuring Exclusive Conversations with John Lennon and George Harrison, published by the Bhaktivedanta Book Trust, Los Angeles, CA, 1997.

Comfortable with Uncertainty, by Pema Chödrön and Emily Hilburn Sell, Shambhala Publications, Inc., 2002.

Conscious Loving, The Journey to Co-Commitment: A Way to Be Fully Together Without Giving Up Yourself by Gay and Kathleen Hendricks, Bantam Books, New York, NY, 1992.

Crest-Jewel of Discrimination, by Shankara, translated by Swami Prabhavananda and Christopher Isherwood, Vedanta Press, Hollywood, CA, 1975.

Embracing the World: Images and Sayings of Sri Mata Amritanandamayi Devi, Mata Amritanandamayi Mission Trust, M.A. Center, San Ramon, CA, 2003.

For Love of the Dark One: Songs of Mirabai, translated by Andrew Schelling, illustrated by Mayumi Oda, Shambhala Publications, Inc., Boston, MA, 1993.

Frida Kahlo: Pain and Passion, by Andrea Kettenmann, Benedikt Taschen, Germany, 1993.

Great Swan: Meetings with Ramakrishna, by Lex Hixon, Larson Publications, Burdett, NY, 1996.

Hindu Gods and Goddesses, by Swami Harshananda, Sri Ramakrishna Math, Madras, India, 1982.

Holy Mother: Being the Life of Sri Sarada Devi, Wife of Sri Ramakrishna and Helpmate in His Mission, by Swami Nikhilananda, Ramakrishna-Vivekananda Center of New York, 1962.

I Ching: Book of Changes, An Interpretation by Blythe Lasley, Photographs by Diane Fassler Chasmar, Momentum Publishing, Ashland, OR, 2005.

I Heart Huckabees, film by David O. Russell and Jeff Baena.

In Days of Great Peace: The Highest Yoga As Lived, by Mouni Sadhu, Allen & Unwin, London, 1953.

Kirtan!, double CD by recording artist, Jai Uttal.

Lalla: Naked Song, translations by Coleman Barks, Maypop Books, Athens, GA, 1992.

Lalla-Vakyani, the Wise Sayings of Lal-Ded, A Mystic Poetess of Ancient Kashmir, by Sir George Grierson and Lionel D. Barnett, Royal Asiatic Society, London, 1920.

Meditate, by Swami Muktananda, State University of New York Press, Albany, NY, 1980.

Medicine Cards, by Jamie Sams and David Carson, Illustrated by Angela C. Werneke, Bear & Company, Santa Fe, NM, 1988.

Miracle of Love: Stories about Neem Karoli Baba, by Ram Dass, A Dutton Paperback, E.P. Dutton, NY, 1979.

Mother of Sweet Bliss: A Book for Young Readers and for the Young at Heart, by Swami Amritaswarupananda, Mata Amritanandamayi Center, San Ramon, CA, 2003.

Navigating the Tides of Change: Stories from Science, the Sacred, and a Wise Planet, by David La Chapelle, New Society Publishers, BC, Canada, 2001. Go to **umya.com** to view David La Chapelle's inspirational artistic works.

Prem, *Shanti*, and *Grace*, CDs by recording artist, Snatam Kaur.

Ramayana, by Ranchor Prime, Mandala Publishing, San Rafael, CA, 2004.

Returning and *Praises for the World*, CDs by recording artist, Jennifer Berezan.

Sacred Transitions, CD by recording artist, Prema Mayi Dasi.

Songs for the Inner Lover, CD by recording artists, Deva Premal and Miten.

Tantrika: Traveling the Road of Divine Love, by Asra Q. Nomani, HarperSanFrancisco, a Division of HarperCollins Publishers, Inc., NY, 2003.

The Adventures of Young Krishna, The Blue God of India, by Diksha Dalal-Clayton, Rupa & Co., Calcutta, India, 1992.

The American Heritage College Dictionary, Third Edition, Houghton Mifflin Company, Boston, MA, 1993.

The Bijak of Kabir, translated by Linda Hess and Shukdev Singh, North Point Press, San Francisco, CA, 1983.

The Divine Consort: Radha and the Goddesses of India, edited by John Stratton Hawley and Donna Marie Wulff, Beacon Press, Boston, MA, 1986.

The Divine Life: An Interview with Swami Chidananda, by Bill Eilers and Susan Eilers, *What is Enlightenment (magazine)*, Lenox, MA, issue 13, Spring-Summer 1998.

The Essential Rumi, by Jalal Al-Din Rumi (Author), Et Al Coleman Barks (Translator), HarperCollins Publishers, New York, NY, 1995.

The Essential Teachings of Ramana Maharshi: A Visual Journey, edited by Matthew Greenblatt, InnerDirections Publishing, Carlsbad, CA, 2003.

The (2004) Gita Journal: A Weekly Inspirational Calendar from the Bhagavad Gita, Mandala Publishing, San Rafael, CA, 2004.

The Illuminated Rumi, by Jalal Al-Din Rumi (Author), Michael Green (Illustrator), Coleman Barks (Translator), Broadway Books, NY, 1997.

The Molecules of Emotion: the Science Behind Mind-Body Medicine, by Candace B. Pert, Ph.D., Touchstone of Simon & Schuster Inc., New York, NY, 1997.

The Prophet, Pocket Edition, by Kahlil Gibran, Alred A. Knopf, Inc., NY, 1973.

The Spiritual Teaching of Ramana Maharshi by Sri Ramanasramam and Shambhala Publications, Inc., Boston, MA, 1998.

The Storyteller's Daughter, by Saira Shah, Anchor Books, New York, NY, 2003.

The Wild Parrots of Telegraph Hill, film by Judy Irving, starring Mark Bittner.

What Should I Do With My Life? The True Story of People Who Answered the Ultimate Question, by Po Bronson, Random House, Inc., NY, 2002.

What the Bleep Do We Know?, film by William Arntz, Betsy Chasse, and Mark Vicente.

Wisdom: 365 Thoughts from Indian Masters, by Danielle and Olivier Föllmi, Harry N. Abrams, Inc., New York, NY, 2004.

Women of Power and Grace: Nine Astonishing, Inspiring Luminaries of Our Time, by Timothy Conway, Ph.D., the Wake Up Press, Santa Barbara, CA, 1995.

Acknowledgements

I offer sweet flowers of gratitude to the many beings who have lovingly supported my journey, including: Julianna, Dana, Luna, Basil, Baron, Randi Jan, Raya, Sallamae, Paulina, Grace, Shannon, Gaelyn, Baba Rampuri, Shoshana, David Hodges, my sons Joshua and Benjamin, their papa Bryan, my brothers, my parents, my sisters-in-law, my dear friend Thomas... and Karl ~ wherever you may be.

I send healing sound vibrations from the tiny gold bell in the center of my heart to my dearest teacher, Basil. Words cannot express the depth of my appreciation for the teachings that you gave so selflessly.

I thank you, dear Luna, for keeping your heart open to me throughout it all. I am inspired by your level of *presence*... and I am ever-grateful for our enduring connection.

I thank my dear family for our wonderful closeness. I look forward to sharing many more colorful meals and invigorating hikes together.

I thank you, dear Randi Jan, for the purity of love in your big heart.

I thank you, dear Dana, for your wise, loving, earth-mama support. The beautiful way you mother your daughters inspires me to be a better mother myself.

I thank you, dear Baron, for joining me in the dance that swung me so much deeper into Faith in the Self... *There is only Rama.*

I thank you, dear Gaelyn and dear Constance, my elder sisters on this life journey... your love nourishes my heart.

I thank you, dear Ramas, for showing up in the ways that you are – our friendship supports me on so many levels. Thank you for holding integrity as you teach me (again and again) the importance of staying in my power.

I thank you, dear Prema Mayi, for the sweetness that you radiate.

I thank you, dear Julianna, my sadhana sister – yogini sister – gopini sister! I so appreciate the ways we support each other's heart openings.

I bow again and again to my beloved Gurus,
Amma and **Neem Karoli Baba**.
I offer Them my whole self and I rest in the Bliss of Their Grace.
Jai Ma! Victory to the Divine Mother...

241

About the author

Rita Ann Shankara, named *Tejaswini* by her Guru, Ammachi, is awakening her inner bliss through Yogic spiritual practices. A mother of two bright boys, she lives in a cozy little cottage where she enjoys reading, writing, and cooking mantra-infused meals. Together with her greatest teachers – her sons, Josh-ji and Benji-ji – she is learning to slow down and flow with what is arising in each moment of life.

Rita has always loved religion and ritual. Born Catholic, she remained devoutly Catholic until she was twenty-three years old. Then she switched to Judaism for ten years, during which time she also studied Daoist, Buddhist, Native American, and Muslim traditions.

At age thirty-three, she was suddenly strongly drawn to India, Hinduism, and the Yoga Path, and now, as a practicing raja yogini, Rita finds that regular chanting and meditating are leading her Home to the Bliss of her true Self. With an ever-increasing heart openness, she intends to serve many beings through a myriad of roles, including author, spiritual teacher, caregiver, social worker, counselor, and cook.

Also by Rita Ann Shankara:

Love Soups: A Vegetarian Soup Cookbook Inspired by the Soup Devas

www.ingramcontent.com/pod-product-compliance
Lightning Source LLC
Chambersburg PA
CBHW030920090426
42737CB00007B/266